WU YUBI

# The Journal of Wu Yubi

## The Path to Sagehood

Translated, with Introduction
and Commentary, by

M. THERESA KELLEHER

Hackett Publishing Company, Inc.

Indianapolis/Cambridge

16 15 14 13      1 2 3 4 5 6 7

For further information, please address
    Hackett Publishing Company, Inc.
    P.O. Box 44937
    Indianapolis, Indiana 46244-0937

    www.hackettpublishing.com

Cover design by Abigail Coyle
Interior design by Elizabeth L. Wilson
Composition by Graphic Composition, Inc., Bogart, Georgia.

**Library of Congress Cataloging-in-Publication Data**

Wu, Yubi, 1391–1469.
  [Kangzhai xian sheng ri lu. English]
  The journal of Wu Yubi : the path to sagehood / translated, with introduction
and commentary, by Theresa Kelleher.
    p. cm.
  Includes bibliographical references.
  ISBN 978-1-62466-042-9 (pbk.) — ISBN 978-1-62466-043-6 (cloth)
  1. Wu, Yubi, 1391–1469—Diaries. 2. Confucianists—China—Diaries. 3.
Neo-Confucianism. I. Kelleher, M. Theresa, 1949- II. Title. III. Title: Path to
sagehood.
  B128.W844A3 2013
  181'.112--dc23                  2013017628

# WU YUBI

# The Journal of Wu Yubi

## *The Path to Sagehood*

*For Charlie and Clare*

# Contents

# Preface

The early days of May this year have been unusually beautiful, with crystal clear blue skies and lush blossoming of cherry trees and dogwood. A few mornings ago, as I was sipping my breakfast tea and watching the birds at our feeder, I found these lines of Wu Yubi coming to me: "Today, the twenty-eighth day of the second month, is such a beautiful, clear day. I have been composing poetry in my outer southern studio. The sunlight reflecting through the mountain mist shines on the flowers and trees, while birds flutter up and down in song. What a joyful mood I'm in!" (entry no. 26). There he was again, making his way into my mind as he has done so often. He and I go a long ways back, to my graduate school days at Columbia University in New York City in the late 1970s and early 1980s. We kept steady company for several years, as I worked to translate his Journal to fulfill the requirements for my doctorate. I was drawn to his open confessional manner.

In the years after graduating, I continued some work on his Journal. When the journal *auto:/biography* had a special issue dedicated to the theme of Autobiography and Mysticism (Vol. 6, no. 2, Fall 1991), I contributed a piece, "Writing One's Way to Sagehood: WuYü-pi and his Journal." Around the same time, I presented a paper (still unpublished) on "The Use of Religious Diaries in Self-Cultivation: The Case of WuYü-pi," that included comparisons with Baptist and Quaker diaries of sixteenth-century England.

But other research interests (educational texts for women, children's education, Catholic nuns working with Hakka women in early twentieth-century China), a full teaching load, and family life consumed my time and Wu was left behind on the shelf. He, however, was never completely absent from my life. Students and I pored over his writings in the photocopies I made of my translations. And every once in a while, one of his lines would just come to me, often at the oddest times. (The most frequent being, "Difficulties I am willing to accept as part of life, / But I never thought they would be as extreme as this!" entry 153.)

Several years ago, I finally decided that I really must give Wu the full treatment in book form that he deserved. It has taken me a long time to complete the book—I am more of a turtle than a hare (our family has a thing for turtles; my daughter is training to be a herpetologist). I hope the reader will find Wu as engaging as I have. What I have discovered is that readers react to him along a spectrum of two extremes: some cannot tolerate his negative complaining and find him an incredible whiny bore; others are moved by what they regard as his wonderfully sensitive soul. There are grounds for both reactions. The value I have found of using it in a classroom is that students are given the chance to respond to him first hand, as they will, and also to see that the people trying to put Confucianism into practice were ordinary human beings like themselves.

Before proceeding, I would like to pay tribute to the sage models of my past, those who shaped my intellectual life and inspired my understanding of Confucianism. The first is Thomas Berry, my uncle, who started me on my way in Asian Studies. Next are the outstanding scholars at Columbia University that I had the privilege of studying with, most especially Wm. Theodore de Bary, Wing-tsit Chan, Pei-yi Wu, and Irene Bloom. My debt of gratitude to all of them is immeasurable.

I also wish to express my deep gratitude to Deborah Wilkes, my editor at Hackett, who has been so patient and supportive of me in seeing this book through to its completion. I owe a lot to the steady encouragement she has extended to me over the past two years. I also want to thank Liz Wilson who has overseen the production end of this book, and who too has shown great patience with me.

## Conventions

1.  I use the pinyin system of romanization throughout the book. The one change I make is to hyphenate two-character Chinese terms, instead of putting them together as what appears to be one word. For example: *fu-ren*, instead of *furen*. When it comes to book titles, however, I do not hyphenate.
2.  Because much of the material on Neo-Confucianism was done with the Wade-Giles system of romanization, to help the reader convert the names of people and books according to that system,

I have provided sections in each glossary that convert them into their pinyin rendering.

3. Chinese scholars usually had at least three names. For the sake of simplicity, I refer to each only by one name. Take the case of Zhu Xi, for instance. Wu refers to him by several of Zhu's names, but I refer to him as Zhu Xi all the time.

4. Unless otherwise indicated, all translations from Chinese texts are my own.

# Introduction

In most general studies of Neo-Confucianism, the focus tends to be on the leading thinkers of the Song (960–1279) and Ming (1368–1644) dynasties, such as the Cheng brothers (Cheng Hao and Cheng Yi), Zhu Xi, and Wang Yangming. The dominant emphasis for these major figures is their key philosophical ideas as expressed in their various writings. Except for some personal accounts of Wang Yangming, readers seldom get a glimpse of how scholars struggled with putting their ideas into practice, as there are few extended firsthand accounts of anyone engaged in the daily pursuit of the Neo-Confucian goal of sagehood.

One of the few examples is the Neo-Confucian Wu Yubi (1392–1469) who lived in the early Ming dynasty. He kept a diary that chronicled his pursuit of sagehood, detailing its ups and downs and his progress and backsliding in over 300 entries. His Journal is considered a rare instance of confessional literature in China before the sixteenth century when that genre became the rage. One expert on Chinese autobiographical writing, Pei-yi Wu, attributes the paucity of self-revelatory writing in China before the sixteenth century to the "general inhibition against writing about one's inner life for a public audience" on the part of Confucians. He notes that many Song figures kept diaries, but that they "were nothing more than logbooks of external activities, receptacles of reading notes and anecdotes. For any record of self-examination and self-cultivation, we have to wait until early Ming when Wu Yü-pi wrote what might be described as a subjective diary."[1]

Wu spent most of his life in Jiangxi province, away from the centers of cultural and political activity, engaged in a life of farming and teaching. One of the prime motivations for his keeping a diary stemmed from an earlier experience as a teenager while studying for the civil service exams in

---

1. Pei-yi Wu, *The Confucian's Progress: Autobiographical Writings in Traditional China* (Princeton: Princeton University Press, 1990), p. 93. Wu Yü-pi is Wu Yubi according to the Wade-Giles romanization system.

the capital, Nanjing, where his father held a high position at the National University. While reading a book that might be called a kind of "lives of the Song dynasty Neo-Confucian saints," Wu was seized with an urgency to become a sage just like them. He gave up his academic studies, which would have led to a career as an official, in order to concentrate on the study of the Song masters that would help him realize his own sagehood. His father, enraged at his son's decision, sent him back to the family farm and disowned him. Wu's immediate self-righteousness and fervor soon faded once he was home. With no outer evil to protest, he was faced with the struggle within himself, forced to face his own wayward nature.

Wu floundered for ten years, never, however, giving up the cause. He was finally reconciled with his father, and then, several years later, turned to the practice of keeping a written record of his efforts in the form of a journal. He used it for a variety of reasons but mostly to keep track of his behavior, his progress and his setbacks, his highs and lows. And highs and lows there were. Wu reveals himself to be a high-strung, at times overly emotional person, whose moods shift between darkness and light, depending on his behavior and external circumstances. Wu shared the tendency of many idealists, that is, impatience with the shortcomings of others and, even more so, himself. Judging by the change in tone over the course of the Journal as he aged, the cycling back and forth between moods modulated with time. The Journal, although it did not make him a sage on the level of the Song Neo-Confucians and Confucius, nevertheless contributed to his sense of deeper involvement with life. It wasn't that he ceased having dark moments but that they became less frequent and less intense.

What emerges from the reading of the Journal is the picture of a fascinating Neo-Confucian personality with a lifestyle that was more devotional, confessional, and nature-oriented than we usually associate with Neo-Confucians. As Wu became well known as a teacher in his home province of Jiangxi, he attracted more and more students from a wide range of backgrounds who came to study under him. Among them were three of the leading Confucian thinkers of the next generation, Lou Liang, Hu Juren, and Chen Xianzhang. Students attributed his attraction as a teacher to his skill at opening up students to the material and making his teachings clear, but part of the attraction lay in his frank admission of his own difficulties. In Wu, students found someone who affirmed that their own struggles were not something indicating a defect on their part but were an expected part of the pursuit. He did not present himself as a more accomplished practitioner with quick answers, as the Song Neo-Confucian Zhu Xi had. As Wu's fame grew, he was invited to court to be an advisor to the throne, but he declined. He spent the rest of his life as a teacher, dying at the age of seventy-seven.

Wu was not an intellectual figure of the same heft as the Neo-Confucian masters Zhu Xi and Wang Yangming. He made no contributions to Neo-Confucianism in the areas of philosophy, statecraft, scholarship, or literature. And yet, despite the low-key, unobtrusive, quiet way he went about his practice and teachings, he was chosen by the early-Qing historian of Ming thought, Huang Zongxi (1610–1695), as the first major figure of the Ming in his groundbreaking anthology, *Case Studies of Ming Confucians*: "Just as the Imperial Chariot had its origins in the oxcart, and thick ice comes about by an accumulation of water, so Ming thought could not have flourished without Wu Yubi."[2] Huang saw Wu as the one who provided the link to the transmission of the Confucian Way from the Song to the Ming dynasties, and as someone who merited consideration for his achievements as a teacher.

## Brief Introduction to Neo-Confucianism and to the Ming Dynasty

When we speak of Neo-Confucianism[3] we are referring to the revival in the Song dynasty of the classical Confucian tradition, which had been superseded in influence—though never entirely replaced—by Buddhism and Daoism from the third to the tenth century. The revival was led by

---

2. "Introduction to the Congren School," in *Case Studies of Ming Confucians* (*Mingru xuean*)1:1a.

3. The term Neo-Confucianism is a more recent term of Western origin, and not something that the men we are discussing would have been familiar with. They would not have described themselves as Neo-Confucians. As such, some contemporary scholars shy away from using the term. I use the term for want of a better one and because of its wide usage in the West. But the reader is advised that it is not without its problems. What is more, the revival of Confucianism in the Song was multifaceted and encompassed literature, statecraft, and economics as well as thought. I focus on the Cheng-Zhu school, which is often referred to as *li-xue* 理學, School of Principle, or as *dao-xue* 道學, Learning of the Way. For more on these topics, see the Suggested Further Reading section.

a newly emerging class of literati, a group brimming with talent, energy, idealism, and self-confidence. Partly as a result of the strong challenges posed by Buddhism and partly of the changing political situation in which this new class had emerged, these men sought to reassert the Confucian Dao or Way, a new Confucianism, or, as it has come to be known in the West, Neo-Confucianism. For them, the articulation of this Way had to be broad and comprehensive enough both to answer the competing claims of Buddhism, and also to support the grand enterprise of building a new society they envisioned. It had to be a Way that successfully integrated the social, political, intellectual, cultural, and religious concerns of the human. Over and against the Buddhist notions that this world is illusory and the source of all suffering, it had to assert the reality of this world, especially human society, and the validity of human efforts to build up that society.

The Way that they articulated was that of a cosmic organism, essentially one in nature, in which the heavenly, the natural, and the human realms cohere and are identified with each other. This oneness was spoken of as *li* 理, or principle, when referring to its aspects of rationality, order, and harmony; and as *ren* 仁, humaneness or benevolence, when referring to its affective life-giving and life-connecting qualities. The cosmic Way, like the human mind, is both rational and affective, principle and love, perfect objectivity and perfect subjectivity. Thus a Neo-Confucian would proclaim: "Heaven is my father and Earth is my mother, and even such a small creature as I finds an intimate place in their midst. Therefore that which fills the universe I regard as my body and that which directs the universe I consider as my nature. All people are my brothers and sisters, and all things are my companions."[4]

Corresponding to the reassertion of an all-embracing Way was a new sense of the human person and his role in this Way. Reflecting the great optimism and self-confidence of the new literati class, the human person was seen as having a key role in the proper functioning of the Way: he was no less than a partner with Heaven and earth, no less than a sage. All human beings have the potential for sagehood. Sagehood is what describes the fullest identity of what it means to be human; it is what every person has the innate capacity for, what every person is called to be. The human person has the capacity for sagehood because his mind has been bestowed

---

4. Zhang Zai, "Western Inscription," trans. by W. T. Chan, *Source Book of Chinese Philosophy* (Princeton: Princeton University Press, 1963), p. 497.

by Heaven and earth, and shares in their fundamental rationality and life-giving creativity. The human mind is the source of a person's power to know the oneness of his own being and that of the cosmos, as well as to effect that oneness in the human society around him.

Sagehood was not just a personal matter of the individual but had broad implications for the well-ordered and just society these men sought to bring about. Borrowing a passage from the classical text the *Great Learning*, they insisted that, "From the Son of Heaven (ruler) down to the common people, every single one should regard cultivating the self as the foundation." Even the emperor must regard the pursuit of sagehood and the self-discipline that it entails as his personal responsibility.

In their formulation of these ideas, Neo-Confucians borrowed a good deal from Buddhism, even as they criticized Buddhism and denied any such borrowings. This was especially so in the areas of meditation and meta-physics. In effect, they argued, these ideas had been part of Confucianism all along. The Way is the Way because it is eternal, it operates in all times and in all situations. Just look at the sages and the classical writings of the past, they said. The problem was that the Way has not been transmitted, as it should have been, since the time of the philosopher Mencius (372–289 BCE). Buddhists and Daoists had fooled the people for a long time. But right here and now, they asserted, we can revive it by going back to the sage models of the past and the perennial truths of the written word found in the classics.

So to underscore these assertions, they presented a version of Chinese history that emphasized what they called the "transmission of the Way" (*daotong* 道統) that went like this. Back in ancient times, the sage rulers like Yao and Shun embodied the Way and started benevolent government, ruling wisely and kindly, making sure the people were educated and well-taken care of. The Way revolved around human relationships and the moral conduct appropriate to each. Yao, around 2300 BCE, transmitted this Way to the next ruler, Shun, and Shun to Yu, who became ruler of the first dynasty, the Xia (c.2205–c.1766 BCE). When that dynasty descended into chaos and misrule, King Tang (c.1675–1646 BCE) founded the Shang dynasty and was able to regain the Way; when the Shang was conquered by Kings Wen and Wu of the Zhou (c.11th century BCE), the same thing happened. When the Zhou fell into chaos and seemed to have lost the Way, Confucius (551–479 BCE) came along and did all he could to revitalize it. He had a strong sense of mission to keep alive the work of King

Wen, as seen in this passage from the *Analects:* "The Master was surrounded in Kuang. He said, 'Now that King Wen is gone, is not culture (*wen*) now invested here in me? If Heaven intended this culture to perish, it would not have given it to those of us who live after King Wen's death. Since Heaven did not intend that this culture should perish, what can the people of Kuang do to me?'"[5] After his death, as the Zhou descended into further bloodshed and fighting, Mencius took up where Confucius left off, traveling around to different feudal lords to get them to adopt Confucian measures for humane government in the spirit of Yao, Shun, and Confucius. The very last passage of the *Mencius* text ends with a question: "Is there indeed no one? Again, indeed is there no one?"[6] Commentators are not all in agreement about what exactly Mencius meant here, but the Song Neo-Confucians took it as both a question and a challenge about the transmission of the Confucian Way.

For them, although there were Confucians who tried to practice the Way after Mencius, their efforts were insufficient and the harm done by Buddhism and Daoism too great. They felt called to embrace Mencius' challenge, even though reviving the "real" Way and guaranteeing its pivotal place in society were arduous struggles of epic proportions. Since the amount of time passed had been so long—a thousand years—they were up against great odds. They felt they were up to the task, but doing so would be the stuff of heroes.

The principal architects of the Cheng-Zhu tradition[7] in the early Song were Zhou Dunyi (1017–1073), Zhang Zai (1020–1077), Shao Yong (1011–1077), Cheng Hao (1032–1085), and Cheng Yi (1033–1107). The last two made the greatest contributions in the area of thought. It was Zhu Xi (1130–1200) in the Southern Song who pulled together the various strands of these thinkers' ideas and shaped a comprehensive, multifaceted philosophy of life. He threw himself into a wide range of writing projects to spread these teachings: commentaries on almost all of the classics, reordering the content of some of the classics, editing collections of sayings and biographies of earlier Confucians, devising curriculums of study, and com-

---

5. *Analects* 9:5, trans. by Edward Slingerland, *Confucius Analects, with Selections from Traditional Commentaries* (Indianapolis: Hackett Publishing, 2003), p. 87.

6. *Mencius* 7B:38.

7. Neo-Confucianism was a much broader, multifaceted tradition than I can cover here, so I focus on the Cheng-Zhu school.

posing guidelines for private academies, among other things. He ran afoul of court politics late in his life, and his teachings were proscribed. He died without knowing that his writings would become the basis of all Chinese education and the civil service examination system from the fourteenth to the early twentieth century.

It was the Mongols who conquered Song China and ruled as the Yuan dynasty,[8] who first adopted Zhu Xi's writings. Its founder, Kublai Khan (1215–1294), made use of Neo-Confucian advisors at court. Although he toyed with the idea of reinstituting the civil service examination system, he never did. One of his successors did in 1313 and the required content of the exams was the Four Books[9] and Zhu Xi's commentaries on them. It would be the following Ming dynasty when the Cheng-Zhu school of Neo-Confucianism would take root, from the emperor himself down to the lowest class of people.

The Ming dynasty (1368–1644) was the last dynasty to be ruled by native Chinese, sandwiched between the Yuan dynasty when the Mongols ruled and the Qing dynasty (1644–1912) when the Manchus ruled. It lacked the grandeur of the great Han and Tang dynasties in terms of empire and wealth, but it had its own distinctive flavor. It was one of the more colorful dynasties and exuded a modern energy. It was a period that saw grand ocean expeditions that went as far as east Africa, an expansion in the production of exquisite Ming porcelains, the building of the Great Wall, and the rise of a wealthy merchant class. It was the great age in book publishing, responding to the insatiable demand for books, especially those with color illustrations. In the areas of religion and literature, it witnessed a great celebration of the "self" and human emotions.

Its founder was Zhu Yuanchang (1328–1398), one of the most colorful emperors in Chinese history. Rising from extreme obscurity and poverty to power, he was one of only two emperors who came from the peasant class, the other being the founder of the Han dynasty, Liu Bang. Orphaned as a child, Zhu spent part of his childhood in a Buddhist monastery and rose to power as a participant and then leader of the messianic, anti-dynastic White Lotus rebellions of the 1350s. In 1368, he declared himself emperor

---

8. They conquered north China in 1234 and the rest of China in 1279. The dynasty lasted until 1368.

9. These included the *Great Learning*, *Analects* of Confucius, *Mencius*, and *Practicing the Mean*.

of all of China, calling his dynasty the Ming 明, or "bright," dynasty. Known by his temple name, Ming Taizu 明太祖, he fully embraced the cosmic identity of the role of emperor, the appointed Son of Heaven, who was invested with both secular and sacred responsibilities. More than most founding emperors, he drew heavily upon this status to articulate a new state ideology that effectively legitimized and enshrined his absolute power. He made use of Neo-Confucianism for its public philosophy as well as its institutional framework of schools and the examination system. To his credit, he was a conscientious administrator and did much to alleviate the suffering of the peasants.

For Confucians, there was one major problem. The all-important relationship between ruler and minister, which required a sense of respect and reciprocity on both sides, was not honored. Taizu discarded this relationship insofar as he felt himself to be beyond the demands of reciprocity, accountable to no one. This was most dramatically demonstrated in 1380 when he abolished the whole upper-echelon of the central government, including the prime ministership. He, in effect, became the government. Besides diminishing the power of ministers, Taizu set in motion dynamics of force and terror that once unleashed were never checked throughout the dynasty, including the public humiliation of officials, court beatings, secret police, and purges of officials numbering in the thousands. He visited his cruelty indiscriminately. Few of his advisors enjoyed a natural death. Even the military men who had risen with him to power and to whom he had shown special favors early in his reign were in the end subject to his wrath.

Taizu's death in 1398 created new problems. Early in his reign, he had appointed his eldest son to be his successor. But this son died six years before Taizu did. Operating on the premise that the line of succession must proceed from one generation to the next, he chose his grandson, the oldest son of his oldest son rather than any of his living sons, to succeed him. When he died, his grandson took office as the Jianwen emperor, something Taizu's oldest living son Zhu Di (1360–1424) greatly resented. Under the influence of Confucian advisors, the new emperor tried to move away from the harshness of his grandfather's rule, but his attempts were cut short by the usurpation of the throne by Zhu Di, who installed himself as the Yongle emperor. Following his seizure of power, he had the court scholars rewrite the official court records to fit his account that he was the true heir to the throne. In his reaction to scholars who protested his actions, he proved himself as heavy-handed as his father in their widespread execution. Eager to win over other scholars, he sponsored several large scholarly compilations that he hoped showed himself to be a patron of Neo-Confucianism. As we shall see, Neo-Confucians such as Wu Yubi were faced with the moral issues posed by these two Ming emperors who presented themselves as Confucian sage rulers but whose actions belied their claims.

## The Life of Wu Yubi[10]

Wu Yubi was born on January 6, 1392, in Fuzhou prefecture, Jiangxi province in central China. It was an area with a strong tradition of Neo-Confucian learning, dating from the days when Zhu Xi's disciple and son-in-law, Huang Gan (1152–1221), served as magistrate there. Wu Cheng, the most important Neo-Confucian during the period of Mongol rule, (1249–1333) who lived in this area, noted its tradition of Neo-Confucian learning in a piece entitled, "Record of the Learning of Linchuan County."

Wu Yubi's family proudly traced its identity as Confucian several generations back. Wu's great-great-grandfather was a literary man whose collection of poetry was given a preface by the renowned Wu Cheng. His grandfather moved the family to Chongren county, the next county to the southeast, because the family's fortunes had fallen. It was this grandfather, according to Wu Yubi's *Biographical Account*, who, the night before Wu's birth, dreamed of a vine winding up and around the ancestral graves. When he asked an old man standing near the graves what kind of vine it was, he was told it was "pulling-the-official cart" vine, an allusion to a person who achieves high official rank in government. When Wu Yubi was born the following day, his grandfather gave him the name of Mengxiang (夢 祥) ("Auspicious Dream"), thinking the dream meant that the boy would become a great official. Later this name was changed to Yubi (與 弼), meaning "one who concerns himself with helping and guiding

10. The primary source for Wu's life is the *Biographical Account of Wu Yubi* (*Kangzhai xiansheng xingzhuang*) by Lou Liang upon which most other biographies, such as the ones in *Case Studies in Ming Biographies* and in the *History of the Ming (Mingshi)*, are based. The most extensive biography in English is the entry on him found in the L. Carrington Goodrich and Chao-ying Fang, eds., *Dictionary of Ming Biography* (hereafter DMB) (New York: Columbia University Press, 1976) pp. 1497–1501, which was co-written by Chaoying Fang, Julia Ching, and Huang P'ei.

others."[11] In actual fact, Wu never did become an official; indeed, in his late teens he made a dramatic gesture of rejecting that option. Instead, he became a noted teacher and, not incidentally, a great dreamer of dreams himself.

Although this grandfather did not serve in government, his son and Wu's father, Wu Pu (1363–1426),[12] not only served in office but did so successfully as a high government official in the capital, Nanjing. In 1390, two years before Wu Yubi's birth, Wu Pu was recommended as an examination candidate from Jiangxi province to go to the capital to study for the highest level of the civil service examination. Illness kept him from being able to take advantage of the opportunity. It was three years after Wu's birth, in 1395, that Wu Pu finally was able to go to Nanjing and enroll as a student at the National University, leaving his wife and three children (two daughters and a son) with his wife's family. Wu Yubi's emotional ties remained with his mother's family long after this. Wu Pu won quick notoriety when, in 1400, five years later, he passed first in the metropolitan examinations and fourth in the *jinshi* examination (highest degree possible), two impressive accomplishments that guaranteed him a successful government career right there in the capital at China's power center rather than out in the provinces. His first assignment was as a compiler in the Hanlin Academy, a group of elite scholars that served the emperor for secretarial and scholarly projects. After the usurpation of and then accession to the throne of the Yongle emperor in 1402, Wu's father took part in the rewriting of the imperial annals of the Jianwen reign that, in effect, rewrote the history of the past four years. Later, in 1405, he was promoted to work as one of the assistant editors of the *Great Encyclopedia of the Yongle Era*.

Wu Pu's successes continued when, in 1408, he was appointed to the prestigious position of Director of Studies of the National University by its chancellor, Hu Yan (1361–1443). When the position came open, the emperor is said to have stressed the importance of the position and urged Hu Yan to choose a person whose learning and practice would prove

---

11. Wu's name was probably changed after the remarriage of his father and the birth of three half-brothers, all with the initial name of "Yu."

12. Sources for Wu Pu and his father are "Elegy for the Director of Studies of the National University, Master Wu Pu," by Yang Rong, in *Collected Works of Yang Rong* (*Yang wenmin gong ji*), and "Elegy," by Yang Shiqi in Xu Hong, *Records of the Noble Conduct of Famous Officials of the Ming* (*Ming mingchen wanyan lu*).

exemplary to students. When Wu Pu took over the position, it is said that he restored a seriousness and dedication to the job that his immediate predecessors had not given it. In contrast to those who had only showed up for work every now and then, and had not seriously taught or examined the students on their progress, Wu Pu was there each day from early morning, "sitting in a dignified posture without any unbecoming comportment. The various students all had great respect for him and gave their hearts to him."[13] In his lectures, he not only sought to explain the principles of things but also to encourage a questioning attitude that would lead to self-reflection and self-appropriation of the material on the part of the student. Wu Pu would remain Director of Studies for eighteen years, until his death in 1426.

In 1402, after having passed his exams and gained an official position, Wu Pu sent for his son, Yubi, to come to Nanjing to live with him. Wu Yubi, by Western reckoning, was ten at the time.[14] The Nanjing that he came to was not a city of peace and tranquility—just the opposite. As discussed earlier, a civil war had raged there between 1400 and 1402, when the uncle of the reigning emperor rebelled in an attempt to usurp the throne. With his success in doing so, he proclaimed himself the Yongle 永樂 emperor, the emperor of "lasting peace." But he was vengeful in victory, carrying out bloody purges of those Confucian scholar-officials who protested his usurpation of power and who defiantly asserted that his rule was illegitimate. Aware of the need not to alienate the whole Confucian community but rather to enlist their support to overcome the shadow of illegitimacy, Yongle cast himself in the role of patron of Confucianism by sponsoring large scholarly projects, involving the compilation of authoritative editions of Confucian classics. These big projects, he reasoned, would keep scholars too busy to criticize him. This divided Confucians among themselves: Could one in good conscience serve this emperor or not? This was to be a hot issue that divided Wu Yubi and his father, who was part of the inner circle that worked for Yongle.

---

13. Yang Rong, "Elegy," *Collected Works of Master Yang Rong*, p. 954.

14. By Chinese reckoning, Wu Yubi was twelve. In China, a person is considered one year old at birth. Everybody is considered one year older on New Year's Day. Since Wu was born near the end of the year, he was actually considered two years old when he was only about a month old by Western reckoning.

With Nanjing astir with controversy, Wu Pu must have been anxious to start taking a more active role in his son's education to pick such a time to have his brother, Wu Chongxue, escort his son to the capital to live with him. He had high hopes for his son in terms of his future career prospects, but he was just as concerned to be personally involved in his son's moral formation. When Yubi was much younger, his father had written him this poem when he was leaving for Nanjing in 1395.

> You, Mengxiang, are just now five years old,[15]
> And already know how to recite passages from poetry and literature.
> Though affection among brothers is important,
> Teacher-student decorum must be strict.
> Engaging in study requires that one be intimately involved.
> The path can have no circuitous ways.
> Hence, if you can be diligent in your learning,
> In the end, you should become a noble Confucian.[16]

When Yubi and his father were first reunited, according to Yubi's account, it was highly emotional for both father and son in that neither recognized the other at first.

> It was only when I was twelve years old that Uncle took me to the capital to be with you. But you and I, father and son, didn't recognize each other at first. During the time I lived in the capital, you once told me at night in bed, "In the past, while I was away from home, I often thought of you, but not being able to see you, I was moved to shed many tears. Now that you are here with me, you must exert your efforts to advance in your learning, striving to become a mature and accomplished person." (CW 8:13a, Letter 1)

Soon after his arrival in Nanjing, Wu Yubi got word of his mother's death. Having spent much time with his mother's side of the family after

---

15. Recall that Mengxiang was the name given to him at birth by his grandfather and used by the family while he was very young, and that by Western reckoning he was only three years old.

16. *Collected Works of Wu Yubi* (hereafter CW) 4:31a–b. Wu included this poem in a note appended to a New Year's day poem he wrote in 1457 remembering his father.

his father left for the capital, he was much more emotionally attached to that side of the family. It grieved him that he was not able to see his mother's grave until his return home much later. He remained close to his maternal grandmother, who outlived his mother, as can be seen by the concern he shows about escorting her home in his famous 1421 letter to his father (Letter 1), and also in an elegy written upon her death where he expressed his deep gratitude for the boundless affection she had shown for him since his childhood. His father remarried not long after Wu's mother's death and had three more sons, half-brothers to Wu. Wu Yubi's biographer commented, "He served his father with perfect filial piety, he served his step-mother as if she were his own mother, and he treated his half-brothers as if they were friends."[17]

From 1402 on, Wu Yubi pursued his studies, as all young men at the time, with the goal of passing the civil service exams with high scores in order to secure a prestigious job in the government hierarchy. With his father's connections at the National University, he had the benefit of some of the best teachers around. One of them, Yang Pu (1372–1446), would eventually become one of the top officials in the whole government. These years were fraught with tension in the relationship between father and son. In temperament they were as different as day and night: the father was scholarly, ambitious, and highly disciplined; the son was dreamy, highly emotional, and mercurial. From Wu's own accounts of these years as a teenager, he says he was pulled between the noble ambitions of his father and a rebellious spirit that flouted Confucian values.

> When I got to be eighteen and nineteen, even though I was fairly good at my studies, still, since I was overly self-confident and pushy, I would boast to myself that to match the achievements of the ancients was not all that difficult. I would frequently slight the men of the past and carry out my affairs carelessly and disrespectfully. (CW 8:13b, Letter 1)

This kind of behavior occasioned frequent rebukes and punishment from his father.

As for the exams he was studying to pass, Wu struggled to make sense of them and the civil service system itself. These exams required mastery

---

17. *Records of the Words and Deeds of Ming Confucians* (*Mingru yanxinglu*) 13:10b.

of the Confucian classics, the underlying rationale being that government officials need to be smart, capable, and, most importantly, moral. If they studied the classics and knew them backwards and forwards, it was assumed that the moral teachings of the classics would rub off on them, making them noble in character. In fact, the competition to pass was extremely great and a fair amount of cheating took place. Wu increasingly became alienated from both the city of Nanjing and the "exam game."

At the beginning of 1410, everything dramatically changed for Wu. Near the end of 1409, as Wu later described it,[18] he came across a book of Song biographies, *Record of the Origins of the School of the Two Chengs*, which someone had sent his father. Casually picking the book up for a quick glance, he found, much to his surprise, that he was drawn into it. The more he read, the more absorbed he became. Here were the courageous heroes who had rescued the Way from a thousand years of oblivion when Daoism and Buddhism had dominated Chinese philosophical and religious life. They had responded to Mencius' question, "Is there anyone who will continue the transmission of the Way?"

Of all of them, Cheng Hao was regarded by many as the most heroic in this regard. But what was Wu reading about him? Cheng Hao had a love of hunting, something he wasn't proud of and wished to overcome. He was fairly confident that he had done so. But his teacher, Zhou Dunyi, voiced his doubt that he had indeed eliminated it, suspecting he had merely repressed it. Sure enough, sometime later when Cheng happened upon a group of men out hunting, he felt the tug of his old passion, and realized how perceptive his teacher had been and how foolishly he had assumed the ease of overcoming personal weaknesses.

This came as a bolt of lightning for Wu. Could it really be that the sages he regarded as having been born perfect had actually started out no different from himself? That they had had to struggle and became sages only after much study and effort? Suddenly, the crassness of spending one's life trying to pass exams and compete for official positions repelled Wu. He felt that his life had changed dramatically and his life's purpose was now clear. He would devote all his time and efforts to the pursuit of sagehood. He abruptly announced to his father that he was giving up all attempts to study for and sit for the exams. In a grand gesture, he burned all his

---

18. See "'Colophon' to the *Record of the Origins of the School of the Two Chengs*" where he describes this experience.

practice sheets and essays and shut himself upstairs in his father's house. There he obsessively pored over the writings and biographies of the Song Confucian masters:

> Thereupon he abandoned his study for the civil service examinations, gave up involvement in worldly affairs, and secluded himself in an upper room. He exhaustively pored over the Four Books, the Five Classics, and the recorded conversations of the Song masters, trying to comprehend them experientially with his whole self—body and mind.[19]

Finally, when his father had had enough of Wu's behavior, he sent him home and ordered that he get married. He was furious at his son's decision and went so far as to disown him. To Wu Yubi's distress, his father broke off all communication with him. Ten years would pass before Wu Pu agreed to see him and they reconciled. Part of Wu's behavior was no doubt motivated by a fear that his son's decision was a veiled criticism of the Yongle emperor and a refusal to serve an illegitimate ruler (and not so indirectly, a criticism of Wu Pu himself for having served this emperor). If so, or even if simply perceived as so, Wu Pu's own life and that of his family would be in jeopardy. According to Ming scholar Fang Chao-ying, "His father must have been thoroughly alarmed by this declaration (of Wu Yubi's not to serve), which, if discovered, could mean death to the entire family. So he kept Wu Yü-pi secluded for two years, and when the son would not repent, sent him home, and severed the relationship."[20]

Wu himself, however, never explicitly mentions the usurpation as his reason for giving up public life, which, if true, could not have been spoken openly as long as Yongle was still alive. Some indication that an element of protest may have been involved can be found in the third entry of his Journal: he raises the question of the culpability of Emperor Taizong (r. 976–997) of the Song dynasty for the death of his elder brother, Song Taizu,

---

19. *Case Studies of Ming Confucians* 1:1a, and *Biographical Account of Master Wu Yubi* 10:7b. Elsewhere Wu Yubi also attributes his decision to heeding the last passage of the *Mencius* text, "Is there no one to continue it?": "When I was around eighteen or nineteen, I read about Cheng Hao's love for the hunt and realized my path of error had to be changed. I read the last section of *Mencius* and realized that keeping up with the swift-moving carriage of the Way was a difficult challenge" CW 10:14b.

20. Fang Chao-ying, "Wu Yü-pi," in DMB, p. 1498.

and his subsequent accession to the throne in the place of the heir apparent. Yongle had died the year earlier in 1424 and been given the temple name of Taizong, which would give some weight to this being a veiled criticism.

Wu returned to the countryside anxious to embrace his new life, dedicated to realizing this vague and dreamy ideal of becoming a sage. He had his lofty ambition before him, and now he was away from the evil influences of the capital with all its political intrigue and hypocrisy. But to his shock and dismay, things were not as he expected them to be. He came face-to-face with the demands of making a living for himself and his new wife with very limited financial resources. His sole recourse was to farm his family's land. At the time he had only a smattering of the "will" and the "know-how" to make a living. He was deeply naive about life and its realities. It was as if he assumed that having committed himself to becoming a sage, all of life's messiness would disappear and he would not have to be pestered by all the tiny irritating details of daily life. Giving up life as an official had economic repercussions. Chinese officials were granted regular stipends of grain, had their taxes reduced, and were not liable for corvée labor.

Even more distressing were the realities of his own disposition, which did not take easily to the discipline necessary for pursuing a life of sagehood. He couldn't believe he was unable to get hold of himself as he thought he would: "At that time, I hardly understood the methods of learning to be a sage or worthy, yet I bragged to myself that there was no great difficulty in reaching the level of the ancients" (CW 10:2a). He found himself pulled back and forth between the ideal life that was so tantalizing and the realities of everyday life that were so prosaic. As unforeseen problems emerged in the actualization of his new commitment to becoming a sage, Wu spent the first nine years struggling between the realities of having to make a living and the desire to be a sage, bouncing back and forth between what might be considered vague, dreamy goals and the very concrete struggles to keep a roof over his family and food on the table. He expresses this tension in a poem he wrote:

> Engaged in my studies, I neglect my hoe and plow;
> Working at farming, I am remiss with my reading.
> When idle in my studies, my mind and nature are thrown into disorder;
> When lazy about farming, I find starvation and the cold press in on me.
> Of these two responsibilities, I must regard both as important,

With the hope that I might each day make progress in both.
What shall I do about these ailments that tie me up?
I stumble along as the night turns to day. (CW 2:4a–b)

The year 1421 marked an important breakthrough for Wu in several areas of his life. We have a number of letters he wrote in this year to former teachers and friends,[21] stating his new understanding of what the sagely enterprise is all about, and the fruitful progress he has made by focusing on the Four Books. In these letters he shares his struggles and successes with these men, grateful for their help and support. In his first poem of the New Year, he speaks of making Yan Hui, Confucius' favorite disciple, his model. Confucius' admiration for Yan Hui stemmed from the fact that Yan lived in mean circumstances yet loved to learn and maintained a joyful appreciation for life. But Wu is sad that he operates with the twin handicaps of having been born so much later in time and having such a weak disposition.

The other important milestone in Wu's life, which is also related to his newfound understanding of himself and sagehood, was his reconciliation with his father. Of the many challenges Wu had faced since returning to the country, one of the heaviest burdens was the continued alienation of his father. In 1420, nine years after Wu had been sent home, he got up the courage to travel to Nanjing to make a personal appeal for reconciliation with his father. Despite the distance Wu had traveled and his daily pleadings once he arrived, Wu Pu remained adamant in his refusal to see his son. Wu Yubi was forced to give up:

> Last year, in the sixth month, I came to wait upon you, hoping to get one glimpse of your face. I wished to report in full what had been happening these past ten years since I had left the capital for home, thinking I would rouse myself to action from that time on. But my offenses were so great that your mind remained unchanged and you refused to see me. Filled with great sorrow, I returned home. Is there any place in the world were one can be without a father? Truly I was like "a poor man who has no real home to which to return." (CW 8:13b–4a, Letter 1)

---

21. See "Letters and Miscellaneous from Wu Yubi's *Collected Works*" for translations of these letters.

Wu set out again in the spring of 1421 to make another attempt at reconciliation, using the excuse of escorting his maternal grandmother home from Nanjing. Before he left, he had a dream of his father that left him crying. He wrote this poem:

> Rivers and mountains have separated me from home for a long
>     time.
> How could I have been able to care for you in even the
>     simplest way?
> Right now I am confused as to where I am.
> In my dream, I stand before you, catching a glimpse of your face.
> I doubt not that your natural disposition is a loving one.
> This makes my deep love for you start me crying.
> I weep and weep and cannot stop.
> Rising at dawn, I find my gown is still damp from tears.
>     (CW 1:22a)

En route to Nanjing, Wu got cold feet, fearing another rejection. He got as far as the point of transfer for a ship on the Yangzi River bound for Nanjing when he froze. Indecisive about what he should do, he neither boarded the ship to Nanjing nor returned home. Instead he took a ship going west, in the opposite direction. His dreams of his father continued, like this one that he described in a poem:

> I wish to write down the painful feelings of separation,
> Without words, it is hard to begin to write.
> What day will I finally receive the joy of seeing you?
> In my dream I catch a brief glimpse of your face. (CW 1:24a)

Soon he realized that it was harvest time and he must return home in time to harvest his crops. He found a friend on board headed for Nanjing who promised to deliver a letter to his father in person, a letter that was both lengthy and highly emotional.[22] It included a report on his behavior and his admission that he had often been at fault in the past:

---

22. For a full translation of the letter, from which I have been quoting sections of, see Letter 1 in "Letters and Miscellaneous."

> Since the beginning of this year, I have been reading the Four Books a great deal, not letting up for even a moment. I have some sense that my whole self—body and mind—has benefited from this in its own rough way. In my efforts at sharing the lot of the sages and worthies, I have made a good beginning. Only now do I realize why Heaven inflicted poverty and sickness on me and why you scolded and admonished me for my behavior. What a great blessing for me! (CW 8:14a–b, Letter 1)

The way Wu Yubi reports to his father suggests that part of the disaffection between father and son stemmed from Wu's somewhat erratic and half-hearted ways upon his return home to the country. Wu Pu's reputation as Director of Studies was that of a stern and exacting teacher, and he no doubt was even more exacting with his own sons, especially his eldest who had publicly professed his pursuit of sagehood. That Wu Pu was concerned about Yubi's behavior is also suggested by a letter from a friend of Wu Pu's which Yubi came across late in his life. The friend had written Wu Pu to assure him about his son:

> Some time ago, I had a talk with your son, Yubi, for several hours. In searching out his inner state of mind, I discovered he was the type of person, described by Mencius, who could not be bent or moved by force or might, poverty or riches. While at the present moment, he is beset with difficulties, at a later time he certainly will achieve something great. So don't worry about him. (CW 11:38b)

At the end of 1421, Wu went again to Nanjing. This time he was received by his father in a happy reunion. Wu's poems at the end of the year reflect a joyful, optimistic tone. He speaks of the progress and good fortune he has experienced in the year just ending and his desire to leap into the New Year, fresh with new resolve to make even greater progress in his moral cultivation.

Wu's relationship with his father continued to improve in the ensuing years as is evident in the four letters he wrote his father (see Letters 12a–d) until Wu Pu's death in 1426. The most striking evidence is that Wu Pu sent his three younger sons, Yubi's half-brothers, to the country to study with him in 1423. He also entrusted Yubi with the family genealogy, his books, and his personal papers, including letters from relatives and friends. Wu Yubi, for his part, continued to record dreams about his father in his poetry and took on the education of his brothers. When his father died, Wu Pu's biographer noted, "Known to have had little money and to have shared even that little bit with less fortunate relatives, his family had to depend on his colleagues to help pay for his burial."[23] It was a great source of embarrassment for Wu and his brothers that they could not do better for their father in terms of his burial.

Wu started keeping his Journal in 1425, although he gives no indication why he started it at that particular point in his life. Indeed, he never says anything about why he decided to keep one at all. In 1428, he moved to a place called Xiaopo, which remained his home until his death (except for the years 1440–1442). In the late 1420s and 1430s we begin to hear mention of his children. He had one son and three daughters. From the evidence of his poetry, his relationship with his children was much closer than what he had shared with his father. He speaks of taking his daughters on outings in the fall to pick fruit, of listening to them playing the lute, and of teaching them the *Analects*.[24] His son, Xuanqing 璿慶, is even more frequently mentioned. Wu describes the joys of teaching him lessons and harmonizing on the lute with him. One of the earliest poems about his son is entitled, "Xuanqing Reads at Night. In My Joy, I Wrote This Poem to Encourage Him in His Studies":

> At eight years old, you understand about being earnest in study.
> Burning the night oil, we find it is past the second watch (9:00–11:00 p.m.).
> Sagely results come from beginnings like this.
> As Confucius said, "The Way is only made great by us humans." (CW 2:28b–29a)[25]

When traveling, Wu kept his son close by his side. On one occasion when his son lost some money on a trip, rather than scold him Wu tried to console him, telling him that the learning of the former sages was more important than money (CW 2:42a–b). In Wu's old age, he entrusted much of his teaching responsibilities to Xuanqing.

---

23. "Elegy," in *Records of the Noble Conduct of Famous Officials of the Ming* 23:18b.

24. For references to his daughters, see CW 2:24a, 2:25a, 2:24b, and 11:18b.

25. Reference to *Analects* 15:29. For other poems about teaching his son, see CW 2:35b, 2:40a, 3:15b, and 3:16a.

As a rule, Chinese men made little mention of their wives in their writings, and Wu is no exception. But his biographer noted, "He loved his wife and treated her with great respect, that is, with the manners befitting a guest. There was no rudeness or overfamiliarity."[26] Among the times he mentions her in his writings, once was for her help in allowing him to maintain his studies: "The past several nights we have lacked oil for the lamp, so my poor wife has been burning firewood to provide light for my reading" (no. 117). Another time, he writes a letter to his best friend Hu Jiushao to ask him to accompany him to take his wife for medical help in the next town over.

The years until 1440 remained more or less quiet ones for Wu, preoccupied as he was with his family, farm, and students. One biographer describes these years thus:

> During his middle years, his household was poor. He had inadequate food and clothing, and no protection from inclement weather. Engaged firsthand in the farming, he had calluses on his hands and feet.[27]

Another account mentions that "In his coming and goings, the Master wore coarse garments and old shoes such that people didn't even know that he was the son of the Director of Studies of the National University. He lived in the country, did his own plowing, and ate by the means of his own labor. If anything was not in the least bit according to moral principles, he would not do it. If it wasn't from his own labor, he wouldn't eat it."[28]

In 1440, Wu moved temporarily to Chonghu, his family seat in the next county, to tend the family graves and to lecture in the local schools. By this time, he was beginning to emerge as a public figure and respected teacher and was thus honored at his arrival by a formal greeting by the magistrate of Linchuan. In this period we find a dramatic increase in the number of prefaces and commemorative and occasional pieces and poems, given to officials, students, and families of students, accompanied by a definite shift in tone from a more private and reflective to a more public, formal one. Already in 1421, we have evidence from the letters he sent to friends and

---

26. *Records of the Words and Deeds of Ming Confucians* 3:10a–b.

27. *Biographical Account of Wu Yubi* 10:8a.

28. Ibid.

local education officials that he was interested in the role of teacher. Both of his sisters were married to education officials with whom he exchanged letters about programs of self-cultivation. He seemed to have begun his career as a teacher gradually, with no specific starting date. Students from his local area started coming to him. Gradually, as his reputation spread, he began attracting a greater number of students from a wider area. Students often came to him upon the recommendation of officials in their home areas, as was the case with Lou Liang and Zhou Wen, who were sent in 1448 by the Prefect of their hometown to study under Wu.

In the years following his return to Xiaopo late in 1442, Wu devoted much of his time to his son, students, and visitors, teaching them and taking them on outings to local scenic spots, family graves, and Chan temples. In his poems, there is a note of joy and celebration of life not found in such abundance in his earlier life. Nevertheless, he continued to complain about poor health and frequent illnesses, though rarely mentioning anything specific. In 1453, he undertook a major trip to Nanjing for medical care. He gives us no details about his condition. There are no Journal entries for these middle years.

As Wu became well known as a respected teacher, he began to receive recommendations for public office. While the principal access to government positions was through the civil service examination system, some positions were filled on the basis of strong recommendations by noted officials. The first recommendation Wu received came in 1446 from Mr. He Zixuan, Assistant Surveillance Commissioner for Shanxi province. In his letter petitioning the emperor, He noted that Wu Yubi was the son of the former Director of Studies of the National University, was a master of classical learning, and a man of impeccable conduct. Wu had not been ambitious for public office, He wrote, but now that he was over fifty years of age, the government should avail itself of his services before he became too old to serve. The emperor should also note the fact that Wu ran a private school that charged no tuition and that his students all tried to emulate him out of admiration.[29]

---

29. The text of this and the other four recommendations for office can be found in the *Collected Works of Master Wu Yubi, with Appended Sources*. The Appended Sources section contains various primary materials associated with Wu's career. Hereafter I will refer to it as "Appended Sources," CW. The summary of He's recommendation here is from 8a–b.

Although the Imperial Court responded positively to this and subsequent recommendations by other officials made in 1450, 1452, and 1454 by sending Wu official invitations to court, Wu turned them all down. Finally, when recommended in 1457 by the general Shi Heng (d. 1460), he decided to accept. The Chinese political situation in the 1450s found the Imperial Court in an awkward situation. When Emperor Yingzong had been captured in battle by the Mongols in 1449, the government did not fight to get him back. Rather, they put his brother on the throne as the Daizong emperor. When the Mongols decided they did not want the emperor, they sent him back. The court did not know what to do with him, however, since his brother was now the emperor. The government solved the problem by putting the Yingzong emperor under house arrest. General Shi Heng had been one of the prime movers in the coup of 1456 known as the "forcing of the palace gate," in which the Yingzong emperor was restored to the throne and the Daizong emperor put under house arrest (where he died soon afterward). The Yingzong emperor then, in a surprise move, turned on many who had helped restore him to the throne. "Early acts of injustice made the first years of his reign unpopular. It seems he tried to improve his image. His choice of Hsüeh Hsüan and Li Hsien as grand secretaries met with approval. After Hsüeh Hsüan retired in the middle of 1457, the emperor sought another respected Confucianist and found him in the person of the country teacher Wu Yü-pi."[30]

The imperial invitation to court arrived at Wu's home late in the year of 1457.[31] After a round of formalities with local officials, friends, and family, Wu set out for Beijing (the capital had changed from Nanjing to Beijing in 1421) in the third month of 1458 and arrived there two months later. The day after he arrived, he had his first audience with the emperor and was offered the position of Tutor to the Heir Apparent in the Directory of Instruction, a largely ceremonial job. He declined the offer. The emperor is then said to have remarked to Wu, "For a long time now, I have heard

---

30. DMB pp. 292–93. In the pinyin romanization system, Hsüeh Hsüan is Xue Xuan, Li Hsien is Li Xian, and Wu Yü-pi is Wu Yubi.

31. Text of the invitation letter can be found in "Appended Sources," CW. The following account of Wu's trip to court is based on material from *Biographical Account of Wu Yubi* (10:9b–11a), Wu's biography in the *History of the Ming* 282:3171, the *Case Studies of Ming Confucians,* and Li Zhi's biography of Wu in the *Continuation of the Book to Be Hidden Away (Xu cangshu).*

about your lofty virtue and have especially invited you to come here. Why won't you accept the office?" Wu responded:

> Your humble servant is just a common, lowly person. I have had many infirmities since my youth and so have hidden my traces away in mountains and forests. Basically I have no lofty behavior of which to speak. It was only due to the spreading of a reputation which exceeds the reality that I have been mistakenly put forward in the recommendation papers. That you should have been misled by these reports, sending me an official invitation with gifts of silk right to my door, has caused me unbearable shame. I must firmly decline your generous offer. This year I am sixty-eight years old and really cannot assume the duties of office.[32]

Reassuring Wu that the office provided plenty of leisure and was not too taxing, the emperor showered Wu with gifts and had him escorted to the government hostel. Among the gifts were eight bolts of silk, wine, lamb, and grain. He then turned to Li Xian, his grand secretary, and remarked, "This old fellow is not so out of it as people say. Convince him to accept the office." Wu continued to send memorials to the throne,[33] declining the office and asking for permission to return home. A week after his arrival, Wu gave a lecture to the inner court on his favorite text, *Practicing the Mean*. After this he submitted another memorial in which he requested leave to return home as well as permission to see the books in the Imperial Library before he left. Neither request was granted.

Finally, after two months in the capital, physically ill and homesick, Wu had his son appeal to the Board of Civil Office on his behalf. The grand secretary, Li Xian, thereafter convinced the emperor that Wu could not be forced to stay, and that the proper thing to do would be to let him memorialize once more for permission to return home. Wu did so early in the eighth month, and his request was granted. In his last audience, the emperor presented him with an imperial letter ordering that he be provided with a stipend of grain for life, and had an imperial messenger escort him back to Jiangxi. One account describes how the emperor impressed upon the messenger the need to take special care of Wu on the trip back

---

32. Li Zhi, *Continuation of the Book to Be Hidden Away, juan* 21, pp. 416–17.

33. All of his memorials to the throne, four in number, are included in CW 8:1a–4a.

since he was old and sickly, and since the weather would be getting colder, travel would be more difficult. Before Wu left, he submitted a memorial of Ten Maxims for Sagely Government. Drawing on passages from the classics and the works of the Song masters, Wu appealed to the emperor to take seriously his responsibility to be a sage emperor like Yao and Shun, and to put these maxims into practice right away.

Wu arrived back home in Jiangxi in the middle of the tenth month of 1458, after a short stay in Nanjing along the way. Once home, there followed another round of ceremonials with the imperial messenger, friends, and officials. In the following year, Wu sent a student with his formal letter of thanks to the emperor.

Wu's journey to Beijing and his refusal of office generated controversy both during his lifetime and afterward.[34] Some criticized him for accepting the invitation, citing Zhu Xi's criticism of Yang Shi in the Song dynasty for having emerged from retirement late in life to serve under the much criticized minister Cai Jing. To this, the most famous Ming Neo-Confucian, Wang Yangming countered that neither Yang nor Wu Yubi had anything to be ashamed of in going to court.[35] Others attacked Wu for accepting the patronage of a person like Shi Heng, as he implicitly did when he wrote a colophon for Shi's family genealogy in which he declared him his patron.[36] Shi fell in disgrace shortly after Wu left the capital and died in prison in 1460. To these critics, the late–Ming radical Li Zhi (1527–1602) responded that at least Shi appreciated Wu:

> Some regard the Master's recommendation for position by Shi Heng as a shameful thing. They do not realize that during the previous reign of Jingtai, others had dispatched official messengers to invite the Master to court. Shi Heng was not the first. That Shi Heng even appreciated the Master's virtue was better than later people who were envious of his virtue.[37]

---

34. The other major criticism about Wu had to do with the family's ancestral grave property. Stories circulated that Wu had sued his younger brother and had appeared in court, disrespectfully dressed in commoner's clothes. See DMB pp. 1499–1500 for a discussion of the accusations and the realities of the situation.

35. Mentioned in *Records of the Words and Deeds of Ming Confucians* 3:13a–b.

36. This colophon appears in CW 12:2a–b. In it Wu signs himself a *men-xia-ren* 門下 人, or protégé of Shi Heng.

37. *Continuation of the Book to Be Hidden Away*, juan 21, p. 417.

Still others, the most strident of whom was Yin Zhi (1427–1511), criticized Wu for going and not accepting office. They claimed he was holding out for a position more prestigious than Tutor to the Heir Apparent. When he was not successful in his attempt, according to Yin, Wu refused to have any position at all, returning home more arrogant and proud than before.[38]

Wu's own explanation was that he had gone to court to express his gratitude to the emperor, not wishing to be thought ungrateful for the favors bestowed on him. His refusal to stay was only because of sickness and old age. Some of his biographers added that Wu was also not so naïve about the political situation and what his acceptance might entail.

> Now the Master realized that Shi Heng would inevitably fall from power. Therefore he maintained his purity and aloofness from the situation. When he returned to the south, people asked him why he had not stayed. He answered, "I merely wished to preserve my nature and destiny."[39]

Wu's student and biographer Lou Liang commented that Wu had earnest affection for the emperor and that declining office was not a matter of refusing to spread the learning of the former sage kings, but that it was the only possible thing for him to do at this time. Wu was immensely affected by the whole event, as is quite evident in the number of poems written in the two to three years afterward with titles that ran along the line of "Recalling What Happened on This Day in 1458 While in the Capital."[40]

Wu returned home with even greater prestige and a guaranteed income, enabling him to spend the last eleven years of his life in more comfort and leisure. Even so, it was said that he continued to wear commoner's clothes and plow his fields. During this time, he continued to accept students, placing his son in charge of them during his absences. He had the added joy of becoming a grandfather, taking delight with his grandchildren on outings with his students and relaxing with them in his Pavilion of the

---

38. Yin Zhi, *Record of Bits and Pieces Put Together by Yin Zhi*, p. 891. See DMB, p. 1500, for a rebuttal of Yin's claim.

39. *Case Studies of Ming Confucians* 1:2a. That is, to preserve his integrity from the corruption of court life. Here "nature" refers to his personal integrity and "destiny" to the context in which his nature is developed and expressed.

40. See his poetry for the years 1459 and 1460, CW 6:1a–12b, especially 6:2a–b and 6:7b–10a.

Self-at-Ease. From 1461 to 1466 he traveled extensively, surely made possible by his greater wealth and prestige. The most emotional and fulfilling of these trips was in 1462 to pay his respects at the birthplace of his hero Zhu Xi in Qianyang, Fujian province. He also did a great deal of traveling in his own locality in central Jiangxi, visiting friends, officials, and ancestral graves.[41]

From 1467 until his death in 1469, Wu stayed close to home. As his eyesight was failing (he had always had trouble with his eyes), he reported that he was unable to do very much reading. Instead, we find once again a more reflective tone and a sudden increase in the number of entries in his Journal. A certain somber tone is present, due in part to the death of several of his good friends during this period, especially Hu Jiushao.[42] Wu himself died late in 1469, at the age of seventy-nine (seventy-seven, by Western reckoning). He was honored by the locals as Master Pingjun ("Invited Scholar" 聘君), a reference to his having been invited to court in his lifetime, an honor that bestowed prestige to the area. He was buried in the family graves in 1472.

As was usually the case when a Chinese scholar died, his various writings were collected and published as his *Collected Works*. In addition, someone, usually a person close to the scholar, would write a "biographical account" (*xingzhuang* 行狀). Wu's student Lou Liang published the *Biographical Account of Master Wu Yubi* at the request of Wu's son in 1488, nineteen years after his death. Lou's work provided the basis for most of the later biographies of Wu. As for the collection of his writings, the *Collected Works of Master Wu Yubi,* the first edition was published around 1494, under the direction of Wu Dai, the prefect of Fuzhou. In his preface to the work, Wu describes how, when he first took his new job as prefect in the area, he went to pay his respects to Wu Yubi's grave and requested Wu's son to collect his father's writings for publication.[43]

This first edition of the *Collected Works* did not fare well, parts were lost and parts had errors. Neither did the shrine at Wu's grave: it burned down, and his family's poverty prevented them from restoring it. In 1526, thirty-seven years after his death, the shrine was rebuilt and designated by

---

41. The poems in CW for 1461–1466 reflect his great joy and delight and include a set of poems for each trip (6:13a–48b, 7:1a–34a).

42. The poems in his last years are also more somber and reflective (CW 7:34a–46b).

43. "Appended Sources," CW 22b–23a.

the Jiajing emperor as "Shrine Honoring a Confucian Scholar." That same year, by order of the governor of the province, Wu's *Collected Works* were republished, in twelve *juan* (fascicle) instead of the original four *juan*. Xu Dai, an Investigating Censor, was commissioned to write the preface to the new edition. In it, Xu describes some of the history of the text and the shrine. He also speaks of the merits of Wu's writings:

> Students who wish to commit themselves to his purpose and study his teachings must examine this collection of his writings. It is a real example of a literary contribution to this age: indeed, it is worthy of being transmitted along with the records of the Cheng brothers and Zhu Xi. With the publication and transmission of his writings, his name will not be forgotten, and the influence of the Master's virtue will be handed down.[44]

For Wu Yubi as a commoner to have received such a designation for his shrine from the emperor was a great honor. Nonetheless, two of his students, Hu Juren and Chen Xianzhang, were given even higher honors. In 1584, they were placed in the official Confucian temple and given posthumous titles, honors not accorded their teacher. According to Zou Yuanbiao (1551–1624), a follower of Wang Yangming, Wu's having been left out of the official Confucian temple was a source of some controversy in his time. His own view was that whether or not Wu was enshrined did not take away from his worth as a moral man. For Zou the whole notion of society even presuming to make such judgments of who was or wasn't worthy of enshrinement ran contrary to the very nature of sagehood.[45] The radical Li Zhi, who had defended Wu Yubi with respect to the Shi Heng criticisms, spoke in Wu's favor in this matter as well. "The Master's character and learning were superior to Hu Juren's a hundred times over, but in the Confucian temple sacrifices, Wu is left out and Hu is included. How could this be?"[46]

---

44. Preface, *Collected Works of Wu Yubi* (Siku quanshu zhenbu edition) 4a–b.

45. *Collected Works of Zuo Yuanbiao* (Yuanxue ji) 4:20a–b.

46. *Continuation of the Book to Be Hidden Away, juan* 21, p. 417.

# Notes on the Translation

## Brief Introduction to the Translations

*This translation section is devoted primarily to that of the Journal of Wu Yubi, but also includes a selection of his letters and miscellaneous pieces.*

As for the specific form the Journal took, it consists of 328 entries, dating from 1425 when Wu was thirty-three to the year of his death in 1469 when he was seventy-seven. It appears as *juan* 11 in his *Collected Works*. Very few entries are dated for the actual day and month. I have numbered the entries, although the original text does not. The bulk of them (201 out of 328) come from the middle period of his life, 1425 to 1436. There are no entries at all between the years 1437 and 1448, nor for the years 1450, 1458, and 1459. Indeed, the entries for the years 1449 to 1466 altogether are few in number. The number of entries picks up considerably for the last three years of his life, from 1467 to 1469. There are forty-nine entries for these final three years compared to seventy-seven for the seventeen-year period from 1449 to 1466. This increase no doubt reflects the fact that Wu had settled down in the last years of his life and, having stopped his travels, applied himself more faithfully to the keeping of this record.[1]

As for the way I have gone about doing the translations, my greatest aim has been to make them readable and accessible. In so doing, I have taken some liberties. For one, I have added the word "today" in many of the entries to give more of a sense of a journal. I have also added extra phrases at times to give the non-specialist some of the context or background

---

1. Since there are a number of years for which there are no journal entries, the question arises as to what, if any, editing was done. If so, was it done by Wu himself, by his son, or by the editor? Were there self-revelatory passages that Wu or his son thought too embarrassing, too personal? As was mentioned in the previous section, the original collection of Wu's writings had to be republished because parts of the original had been lost or had errors. So it could very well be that some of the missing entries were lost.

information without cluttering the text with detailed footnotes. (Glossaries of the names of people and book titles are included in the back of the book.) In making these additions, I have tried not to change the fundamental meaning of the passages. Since a journal is by nature a document of a personal and subjective nature, and, since classical Chinese is terse and allusive, a variety of readings are possible. What I have attempted is to offer one way of reading the text in which I take Wu at his word as much as possible and re-create his particular situation. My particular approach by no means exhausts the possibilities of other readings and interpretations.

The edition upon which I primarily rely for these translations is the *Siku quanshu zhenben* edition, series 4, vols. 335–36. Two other editions I have consulted include: *Kangzhai xiansheng wenji, fulu* (Collected Works of Master Wu Yubi, with Appended Sources), Gest Library photocopy of Naikaku Library 1526 edition; and *Kangzhai xiansheng wenji, fulu,* National Library of Peking Rare Books Microfilm of 1590 edition. There are few textual variations. Most involve a different word with the same meaning. These will be noted at the end of the translation section.

These translations, originally done as part of my doctoral dissertation, had the benefit of readings and corrections by four of the leading scholars of Neo-Confucianism of the 1980s: Wing-tsit Chan, Fang Chao-ying, Pei-yi Wu, and Wm. Theodore de Bary. Each in his own way made the final product more accurate and fluent. They did not always agree with me or with each other. The translations you see here have been revised in the meantime, mostly to make them read more smoothly and less literally. They incorporate responses I have received over years of classroom use with students in my classes.

# List of Chinese Dynasties[1]

Sage Ruler Yao r. c.2357–2257 BCE

Sage Ruler Shun r. c.2255–2205 BCE

Xia Dynasty c.2205–1766 BCE
   Founder: Yu

Shang Dynasty (also called Yin) 1766–1122 BCE
   Founder: King Tang

Zhou Dynasty c.1122–256 BCE
   Founders: King Wen and his son, King Wu

Qin Dynasty 221–207 BCE

Han Dynasty 206 BCE–CE 220

Period of Disunion 220–581

Sui Dynasty 581–618

Tang Dynasty 618–906

Five Dynasties Period 907–960

Song Dynasty 960–1279
   Northern Song 960–1126
   Southern Song 1127–1279

Yuan Dynasty 1279–1368

Ming Dynasty 1338–1644

Qing Dynasty 1644–1912

---

1. These are according to traditional dating. Recent archaeological discoveries have resulted in changes in the very early periods.

# Pronunciation Guide

Chinese names and terms in the book are spelled according to the pinyin system of romanization. Although this system results in the correct pronunciation of most words, it does result in some mispronunciations. Some of the valuation of sounds differs from what English speakers are used to. The five most problematic are:

**c**, which has the approximate pronunciation of *ts* (for example, *cao* is pronounced TSAO, rhymes with "ow")

**q**, which has the approximate pronunciation of *ch* (for example, *qi* is pronounced CHEE)

**x**, which has the approximate pronunciation of *sh* (for example, the *Elementary Learning* text, *xiao-xue*, has the approximate pronounciation of "shiao-shueh."

**z**, which has the approximate pronunciation of *dz* (for example, the author of *Practicing the Mean*, Zisi, is pronounced Dz Sze

**zh**, which has the approximate pronunciation of *j* (for example, the Zhou dynasty is pronounced like the boy's name, "Joe")

In addition, when **ch**, **sh**, and **zh** are followed by an **i**, they sound as if an *rrh* sound is added (something of a growling). That is, *chi* is CHIRRH; *shi* is SHIRRH; *zhi* is JRRH.

When an "**s**" is followed by an "**i**" it is pronounced as "szu," almost like a hissing sound. (See above Zisi.)

In the case of **ong**, it is pronounced as if there were two *o*s (for example, Song dynasty is pronounced Soong).

**ang** is pronounced as if it had an "h" in it, "ahng" (for example, Wang is Wahng).

In terms of the principal Neo-Confucians frequently mentioned in this book: Zhu Xi is pronounced like **JU SHEE**; Cheng Yi – **CHENG EE**; Zhou Dunyi – **JOE DUN–EE**; Zhang Zai **JAHNG DZAI**; Shao Yong – **SHAO YOONG**; Cheng Hao – **CHENG HOW**.

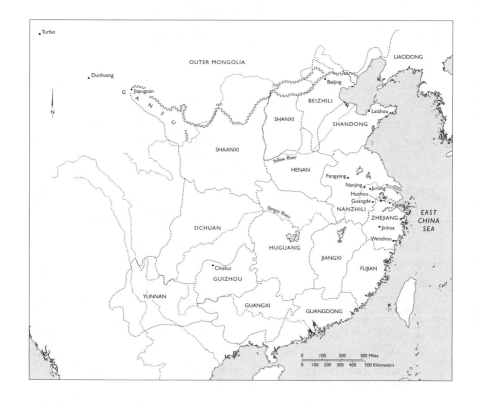

Map of Ming China

# The Journal (日錄) of Wu Yubi

# 1425 (33 years old)[1]

**1.** I had a dream that the two sages, Confucius and King Wen, were standing in the eastern chambers of my father's official residence on Zongli Street in Nanjing.[2] They were standing in the middle of the room while I stood off to the left (literally, west). I could see Confucius' features quite distinctly. I was about to ask the two about how to achieve the mind of intuitive knowledge and natural ease in the practice of the Way (Dao), when it appeared that Confucius had picked up one of King Wen's books off a table and was looking through it. The book seemed to be King Wen's genealogy.[3]

**2.** I had a dream that I was waiting upon Master Zhu Xi.[4] He wore a kind expression on his face and his demeanor was dignified. I made a show of my deep respect and admiration for him.

**3.** Tonight as I lay on my pillow, I was thinking over the "candle-shadow affair" of the second Song emperor, Taizong, who was reputed to have killed his brother for the throne. I felt some regret for him. A person must have the kind of mind, described by Mencius, such that he would not "do even one unrighteous act or kill off just one innocent person in order to gain the empire."[5] Only then can a person succeed in becoming

---

1. I have inserted his age for each year, and done so by Western reckoning, not Chinese. In China, a person is considered one year old at birth. Everybody is considered one year older on New Year's Day. Since Wu was born near the end of the year, he was actually considered two years old when he was only about a month old by Western reckoning. Whenever Wu's age is mentioned in the text itself, the reader has to subtract two years to get his age by Western reckoning.

2. Wu lived in Nanjing from 1402 to 1411 with his father, a high government official.

3. King Wen was the founder of the Zhou dynasty (1122–256 BCE). Confucius (551–479 BCE) was the first great philosopher of the Zhou who had a strong sense of dedication to King Wen.

4. Zhu Xi (pronounced JU-SHEE) (1130–1200), regarded as the primary architect of the dominant Neo-Confucian tradition at that time. Wu had a highly emotional dedication to him.

5. *Mencius* 2A:2.

a sage ruler like Yao and Shun of antiquity. If not this way, then it will be rare that one isn't affected by external influences. Indeed, in responding to every situation, a student committed to following the Way must vigorously examine his motives, completely root out the desire for personal gain, and be purely identified with Heavenly principle. Only then can we speak of the Kingly Way. Truly, if a person is like this, his mind will be greatly liberated and sharp, and he can be said to be a great man.[6]

4. Lately, in handling a certain matter with a neighbor, I have tried to be forbearing with him but haven't succeeded in my attempts. Today I was at the end of my patience, and since he still didn't understand the matter, I couldn't help telling him off. This losing my temper over unimportant matters is something which I later regret. Thinking it over, I see that in order to be a noble person,[7] I must always be willing to be accommodating when interacting with others. Only then will my own actions succeed. To be able to be accommodating is to have patience.

5. Sitting after a meal by the eastern window, I find that my body is relaxed and at ease, my vital spirit (*qi*)[8] clear and bright. I've been making more and more progress with my program of reading books. If I

---

6. Alluding to *Mencius* 3B:2, which describes the "great man" (大丈夫) with heroic qualities. "One who dwells in the wide house of the world, occupies his proper place in the world, and carries out the great Way of the world. . . . He cannot be led astray by riches and honor, moved by poverty and privation, or deflected by power or force. This is what I call a great man." (Trans. by Bloom, *Mencius*, p. 62.)

7. As compared with the "mean and petty person" (*xiao ren* 小人), literally "small" person. Confucius often contrasts the noble person (*junzi* 君子) with the "small" person. Although the literal translation of *junzi* is "gentleman," and the Confucian audience was assumed to be male, I use the more inclusive "noble person."

8. The word *qi* 氣 (pronounced CHEE) here is coupled with the term for the mind, *xin* 心 (pronounced SHIN). Thus it is used as a psychological aspect of the self rather than as a material force in relationship to metaphysical principle, *li* 理. It is used here more in Mencius' sense of *haoran zhi qi* 浩然之氣, a vast, flowing energy. *Qi* indicates the instinctual energies which dynamize the workings of the mind, which, Mencius cautions, should be made subject to one's will but not be harmed or repressed by the will. I have translated it here as "vital spirit," but *qi* is not to be taken as something

could just sustain this over several days, I certainly would be able to break through to the next stage in my practice.

6. What the sages and worthies of the past spoke about was nothing other than preserving Heavenly principle and eliminating selfish human desires. Their actions aimed at the same thing. How other than by these same means can I learn to be a sage or worthy?

7. When Master Zhu Xi was discussing personal practice with his followers, he said, "If it were easy to do, there would be innumerable sages and worthies in the world at any one time." Alas, only one who has actually exerted himself in this regard understands how difficult it is! Overwhelmed, I heave a sigh at these words.

8. Since I have no time left over from strenuously examining myself day and night for my faults, how can I find the time to engage in the practice of checking into the faults of other people? If a person criticizes others in great detail, he will be careless in managing himself. Shouldn't I take this as a warning? Now, two of the three goals mentioned at the beginning of the *Great Learning*, to "manifest the clear character" and "renew the people," are not two separate aspects of self-cultivation. Although this is so, still, if a person has not yet "manifested his own clear moral character" but wants instead to first "renew other people," not only will he have lost the correct sequence of what is primary or secondary, what should come first or later, how could he even succeed at loving others? He would only bring useless worry upon his self and be giving in to his own selfish intentions.[9]

---

disembodied from the self. As Wu gets older and speaks of his *qi* as getting weaker, I often translate it as "vital energies."

9. The third is to rest in the highest good. The text continues: "Things have their roots and branches. Affairs have their beginnings and ends. By knowing what should come first and what should follow one can draw close to the Way."

9. In the midst of poverty and distressed circumstances, I find matters keep coming on me one after another. At the same time, I am suffering from painful boils. I can't help from time to time getting angry and frustrated by it all. At times like these, I slowly try to order my attire and turn to my reading. Often then I immediately become aware of a loosening up within me. As it was said long ago, "If you have not had to cut through twisted roots and gnarled branches, you don't really know how to distinguish a sharp tool."[10] Master Cheng Yi put it this way: "To be mature in your efforts, you must go through this discipline through hardship."[11] Still, how truly difficult this is to do! This being difficult, I can only take care of myself, be patient, and keep on going. Master Zhu Xi said, "If you cannot at last succeed, do not give up altogether but just let up for the time being." How valuable are these words!

10. Zhu Xi said, "My teacher, Master Li Tong, 'never lost his composure in his speech and demeanor.'" I always sigh in wonderment at how Li cultivated himself to reach such a state. Alas, in my own case, even with a whole lifetime of effort, I could not learn how. But Zhu Xi also said, "In the beginning, Master Li was a rather rough-and-ready sort of person. What he became later was the result of 'cutting and polishing.'"[12] From this, I realized that Master Li's self-mastery was not something with which he was born, but was achieved as the result of his efforts at learning. Still, this stupid self of mine is plagued by an inability to control and eliminate the obstinacy of my natural temperament. When things are going well, and my mind and vital spirit are in harmony, I experience a sense of joy with all things. But then, when the least little thing does not accord with my wishes, I lose my temper.

After some reflection, I realized that it was not that Master Li had the benefit of associates who were all sages and worthies, but rather that his capacity "never to lose his composure in speech and demeanor" came from being like the Shang ruler, "Tang the Completer," who "did not demand

---

10. *History of the Later Han* (*Hou Han Shu*) 88:21b.

11. *Written Legacy of the Cheng Brothers* (*Chengzi yishu*) 3:1b. This is a passage Wu quotes over and over again in the Journal. As such, I do not cite its source each time.

12. Both quotations come from *Classified Conversations of Zhu Xi* (*Zhuzi yulei*) 103:1a, b. "Cutting and polishing" is one way Confucians speak of self-cultivation. The *Great Learning* in chapter 3 quotes it from a poem in the *Book of Odes* that refers to King Wen's diligence in cultivating his virtue.

perfection in others but scrutinized himself as if he still had not reached it himself."[13] From this moment on, I became certain that a person is not only able to learn how to be a sage or worthy, but, with study, can also succeed in becoming one. These two facts are true: our deeper nature as human beings is fundamentally good, and our psychophysical nature is capable of being transformed. If I ignore the merits of "starting learning with things close at hand," as Confucius advised, what will I amount to?[14]

**11.** Last evening, sick in bed, I was reflecting on household matters. I couldn't help but calculate and worry about them. The threads of my mind became entangled and my vital spirit became muddled. But then slowly I began to realize that the only thing to which I could apply my efforts is my moral character. Outside of this, I know of nothing else. So what is that which I seek for myself? I seek only to strengthen this moral character of mine. Upon these realizations, I found that my mind had calmed down and my vital spirit had become clear again. This next day, I am writing all this down in order to encourage myself.

**12.** Today in my southern studio, I have been taking great delight in reading *Mencius*. My mind is clear, receptive, and bright, permeated by what Mencius described as the rejuvenating "effects of the calm air of the morning,"[15] unvexed by anything. Amidst the shade of the trees in the clear morning, a warm breeze languidly blows, while the far-off mountains and forests stand so still. Heaven and earth are naturally vast, the sun and moon naturally enduring. This experience verifies what Master Shao Yong meant in a poem:

> One only notices the bright day when the mind is tranquil.
> One only appreciates the blue sky when the eyes are clear.[16]

---

13. First emperor of the Shang dynasty (c.1600) celebrated for his virtue. "Instructions of Yi," *Book of History* (trans. by J. Legge, *The Shoo King or the Book of Historical Documents. The Chinese Classics*, vol. III, pp. 195–96).

14. For Confucius, it was important that students start with the everyday matters of their specific lives before attempting loftier things. Reference to *Analects* 14:37.

15. *Mencius* 6A:8.

16. Shao Yong (1011–1077) is considered one of the five principal Neo-Confucians of the Northern Song dynasty, who is most famous for his work on the *Book of Changes*

13. I have always had a stubborn and irascible temperament. It was only in 1410, when I was eighteen years old studying under Master Yang Pu,[17] that I began to be aware of this. That spring, on my way home from my father's residence, I went out of my way to visit an old friend, Li Yuandao, at an inn along the Qinhuai Canal in Nanjing. We walked together arm in arm along the bank of the river, discussing self-cultivation.[18] Talking to him heart-to-heart about my problem of being stubborn and irascible, I felt for the first time the desire to begin some sort of program to bring my wayward disposition under control. When Yuandao subsequently informed my parents of this, they were overjoyed. He was a person from Luling county, Jian (Jiangxi province), and the nephew of my maternal uncle, who held the position of Secretary in the Supervisorate of Instruction.

After this, however, even though there were times when I made some efforts to control myself, they were still careless and haphazard. In the subsequent fifteen or sixteen years, I continued to be wild and self-willed. Whenever some bit of goodness from my deeper nature emerged, I became so infuriated with myself at my baseness, that I felt there was nowhere to hide in shame. Last winter and this spring, I devoted a great deal of energy to my efforts, yet at the same time was aware of how my daily life had become even more filled with hardships. I began to suspect I was one of the stupid ones who could never in the least bit emulate the sages and worthies, and that there was nothing to prevent me from ending up as what Confucius described as a "mean and petty person."

But then, for these past five or six months, I've noticed some improvement in my disposition. As a result, I've stepped up my efforts and been making daily progress. Both my mind and my vital spirit have gradually been made more peaceful. Although there have been times when, finding

---

and numerology. Wu Yubi was more interested in his poetry. *Songs of Slapping an Old Gourd by the Yi River* (*Yiquan jirang ji*) 16:88a–b.

17. Yang Pu (1372–1446) was the teacher of Wu and a close colleague of his father's. The text mentions the position he held at the time, that is, Librarian in the Supervisorate of Instruction for the Heir Apparent.

18. Literally, "daily renewal" (日新), from the *Great Learning,* chapter 2: "The inscription on the bathing tub of Tang said, 'If you can renew yourself for one day, then do so day after day. Let there be constant daily renewal.'" "Daily renewal" became shorthand for self-cultivation. I put it in quotation marks when it appears in the text.

myself in an adverse situation, I couldn't help becoming agitated inside, still, almost immediately, I was able to get rid of the disturbance. In the end, no great damage was done.

However, on the twentieth of this month, I found myself in another adverse situation, the inner agitation from which I could not rid myself. My mind became more and more discontented. This was because my usual practice was only one of negatively restraining myself and not one of positive nurture. I still lacked the intention of completely eradicating the root of the problem. Only after having reflected back and forth on it did I realize that my recent problem derived from wanting to have my mind and vital spirit at peace, yet at the same time, hating all those external things that go contrary to my wishes and that spoil my inner equilibrium. But this is wrong.

The mind is originally the Great Vacuity, the seven feelings (joy, anger, sorrow, fear, love, hate, and desire) may not be infringed upon. In one's contact with things, there are cases of sweet, sour, salty, and bitter. All things in the world are unalike. How can I hate those things that are contrary to my tastes? The correct thing for me to do, in the midst of the universal diversity of life, is to carefully examine the principle of each thing in order to respond properly to each of them. Upon realizing this, I felt a great unburdening inside. Was this not a case of my "mastering the self and returning to the rites"?[19]

Now the practice of negatively restraining and not positively acting is a rigid and painful approach, whereas using principle to deal with each situation is a flexible and smooth one. Thus, I thought, it is not that I have never before experienced the state of my mind and vital spirit being at peace, but that I have never experienced it uninterrupted for eight to nine days like this. Furthermore, those were times in the past when the household was calm, with not much going on.

Today I know I can deal with the agitation resulting from adverse situations. Still, I worry that my learning will not continue improving along these lines. Therefore, I have taken care to write all this down in a notebook:

---

19. *Analects* 12.1: "Yan Yuan asked about humaneness. The Master said, 'To master oneself and return to the rites is humaneness.'" The Chinese term that is translated as "master" (*ke* 克) has connotations of restraining, disciplining, or subduing the self. Yan Yuan is another name for Yan Hui, one of Confucius' favorite students. As this line is quoted so frequently by Wu, I do not cite its source each time it appears.

"I hope to practice 'daily renewal and further renewal.' My goal is to progress to the point of 'mastering myself and returning to the rites' by means of the practices of reading books and plumbing principle, as well as by devoting myself to the cultivation of reverence and empathy." Whether I succeed right away or it takes a long time, I dare not know. I, Yubi, write this, on the twenty-first day of the seventh month in the year 1425, in my southern studio.

14. A couplet on the pillar in my southern studio reads:

In a state of deep tranquility, I am content with my lot wherever
I am.
In a state of peaceful relaxation, that is the time for reading books.

15. To know where to settle myself, I must eliminate vain hopes.
To be content in poverty, I must restrain extravagant desires.

16. Here are two lines from a poem I wrote:

As placid as the autumn waters is the taste of poverty.
As peaceful as the spring winds is the result of tranquility.

17. On my wall, I've written in large characters to alert myself:

VIGOROUSLY TRY TO ELIMINATE LOSING MY TEMPER
OVER PETTY MATTERS!
FIRMLY MAINTAIN MY INTEGRITY EVEN IN POVERTY!

18. Sick, exhausted, and tied up with household worries, I find I cannot give my full attention to the sacred writings of the sages and worthies. Inwardly, I feel mean and deceitful, lacking in the means by which to extend my knowledge. Outwardly, my manner has become increasingly volatile and rude, with no energy for personal application of effort. Time

flies quickly by! Deep regrets overwhelm me! What am I to do? What am I to do? I write this in my southern studio as the twenty-sixth day of the seventh month draws to a close.

19. For several days now, the demands from household matters have followed one upon the other. I cannot put aside my worries about my parents. My reading schedule has been interrupted and I have been harboring feelings of stinginess inside. It all makes me so ashamed of myself. I reflect on how the sages and worthies followed Heaven's will in all cases with respect to good and bad fortune, without the least bit of inner disturbance. The reason why I am unable to be like them, and cannot help wavering between petty concerns of profit and loss, is that I have not been intensive enough in plumbing principle and not thorough enough in my personal practice. What I should resolve to do is follow the right path and that is all. As for good or bad fortune, calamity or blessing, how can I have any part in determining what I get?

On the whole, favorable situations should not be enjoyed too much, for the emergence of feelings of enjoyment also tends to give rise to those of arrogance and extravagance. Adverse situations should not be disliked too much, for the emergence of feelings of dislike also tends to give rise to those of bitterness and resentment. Both enjoying and disliking things too much cause a disturbance of inner equilibrium that should not be upset. The mind of the sage or worthy is like still water. Whether situations are favorable or adverse, he deals with both using principle and nothing else. How could he let what comes from the outside determine his inner sorrow or joy? Alas! How can I succeed in reaching this state? I must exert myself, yes, exert myself, without any letting up.

Written in my southern studio on the second day of the seventh month.[20]

20. In managing my household affairs, I lack a magnanimous spirit.

---

20. This entry seems to be out of order here. Entry no. 18 is dated the twenty-sixth of the seventh month, and this is dated the second of that month. Perhaps it should read the second of the eighth month.

21. When repeatedly faced with adverse situations, I try to manage in all cases by following what is right.

22. After putting household matters in order today, I read in my southern studio. There is great joy in this, and I am thereby able to gain insight into the original pure mind.

23. On my pillow tonight, I recalled the days when I lived in the capital and could study day and night without interruption, yet never got sick. But for these past ten years or more, various illnesses have followed one after the other, so that I have hardly been able to make the same kind of progress as in those days. I am overcome with deep regrets, though there is nothing I can do about it. All this while, I have been poor and without the medicine to take proper care of myself. All that is left for me to do is to put my mind at ease from anxieties, prevent my obstinate nature from disturbing me, love and nourish my vital spirit—all in the hope of making some small improvement. Alas, the strong young men of this world are not few in number, yet they idly pass their time away. Truly, this is a great pity!

24. I got up from a nap today, my body feeling relaxed and my mind free and untrammeled. Content in poverty, delighting in the Way, what else need I seek?

25. Just when I remember how late the time is getting and how I've still not accomplished anything in my learning, I become apprehensive. Still, I cannot recover what is already past and gone. From today on, I will try to make what progress I can with what energies I do possess, not allowing my will to become lax, that is all. When I look at how the ancients were consistent in their behavior from their youth to old age, I am overcome with great shame.

26. In handling a recent matter, I was short on patience and afterward realized that I acted in error. In cases like this, I must vigorously

increase my efforts at "mastering myself and returning to the rites," so as to make my mind clear, receptive, and bright. Only then can I be without fault in my response to affairs. When tranquil, to nourish the self; when active, to scrutinize the self—I cannot allow for even a moment of "forgetting."[21] If I let the original mind be vexed by things and affairs, and make no effort to make it pure and clear, then my mind will be all the more chaotic and my vital spirit all the more muddled. "This fettering taking place repeatedly,"[22] my failing will be all the worse.

27. Today, I got a hold of an edition of the Neo-Confucian anthology, *Reflections on Things at Hand*, arranged according to categories. Reading it, I heard what I had never heard before and became acquainted with what I had never before been acquainted. My whole being—body, mind, nature, and feelings—derived benefit from it. I felt very grateful that my friend had this book for our mutual edification.

28. Today, while reading *Reflections on Things at Hand*, I could feel that my vital spirit was recollected, and that my body and mind were both restrained. Aware of my deficiencies, I dare not have the slightest intention of "forgetting." Fearful of failure, I am determined to press forward.

# 1426 (34 years old)

29. Today, the twenty-eighth day of the second month, is such a beautiful, clear day. I have been composing poetry in my outer southern studio. The sunlight reflecting through the mountain mist shines on the

---

21. The idea of "not forgetting" is an allusion to *Mencius* 2A:2, "let there be no forgetting nor helping (to grow)" (*wu wang wu zhu* 無忘無助). One cannot forget for a moment the task of self-cultivation. Here it might also mean not forgetting all of his resolves he makes in this entry. He quotes this line so often that I note it only using quotation marks but do not cite the source.

22. *Mencius* 6A:8. This refers to what happens to the self during the daytime, after the "calm air of the morning" effect has dissipated.

flowers and trees, while birds flutter up and down in song. What a joyful mood I'm in! This being late spring, I recall the spring outings to the rain-altars in which countless generations have taken delight. My heart, like that of Confucius back then, resonates with this.[23]

30. I spent this evening reading the *Analects*. I was deeply moved by its discussion of the "nine things" to which the noble person focuses his thoughts: "when looking, he focuses on seeing clearly; when listening, he focuses on being discerning; in his expression, he focuses on being amiable; in his demeanor, he focuses on being reverent; in his speech, he focuses on being dutiful; in his actions, he focuses on being respectful; when in doubt, he focuses on asking questions; when angry, he focuses on thinking about the potential negative consequences of anger; and when seeing gain, he focuses upon what is right."[24] The most important thing is that I put them into practice right this very moment. I must commit myself to doing so.[25]

31. This evening, while observing a young boy torch fishing, I listened in silence to the flowing of the water. I came to understand Confucius' sighing over the continual flowing of water[26] and the meaning of Zhu Xi's teachings about the substance and function of natural ease in the practice of the Way.

---

23. Reference to *Analects* 11:25, when Confucius asked four of his students to tell him their fondest wish. Three of them expressed quite ambitious ways of reforming the world. The fourth student reluctantly told of his wish to enjoy the annual spring outings to the rain-altars, picnicking and laughing with friends. Confucius sighed upon hearing this, "This is just what I too would want."

24. *Analects* 16:10 (trans. E. Slingerland, Confucius, *Analects*, p. 196). These nine are not explicitly mentioned in the Journal. I have included them to give the reader a sense of what they are.

25. Literally, "wear them on my belt," as Confucius' student Yan Hui did, whenever he got hold of something good he wanted to learn. *Practicing the Mean*, section 8.

26. "The Master, standing by a stream, said, 'It just flows along like this, doesn't it, never stopping day or night?'" (*Analects* 9:17). Zhu Xi interprets this to mean the continual creativity of Heaven and earth.

**32.** This evening, I stood on a path between the fields, quietly reflecting on why I have not succeeded in becoming a noble person who has genuinely and purely realized his goals. Truly, it is difficult to do so. It is what my mind deeply yearns for, yet I feel I have no way to reach that realm. Overcome, I heave a deep sigh of regret.

**33.** Today I was out inspecting my fields. On account of an ailment from boils, I lay down on the grass for a leisurely rest. The extreme tranquility I felt there on the path between the fields was as if there were no human world. Today, even though I have not taken a look at any of my books, still, my thoughts have continued uninterrupted in tranquility, and I have had some insight into the principle of things.

**34.** Looking at the water at the mouth of the gorge today, I found everything along the way to be so pleasant. If a person comprehends his original pure mind, then he will be happy in all situations. Success and failure will be all the same to him. But if his mind races outside, then he will be in utter confusion with no rest. How can he then be happy?

**35.** Chao Gongwu said, "Master Shao Yong lived as a recluse but had extensive learning. He was especially proficient in the *Book of Changes*. It is said that he exhaustively explored the origins of that classic, and as a result, had foreknowledge of things to come. However, when he was just beginning his studies, he did not sleep on his pillow for thirty years!"[27] Alas, if the wise men of old went through such hardships in their efforts, what about my own generation?

**36.** Contemplating the flowers and trees around me today, I feel one in spirit with them.

---

27. Chao Gongwu (d.1171) *Memoirs of My Readings in the Jun Studio* (*Chaode xiansheng junzhai dushuzhi*) 1A:22.

37. While out inspecting my fields today, I wandered as far as the Green Stone Bridge and found it all so pleasant. Returning home, I burned some incense and did some reading in the outer southern studio. The weather is clear and mild. Taking in the view, I'm in quite a joyful mood. From my reading, principle has indeed become clearer to me, and my mind and vital spirit have become refreshed.

38. One day recently, I got violently angry over a matter but then right away the anger stopped. But now it has happened that for several days things have not gone well for me. I can't help feeling as though rocks are forming and hardening over and over again inside my chest. I must keep in mind, however, that it is impossible suddenly to make the imbalances of my physical nature and the defects in my learning disappear. I can only gradually diminish them. How could "always be composed in speech and demeanor" come from the efforts of a single day? I must exert myself and not be remiss.

39. Resting on my pillow today, I was thinking how I've had very few idle thoughts lately. This indeed is a sign that I've made some progress.

40. I got out of bed and have been reading in the shadow of the willow trees by the eastern window. All of this holds a subtle appeal for me. This evening, even though I had to contend with two disagreeable matters which caused some inner disturbance, I was able right away to rid myself of it, and feelings of anger never took shape. To steadily follow this kind of "cutting and polishing" should prove efficacious.

41. Returning from having tended the fields, I've set aside my books because of an eye ailment. Instead, I have been leisurely looking over some old papers of mine from the last sixteen or seventeen years. How quickly time has passed, yet I am still finding it difficult to make advancements in my learning and personal practice. Looking back and forth, from past to present, I feel so disappointed with myself. I am also moved by the fact

that my parents are daily growing older.[28] More and more, I find myself overwhelmed by sorrows.

42. In general, students, in putting programs of self-cultivation into action, should test themselves by starting with extremely difficult and challenging situations. Only then will they be successful in whatever they do. If they avoid these kinds of situations, then their other accomplishments are not worth speaking of.

43. Today I was planting vegetables in the garden. Although for a time now I've had to put aside my books, indeed, it is "what poverty and low estate" require. On my way along the road to tend the fields, I chanted some passages from *Mencius*. Coming upon some wild flowers just where lush grasses grow and a stream flows by, I lingered at that spot for a while, allowing my inner state to become quiet and refreshed.

44. A young boy lost one of my ducks and I got a bit angry. Still, compared to my reaction last year to losing a duck, the extent of my anger has been greatly reduced. But all the same, the fact that I failed to remain unmoved inside indicates that my efforts at learning are still not strong enough.

45. Today, I took a look at the "Preface" to the *Collected Works of Wu Cheng*.[29] From doing so, I got the impression that most members of his clan were motivated by honor, rank, riches, and fame. I suspect that our Master Zhu Xi was not like this. My regret is that I've yet to see the actual *Collected Works* itself.

---

28. His father was to die later that year.

29. Wu Cheng (1249–1333) was the most significant Neo-Confucian of the Yuan dynasty, who, as mentioned in the Introduction, came from the same general area in Jiangxi province as did Wu. His Collected Works is the *Caolu wenji*.

46. This morning, in the outer southern studio, I was reading a chapter from *Mencius*, my demeanor solemn and reverent. After the noon hour, because my eyes were sore and my body fatigued, I took a nap. Having nothing special on my mind, I thought back on the very many difficulties I've faced since returning to my native village fifteen years ago. I can't bear to look back on it all!

47. Sitting in the outer southern studio today, I prepared my ink slab and have been writing up my lessons. The shade of the trees in the clear morning creates a lovely scene which pleases me much. My mind open and my vital spirit vibrant, I wonder whether this is what it is like to approach the realm of the worthies. It's a pity my book learning is not more extensive!

48. Tonight on my pillow, I have been silently chanting passages from *Practicing the Mean*. When I got to where it says, "He who has great virtue will certainly receive the mandate of Heaven,"[30] I became greatly alarmed. I reflected that the ancient sage ruler Shun had great moral character and consequently received the mandate to rule. Although Confucius' virtue did not result in his receiving the mandate, still, because he came to be considered the teacher of kings and emperors for countless ages, the end result was the same. Alas, knowing what is due the virtuous person, then one ought to know what is due the person lacking in virtue. How am I to cultivate myself in such a way as to strengthen my own moral character?

49. This evening, slowly walking through the fields, I was silently chanting passages from *Practicing the Mean*. I took my time, going over each word and phrase, chanting them with great feeling. Realized in my mind, verified by my experiences, this book has given me a great deal of insight.

---

30. *Practicing the Mean* 17:5. This is the *Zhongyong*, often translated as *Doctrine of the Mean*. See Glossary of Book Titles for my reason in translating it this way.

50. "The noble person does not complain against Heaven above nor blame other people below. Thus it is that the noble person is quiet and calm, waiting for Heaven's will for him, while the mean and petty person follows dangerous ways, hoping for good luck."[31] By lamplight this evening, I've been reading *Practicing the Mean* and have written down this particular passage in order that I may constantly take it as a kind of highly effective medicine.

51. Today, I was discussing with a neighbor how I have begun to shoulder some heavy responsibilities, and that I have felt somewhat happier with myself.

52. Every day I work hard at my farming. This is my personal lot in life, so why be resentful about it? As *Practicing the Mean* says, "In a position of poverty and low estate, the noble person does what is proper in such a position."[32]

53. My daughter has been sick with boils. I have been so tied up with it that I have been unable to concentrate on my reading. All the while, I am beside myself with irritation and impatience. Even though I am well aware that "in a position of sorrow and difficulty, the noble person does what is proper in such a position,"[33] still, "the years and months wait for no man." Since I've as yet to make any substantial achievement in my learning, I can't help but be upset. The fact is that I wasted time in my youth, passing up good opportunities. Now, as a result, I've ended up with an inadequate understanding of things. The past thirty years I should have been exerting more effort, but what can I do about that now?

---

31. *Practicing the Mean* 14.4 (trans. by Legge, *The Chinese Classics*, vol. 1, p. 396, modified).

32. Ibid., 14.1.

33. Ibid., 14.2.

54. Slowly walking along the road today, I engaged in examining what Mencius referred to as "the four beginnings" of the human heart,[34] and discovered my body and mind were naturally restrained. This is what the Song masters call the "reverence that attends the state of tranquility."

# 1427 (35 years old)

55. If knowledge is not extended and there is no self-mastery, then how can any real learning take place?

56. Upon the occasion of having violently lost my temper today, I slowly reflected that it was all because I judge other people with no sense of empathy. Now, if I wish to judge another person, I should consider whether or not I myself am capable of doing what I expect of him. If I am capable of it, then I should further consider that it was only after I had studied the Way of the sages and worthies that I became capable. How could I then proceed to judge a person who has never exerted any effort at self-cultivation, or a person whose efforts are still immature? How much less should I judge people on the basis of moral principle when I myself am not capable in all cases of fulfilling its demands? Looked at from this perspective, I have been quite reckless in judging others in my life. Stop doing it! Stop doing it! Truly, it is as Confucius said, "If you are hard on yourself and go easy when criticizing others, you will keep resentment at a distance."[35] If I would judge myself in the same spirit as I judge others, I could fulfill the Way.

57. Following the course of affairs in my life, I have come to know the difficulty of dealing with poverty. I think about it but to no avail.

---

34. These are the feelings of commiseration, of shame and dislike, of deference and compliance, and a sense of right and wrong. When nourished, they grow into the virtues of humaneness, righteousness, a sense of propriety, and wisdom. Mencius argues that human nature is intrinsically good because humans are born with these four beginnings (*Mencius* 2A:6).

35. *Analects* 15:14.

So I dismiss it from my mind as something about which I can do nothing. Confucius said, "The dedicated officer does not forget that he may find himself in a ditch."[36] That is not so simple to do. He further said, "To be poor and yet happy."[37] It isn't easy getting to this point. However, perhaps the ancients were not as poor as we are today.

This evening I was reading *Practicing the Mean* where its author Zisi says, "The noble person does what is proper to the situation he finds himself in. He does not desire to go beyond it." I gained much insight from this passage, as well as from the commentaries of two Song Confucians, You Zuo and Lu Dalin. Mr. You said, "One who 'remains quiet and calm' will not necessarily *not* get what he wants, but whether it is good or bad fortune, he behaves correctly. One who 'pursues dangerous ways,' will not necessarily always get what he wants, but whether it is good or bad fortune, he behaves wrongly. If you have never personally experienced this, you will not appreciate its real 'flavor.'"[38] Truly, this You Zuo is our teacher for a hundred generations! He also said, "You must truly believe only in this." From now on, how dare I not truly believe in what he has said!

58. While poring over Zhen Dexiu's *Correct Models of Literature* today, I found myself moved that I haven't made much progress lately in my learning and moral character. As age forty approaches, I'm ending up a mean and petty person. Alas, I am overwhelmed with sadness!

59. A certain recent affair has been difficult for me to deal with. This evening, I was discussing it with my student and friend, Hu Jiushao, trying to look at it from every possible angle. What the situation demands is vigorously eliminating my habit of losing my temper over insignificant matters, and also that I focus solely on the moral demands of the Way. As

---

36. Quoted in *Mencius* 3B:1. The line continues: "the courageous officer does not forget that he may sacrifice his head." (Trans. by Bloom, *Mencius* p. 61.)

37. *Analects* 1:15: "Poor yet free from flattery, rich yet free from arrogance, how would that be?" The Master said, "That would do, but it is not as good as 'poor yet finding joy in the Way, rich yet loving the rites.'"

38. "The Meaning of *Practicing the Mean*" in the *Collected Works of You Zuo* (*Chishan wenji*) 1:35a.

soon as any one of the basic human emotions has disturbed my inner equilibrium, then I have already gone far astray from the Way.

60. Tonight on my pillow, I was thinking deeply over the perennial Confucian concern of public involvement or private retirement. Only learning to be a sage or worthy can be regarded as a way free from defect. With respect to success and failure, gain and loss, I can only entrust myself to the will of Heaven. In this regard, my mind must be without the least bit of shame, and in dealing with myself, I must fulfill my responsibilities in life before I can return what I owe to Heaven. I wish to write down in large characters to help keep a watch on myself:

## WHAT DOES IT MEAN TO BE A SAGE OR WORTHY AS OPPOSED TO BEING A MEAN AND PETTY PERSON?

61. From today on, I must sincerely and genuinely follow the advice of the *Book of Changes*, namely, to "remain lowly to guard myself well," and to "put myself in accord with the Way and its power"[39] like the ancient sages. Only then will I be good enough to get close to realizing the Way. Alas, if a person can succeed in doing these things, even though he die from the cold or hunger, even though he die from capital punishment, these cannot detract from his being a great man. If he cannot succeed in doing these things, even though he be extremely wealthy and well regarded, even though he lives to an extreme old age, he cannot escape the fact of being nothing but a mean and petty person. How can I afford not to reflect on this in my dealings with myself?

62. Today, I was teaching my students the *Analects*. When we reached the passage, "When a person at forty is disliked by others, he will always be that way," without realizing it, I found myself in a state of alarm.

---

39. The first quote is from the *Book of Changes,* hexagram no. 15, "modesty" (*qian* 謙), commentary on the first line; the second is from "Discussion of the Trigrams," chapter 1 (trans. by Richard Wilhelm, *The I Ching or Book of Changes*, trans. by Cary Baynes [Princeton: Princeton University Press, 3rd edition, 1967] vol. 1, p. 81 modified).

Here I am approaching forty[40] and am so much the object of dislike. How can I afford not to deepen my self-awareness in this regard? What I must resolve to do is to lessen the antipathy between myself and others!

63. This evening by lamplight in my outer southern studio, I was looking over three pieces I wrote back when I was twenty. I found myself overwhelmed with sighs of sadness. The reason is that, in the past, my goal in life was clear, based on the belief that the Way of the ancient sages and worthies could be learned, that it could be attained. Now it has been twenty years of vacillating and temporizing. I have been plagued by frequent illnesses and my physical vigor is steadily declining. Not only can I not reach the point of being a sage or worthy, I cannot even succeed in my attempts to become somewhat of a person who has lessened his faults. What am I to do? What am I to do? Where can I find some fine young men committed to learning upon whom I can strongly impress the urgency of persevering in their efforts?

64. I haven't accomplished much lately in my learning and moral cultivation, and I'm getting on in age. My life's goal is not being realized. These feelings of disappointment are inexhaustible. I have no place to hide myself in shame. How distressing!

65. All matters truly have aspects that are hard to bear. The noble person manages each situation no matter what. From this I know how difficult it is to become a noble person.

# 1428 (36 years old)

66. Today, Hu Jiushao was discussing with me how difficult it is to be a good person while actively involved in the affairs of the world. I can deeply appreciate his point. Ah, whenever one observes the good and

---

40. *Analects* 17:26. Actually, by Chinese reckoning, Wu was only 37 and by Western reckoning 35.

bad aspects of other people, one should always turn inward to examine his own self!

67. Today I was reading the *Book of Changes*. When I grew weary, I put it down and started looking through the *Chronological Biography of Zhu Xi*. Moved by the former philosopher's masterful diligence and ashamed of my own good-for-nothing, irresponsible ways, I find myself stupefied and at a loss. What am I to do? I must take my present situation in hand and exert more effort so as to make some headway.

68. On the road today, I was talking with Hu Jiushao about ways of conducting oneself in the world. Hitherto, for my part, I had dared not hope I could reach the ideals of *Practicing the Mean*, yet for the past several days I have been seriously pondering how I really must take them as my personal responsibility. Then and only then can I be unashamed of this life of mine. However, this is a difficult thing to actually do. Still, I cannot let myself be awed by the difficulties and prefer improper ease. I must straightaway undertake responsibility for this!

69. I stopped my reading and have been thinking about the difficulty of repaying my accumulated debts and about the gloomy prospects of my livelihood. All of this ruminating cannot help but give rise to a calculating frame of mind. Slowly, I become aware that whenever this calculating mind emerges, then I am unable to maintain the focus of my commitment to my program of learning. As for what I have been able to achieve in my life, it has never been more than what it is at present. What is more, my physical vigor is constantly declining. If I continue to take the easy path, letting matters drift, then how can my learning advance? How will I be able to endure this life? Thereupon, to alert myself, I write in large characters to be hung on the wall:

STUDY TO THE BEST OF MY OWN PARTICULAR ABILITIES!

In all cases, I must follow the will of Heaven with respect to good and bad fortune, success and failure, life and death, joy and sorrow. This mind of mine must be tranquil and calm, without the least bit of inner disturbance.

70. When I got tired today, I took a nap. During my dreams, I had the same recurring fear of finding myself incapable of learning because it was too late.

71. Today I had stern words for Hu Jiushao to the effect that a person must be courageous in his efforts at learning. But this gentleman himself shows no ambition to energetically rouse himself to action, rise above the vulgar crowd, and be above average. Later, on my way home, I felt disturbed by the whole thing. I heaved a deep sigh as I slowly reflected on my exchange with him. I don't even have enough free time to correct my own faults, how can I correct the faults of others? Alas, does making continual progress depend upon me or upon others? I must exert myself again and again, not allowing myself to be encumbered by external matters!

72. Near evening time today, I went to a neighbor's storehouse to borrow some grain. I remembered then that I had not yet repaid my former debts. This new debt will only add to what I already owe. Oh, what should I do about this life of mine? Slowly reflecting about it even further, I realized that I must "do what is proper in my given station in life," and not find fault with it. As Cheng Hao said, "Unspoiled by wealth or power and happy in poverty and low estate, a person who achieves this state of mind is a hero."[41] To reach that state, however, is difficult! Still, I dare not fail in trying to make the effort. If I can be happy in poverty and low estate, then I will not be dissipated in wealth and honor. To be happy nor dissipated whether I am in poverty, low estate, wealth, or honor, I must continually apply the proverbial whip to enliven my sluggish nature. From the past to the present, I wonder how many people actually have reached this state.

73. Early this morning on my pillow, I was thinking how I have not been active in conducting myself in the world. Before the situation will be exactly right, I must take the capacity of Heaven and earth as my capacity and the moral character of the sages as my moral character. Alas,

---

41. *Collected Works of Cheng Hao* (*Mingdao wenji*) 1:6b. In his talk of the "hero," he alludes to *Mencius* 3B:2.

where am I to find someone of like ambition together with whom I can exert effort in this matter?

**74.** In handling an important matter recently, I was unable to do the best I could and so have been extremely dispirited in thought. At the same time, I have been suffering from chills, the tremors from which at times are strong enough to overwhelm me. As a result, my program of reading has been interrupted. Muddled and dazed all day, I am strongly moved to wonder by what means I can enter the realm of the sages and worthies.

**75.** Early this morning on my pillow, I was thinking how it is my responsibility to take Heaven, earth, and the sages as my standards of conduct. Consequently, it became clear that Zisi wrote *Practicing the Mean* in order to discuss their utmost achievements. He also wrote it to raise up the Way of Heaven and earth, that the sage might be their counterpart.[42] Alas, he who has not reached the Way of Heaven and has not reached sage-hood cannot be called a "complete person."[43] This is the reason why heroes of ancient times persevered in their diligence throughout their whole lives.

**76.** Today after dinner, I handled a matter in a violent manner. Even though the other person was completely wrong, still, I should have been more accommodating in my response. Deliberating on it, I realized that even though he certainly deserved a harsh reproach, still it was not the loyal minister's way of doing things.

**77.** If a person is just able not to fail in his duties to the gods,[44] then he will not begrudge whatever fate brings him, success or failure, life

---

42. Especially in sections 22, 26, 27, 31, 32 of *Practicing the Mean*.

43. See *Analects* 14:13, where Confucius answers Zilu's question about what constitutes a "complete person."

44. The term for "gods" is *shen-ming* 神明, which can also be translated as "spiritual intelligences."

or death. If one wishes to seek to be like this, there is only the way of "being watchful over oneself when one is alone."[45] The Han Confucian, Dong Zhongshu, said, "In human actions, the extremes of good and evil in a person's behavior penetrate, interact with, and mutually respond to Heaven and earth."[46] Alas, how awesome is the boundary point where Heaven and humans meet!

78. A person must order his mind with principle so that it will be bright, pure, and always alert. Only then will all be right. This is the practice of using reverence to straighten the inner life. Alas, if there is no reverence, then there will be no straightening; if there is no straightening, then a person will stumble in confusion, and, as a result, all his affairs will fail. I cannot but be apprehensive about this.

79. I parted from a friend this evening at Xujia Mountain. On my way home, I was thinking that this whole day, I've actually managed to do a few things quite correctly.

80. In all matters, I must make decisions on the basis of righteousness. To calculate on the basis of profit and loss would be wrong.

81. Poverty and illnesses have followed one upon the other. I've yet to get ahead in my reading program. What can I rely on to vigorously practice the Way?

82. In the midst of poverty and low estate, sorrow and difficulty, I must be able to stand firmly on my two feet, subdue and regulate the rough, undisciplined sides of my temperament, and make my mind and nature pure. I must, as Confucius said, "not complain against Heaven

---

45. *Great Learning* chapter 6 and *Practicing the Mean* section 10.
46. *History of the Han* (Hanshu) 56:15b.

me other people,"[47] but forget all distinctions between the self and things, only aware of what pertains to principle and that is all.

83. Today I was reading the *History of the Jin Dynasty* and was struck that whenever Emperor Cheng saw his advisor, Wang Dao, he always bowed to him. Whenever he visited Wang's residence, he always bowed to Wang's wife. I pondered over this many times, then closed the book with a great sigh. This distinguished high official Wang Dao was given such favorable circumstance to serve the ruler as a true Confucian minister, yet his outstanding accomplishments did not go beyond a lackluster fulfillment of duty. The seriousness of his responsibility given to him by his ruler was no less than that of Yi Yin's to King Tang in the Shang and the Duke of Zhou to King Cheng in the Zhou. Yet, in terms of advancing the emperor and benefiting the people, how could Wang Dao be compared to either of them?

Although he lacked ambition and was content with minor achievements, it was more specifically in the inadequacies of his moral training that Wang Dao was not up to standard. Truly, I believe that a person can be without shame only when he studies vigorously right from his youth, aspiring to reach the ultimate in actualizing his intentions. "Confucius said to his students, 'Often you say, "My talents are not appreciated." If your talents were to be recognized, what would you do?'"[48] He also said, "When of use to the country, to serve, when put aside as of no use, to retire."[49] Alas, how can I turn back the westward flying sun of time and vigorously step up my efforts at learning!

84. Today I realized that I have actually benefited somewhat from my poverty and difficulties. It seems people who have never exerted effort in circumstances of poverty and difficulty find that in the end, they don't succeed and they end up weak and timid.

---

47. *Analects* 14:37.
48. Ibid., 11:25.
49. Ibid., 7:10.

85. In teaching others, I must, like Confucius, "by orderly method skillfully lead" them on.[50]

86. While poring over *Practicing the Mean* today, I became deeply aware of the essentials of the learning of the mind, and was moved to lament that one's mind is not so easy to preserve.

87. In my efforts at "mastering myself," I have wavered back and forth with nothing to show for it all. I'm approaching the state whereby "if by age forty, a person is disliked by others, he will always be so."

88. Giving deep thought to the various trials of my life, I find I can't bear thinking back over them all. While leisurely looking over some old papers of mine, I became filled with deep regret that I haven't advanced any further in my learning, and that my body and mind are both so remiss. How sad, how shameful it all is! So this is what I'm resolved to do today: rise early, wash and get dressed, complete the ceremonies at the ancestral shrine, sit very still with my attire in order, read the writings of the sages and worthies, collect my mind, not allow it to be thrown into confusion by external things, and then sleep at night when I am tired. There is nothing beyond this about which I should worry. As for success or failure, short or long life, each person has his own destiny with respect to these. This is what I must sincerely have faith in.

89. For several days, while keeping to a program of self-cultivation for handling difficulties, I find some order has been put into things. I must make my mind composed and transcend the concerns of being poor or rich. Only then will all be well.

---

50. Ibid., 9:11, where the student Yan Hui praises Confucius' teaching methods.

90. Whenever I examine the historical writings of the past and see how lofty in practice were the men of old, I am immensely affected. More and more I am inspired to rouse myself to be like them.

91. It is when I am faced with the difficulty of making progress in my learning that I realize that aspiring to be a worthy is not easy.

92. The mind is a lively thing. If I am not thorough in my nourishing of it, then the mind cannot help but be shaken and moved by things. Only by constantly settling it down by reading books will the mind not be overwhelmed by external things.

93. Reading over the entries of 1425 of my Record of Daily Renewal[51] today, I felt a sense of inner alarm. I followed this up by reading the *Analects*. Observing the way the sages and worthies taught others through repeated, careful instruction, I am more inspired to rouse myself. I must exert myself more strenuously.

94. Today I got violently angry over a certain matter, and then regretted doing so. I must do as Mencius advised, "maintain firm the will and do no violence to one's vital spirit."[52]

95. After fulfilling my duties, then I should spend time reading books, not allowing my mind for even a moment to overstep the bounds of what is proper.

---

51. This seems to be an early name for the Journal, alluding to the line in *Great Learning* about daily self-cultivation. This practice of retrospection is something already evident in his poetry by 1418 when he was 18.

52. *Mencius* 2A:2.

96. For several days now, I have succeeded very well in nourishing my vital spirit. I must continue this on a regular basis, allowing for no interruptions.

97. Above I have no teacher, below I have no friends. As for my program of self-cultivation, I have grown more lax with it. How can I bear this life of mine?

98. Today while carefully reading through the *Reflections on Things at Hand*, I began to understand that the methods used by the sages and worthies to teach people are all included in the prescriptions and strategies of this book. Still, the strength of my own learning is not up to snuff, with the result that there is no limit to my narrow-mindedness. Where can I find a good friend who will read this text with me, clarifying in detail its meaning, so that I can rely upon it to help me restrain myself and deal with affairs?

99. Cut out bad habits and "daily renew" myself!

100. Refine and purify my whole mind in order to face the gods!

101. For the past ten days, I have been neglecting my studies and moral cultivation. Even in my sleep, I let out frequent sighs of frustration. While teaching my daughters the *Analects* today, I was moved by the subtle and profound words of the Sage. Frightened, I found myself moved to step up my efforts. Now where can I find a good friend to help me realize this ambition of mine to reach sagehood?

102. Today I ran into an old friend along the road whose hair was already streaked with gray. Without thinking, I asked his age, with a sense of sadness for him. He replied that he had just turned forty. Then he,

who all the while had been scrutinizing me, noted that my hair too was turning gray. We grew increasingly saddened. It was a long while before we parted. Later I thought how life is so disappointing: there is only this getting old and growing weak. How true the expression that when one is young, one doesn't exert effort, and when one is old, there is only sorrow. When I returned home tonight, I recorded all this, sitting by the eastern window. Alas, it might be impossible to read all the books in the world, but how could it be impossible for me to succeed in becoming a noble person!

103. I was away from home for a few days, cutting bamboo at the site of my new dwelling place. This evening I returned home and my wife informed me that, "Last night I dreamed that an old man leading two followers passed by and stopped at our gate. He ordered one of the followers to enter and inquire whether you, Yubi, were at home or not. I answered that you were not. The follower said, 'Tell him Confucius came here to pay him a visit and teach him how to advance in his learning.'" When I heard my wife recount this, I was at once alarmed and apprehensive, excited and overjoyed. In gratitude, I got up repeatedly to pay my respects to Heaven and earth. I felt shivers go up and down my spine on account of this. From now on, how dare I not make my mind and vital spirit calm, and fully concentrate on my learning and moral character? How dare I be stingy with my energies, worn-out and inferior though they may be?

104. Going to my new dwelling to teach today, I felt extremely pleased with myself that I've made some new progress in my learning.[53]

105. When I heard of the misdeeds of a friend today, I became more watchful over myself and devoted more real effort to my own practice.

106. Today I was reading the *Book of Rites*. When I got tired, I went to bed. There, thinking about the hardships I've experienced in my

---

53. A poem he wrote at this time reflects the great joy he took in finally finishing and moving into this new house. *Collected Works of Wu Yubi*, hereafter CW, 2:6b.

life, I found myself more and more lamenting the fact that learning the way of the ancients is not easy.

# 1429 (37 years old)

107. Today, I was reading the *Digest of the Recorded Conversations of Zhu Xi*. Alarmed, I anxiously worried that if I make no progress in my learning and moral cultivation, then how will I be able to conduct myself in the world.

108. If there is even the tiniest bit of the Way that I have not exhausted, then I have cut myself off from Heaven.

109. Today, I have been sitting outside my gate, my table covered with diagrams and books. Surrounded by my students, I take advantage of the shade of the trees and enjoy the cool breeze. The vital impulse[54] of the manifold things fills my view. The beautiful mountain stands as guest and host. Contemplating this glorious view, I experience a great sense of expansiveness.

110. Early this morning lying on my pillow, I was carefully reflecting on the fact that I have made no recent progress in my learning and moral cultivation, and that the time has suddenly grown late. Looking back over my life, I feel it is all blurred like a dream. How can I bear these regrets? From today on, I must deeply treasure even the smallest bit of time and not repeat my former mistakes.

---

54. The term here is *sheng-yi* 生意, which can be translated either as the "vital impulse" or the "spirit of life" of things. The idea comes from Cheng Hao: "The most impressive aspect of things is their spirit of life. This is what is meant by origination being the chief quality of goodness. This is *jen*" (trans. by Chan, *Source Book in Chinese Philosophy*, p. 539). *Jen* is the Wade-Giles spelling of *ren* (仁).

**111.** Reading the *Reflections on Things at Hand* today, I gained much insight. As a result, the mean and stingy feelings inside me were transformed into a state of expansiveness.

## 1430 (38 years old)

**112.** This evening there was a heavy rainfall that leaked through the roof, leaving not one dry place in the house. Nevertheless, I remained composed in my thoughts all the while.

**113.** This evening, as I was sitting in silence, I thought how I have made no progress recently in my learning. My friends, too, have been unable to advance in their learning. This must be the meaning of the expression that "the Way declines with each day." I remained lost and listless in my thoughts for a long while after.

**114.** If in one's moral practice a person nourishes the fundamentals of the self, that person will be effective in the ordinary matters of everyday life.

**115.** Today, I was harvesting the rice fields around Qingshi Bridge. On my way to and from the village, I felt a tremendous sense of joy with all that was around me.

**116.** The late-year crop of rice has turned out to be a poor harvest. This evening on my pillow, I've been thinking what sore straits I'm in with respect to household necessities and how I cannot concentrate on my reading. After restlessly tossing and turning for a good long time, unable to sleep, I came to realize that extreme poverty and suffering strengthen a person's will and mature his sense of humaneness. I dare not fail to keep exerting myself!

**117.** The past several nights we have lacked oil for the lamp, so my poor wife has been burning firewood to provide light for my reading. This evening I was reading from Zhu Xi's *Collected Works*. I derived great benefit from reciting passages from it aloud. Then I spent time teaching my students the very last passage of the *Mencius* text, where he traces the history of the transmission of the Way from earliest time, ending with the question of who will assume the responsibility for its transmission in the present. I found myself immensely affected by it, wondering what answer I would give. Later, at bedtime, I was reading the *Biographical Account of Cheng Hao*. After all this reading, I found my usual dim-witted nature roused and enlivened.[55]

118. On the road today, I was reading the *Records of the Words and Deeds of Eminent Officials of the Song Dynasty*. On my way home, I lay down in the grass on the other side of the stream. I quite enjoyed sitting by the water, reading my book. It all had the flavor of a quiet existence beyond the dusty world.

119. Tired from reading in the main hall, I strolled around the rear garden and back. Returning, I took up my lute and played a few tunes. At that moment, I experienced a great sense of expansiveness. Today, with the sun so bright and the breeze so gentle, I know of no other happiness between Heaven and earth!

120. Lying on my pillow early this morning, I felt deep remorse for my obstinate and mean ways. By chance, these lines came to me: "The point is not that other people are hard to change, but truly that my own moral character is not up to par."

121. What is required of my behavior is that I dare not fail to fully realize my allotted portion[56] in life. As for considerations of profit or loss, success or failure, they should not enter into my calculations. Rather, I must constantly work on making this mind of mine free and untrammeled.

---

55. I have rearranged the first few lines of this entry to make it read more smoothly.

56. The Chinese term is *fen* 分. Wu often uses it interchangeably with *ming* 命 (fate) or *tian-ming* 天命 (Heaven's will).

122. These are things I should work on: to stay constant and vigorous in my efforts to "hold the will firm" and to devote myself to eliminating the imbalances of my natural temperament.

# 1431 (39 years old)

123. While strolling in the garden today, I found the vital impulse of everything around me[57] especially pleasing to behold.

124. Content in poverty and delighting in the Way—this is what it means to be a noble person.

125. Today I met with an adverse circumstance and got violently angry. Reflecting on it afterwards from the vantage point of moral principle, I realize that all too often I am lacking in moral character and concentrate too much on criticizing others. What is more, people take time to change, and even then, a person cannot avoid there being some occasions of backsliding. Alas, how difficult is the Way of the Mean!

126. Lately I am increasingly aware of the difficulties of being a mature human being. I don't feel like I have made any advancement in my learning and time waits for no man. What am I to do? What am I to do?

127. Tonight on my pillow, I have been thinking how both Zhu Xi's *Collected Works* and *Practicing the Mean* revolve around considerations of cultivating the body, mind, nature, and emotions. All this I find to be of great interest. Yesterday, I wanted to write down a few lines of cautionary advice to myself and so wrote: "With a temperament that is mild and peaceful, I have the means with which to overcome the recalcitrant and narrow nature of my mind. Thereby I can hope to make some slight

---

57. Literally, the ten thousand things (萬物).

progress in my learning." Today I continued writing with this advice: "If I wish to make progress, I know of no way to do so other than practices of 'holding on to reverence' and 'plumbing principle.'" More and more lately, I've felt how apropos these two practices are. Further exploring them in Zhu's *Collected Works*, I find them all the more compelling.

128. This evening, I was thinking about the seriousness of the trust received from my father and teachers, and the depth of the expectations of my colleagues and friends. Trembling in fright, I have become even more apprehensive. I wish to have the means to root out human desires in myself, only I still don't know the exact method.

129. These past several days I have had some feeling of being more effective in handling difficulties. But early this morning on my pillow, the first day of the sixth month, I've been thinking how time is flying by and still I haven't established myself in my life's calling. I can't help but heave a sigh of lament.

130. Today is the fifth day of the seventh month. In my well-lit and tidy studio, I have been practicing the calligraphy of the famous literatus Zhong Yu. Ah, I'm in an excellent state of mind! As long as I am personally engaged with my brush and ink slab, and with the diagrams and writings of the sages and worthies, I am unaware of my actual condition—that of poverty and low estate, of sorrow and difficulty.

131. When a person meets with sorrow and difficulty, he must manage them with a calm mind and relaxed spirit. As soon as any resentment arises, it is certain to result in "complaining against Heaven or blaming other people." It is just at this time that a person sees the strength of his learning. I really must exert myself.

132. In the midst of poverty and distress, I am entangled by all kinds of matters. Although it is like this, I still must exert effort. On one

hand, I must manage the difficulties; on the other hand, I must still try to advance in my learning.

**133.** Since last night, the twelfth day of the seventh month, I have lain awake on my pillow considering what extremely sore straits I'm in with respect to my family's livelihood. I feel so incapable of dealing with the situation. Turning it over and over in my mind, I cannot come up with any solution. Now I find it's already well into the morning and still I haven't gotten up. Ruminating a while longer, I finally came up with something: namely, there is no other clever way out except to follow along with my given allotment in life,[58] economize in my expenses, and be content in poverty—that is all. I vow that even though I "die from the cold or from starvation," I won't dare change this basic resolve of mine. Thereupon I got out of bed with a feeling of joy. I understand even more deeply the meaning of the passage, "To be mature in your efforts, you must go through this discipline through hardship."

**134.** Late last night around midnight, I was thinking how time is passing by and I've made little progress in my life's calling. Tossing and turning in bed, I couldn't sleep until the arrival of dawn.

**135.** In all matters, I must first judge myself!

**136.** This evening I was reciting the *Biographical Account of Cheng Hao* and found myself immensely affected by it. Whenever I came to a place that resonated with me, without realizing it, my hands and feet moved in joyful response.[59]

---

58. The Chinese is *suifen* 隨分, and involves the idea of learning how to discern and follow one's particular path in life, given its limitations and possibilities.

59. Alluding to *Mencius* 4A:27, which Confucians often refer to when they wish to describe the spontaneous and unexpected joy that sometimes comes with their reading. Bloom's translation puts it well: "without realizing it, one's feet begin to step in time to

137. These past several days, I've found my practice of rectifying the mind to be rather meaningful.

138. Last evening, on account of being simultaneously bothered by poverty and illness, I couldn't concentrate my reading and couldn't help feeling restless inside. After deep reflection, I realized that what is required is to direct my moral efforts right at this very problem spot, make myself composed inside, and, in every situation, to progress in my learning according to my given abilities. Then all will be as it should be. Otherwise there will be places where I will fail. *Practicing the Mean* reminds me that, "The noble person can find himself in no situation in which he is not at ease with himself," but this is a difficult thing. And yet, it is herein that one sees the difference between the sage and the ordinary person. I cannot but exert effort in this regard. Whenever I "complain against Heaven or blame other people," it is only because I have not yet penetrated this stage of self-realization.

139. This evening, I was discussing with my students Master Zhu Xi's set of poems entitled, "Letting My Feelings Arise While Resting in My Studio." In the spirit of Zhu Xi's professed aim in composing them,[60] I used them as cautionary guides. The emotion in my voice rose and fell in cadence with the poems' rhythms. We were all immensely affected by them.

140. A wise man of old said, "The body and the mind must have a secure place to settle." For if the body and the mind have no secure place to settle, then in the midst of everyday life, they will be disturbed by

---

them and one's hands begin to dance them out" (trans. by Bloom, *Mencius,* p. 84). The point is that joy in learning registers in the physical body.

60. These are his *Zhaiju ganxing* poems. In the preface to them, Zhu Xi speaks of having written them to alert himself and his friends. He admits that they are not so subtle or profound but are relevant to realizing principle in everyday situations (*Collected Works of Zhu Xi* 4:6b).

considerations of nothing but profit and loss. This indeed is something words cannot fully explain. It is in silence that a person must come to know it.

# 1432 (40 years old)

141. In the late spring, I stroll outside my garden. As the *Great Learning* described, "The mind is expanded and the body is at ease."[61] How apropos these words are!

142. My impoverished situation is already at its extreme and I cannot support myself. At the same time, illnesses add to the difficulties. Even so, I am content with my lot and do not dare permit thoughts of "complaining and blaming." Since I have the means with which to make further improvements in my learning and to strengthen further my resolve, I dare not fail to exert myself to do so.

143. Today while resting, I read some of the poetry of Shao Yong. Subsequently, I fell into a deep sleep. When I awoke, my state of mind was quite excellent, just as Shao himself described in a poem, "no less than had I been enfeoffed or awarded money."[62] Even though I am extremely impoverished, that is my fate. But it cannot destroy this present happiness.

144. Today, I realized that there is a vast difference between my present understanding of the *Reflections on Things at Hand* with that of former days. Inside, I feel free and untrammeled, as if a chronic disease had finally left my body.

---

61. *Great Learning* 6.4: "Riches adorn a house and virtue enriches a person. The mind is expanded and the body is at ease. Therefore, the noble person must make his thoughts sincere."

62. *Songs of Slapping an Old Gourd by the Yi River* 7:84b–85a.

**145.** How lovely it is today to behold the vital impulse of all the various plants!

**146.** Today with the sun streaming in my window, I have been personally engaged with my brush and ink slab. Inside I feel extremely pure and refreshed, such that I completely forget that my body is in such sore straits. Shao Yong said, "Even though I am poor, it does not affect the lofty peace I enjoy each day."[63]

**147.** Whether fate brings success or failure, short or long life, I will follow Heaven in any case. I will behave according to my sense of righteousness and that is all.

**148.** This evening I was chanting poetry in the moonlight, strolling alone in the shade of the trees. From time to time I would rest against a tall bamboo tree, enjoying the pleasant breeze softly blowing my way. The human realm being silent and my mind extremely mellow, there was nothing of what Shao Yong called "matters that assault the mind."

**149.** Today when I got tired, I napped for a while. Then I got up and wrote out some maxims from the wise men of old. In my well-lit and neat studio, with a gentle breeze softly blowing my way, I don't know what further happiness there is between Heaven and earth. How fortunate I've reached this point!

**150.** Yesterday I learned another method of managing difficulties from reading Zhu Xi's *Collected Works*. This evening on my pillow, I have been carefully considering the fact that if I do not go through this discipline through hardship, then truly I cannot succeed in becoming a mature human being and will only increase what I am already incapable of doing. How could these just be empty words!

---

63. Ibid., 8:10a.

151. These past several days, I have been extremely aware of the excellence of the word *zhong* 中, "the mean." However, to realize it in practice is difficult. Nevertheless, I must still exert effort to try. Shao Yong's poem says:

> Those who lift mountains and excel in the world are called talented
>     and powerful
> But when it comes to understanding deeper realities of life, they do
>     not have the least bit of superiority.[64]

# 1433 (41 years old)

152. Evening is approaching on this first day of the new year. I find that both my mind and my vital spirit are at peace. From today on, I must step up my efforts to improve my learning and moral character.

153. Today I wrote this poem, "Difficulty at Its Extreme":

> Difficulties I am willing to accept as part of life,
> But I never thought they would be as extreme as this.
> As for my future, I will follow Heaven in all respects.
> What good would it do to worry too much about it?

I also wrote:

> The original mind is completely responsible for that which comes
>     from the interior self;
> As for what comes from the outside, that is all up to Heaven.

154. Early this morning, how wonderful it was to observe the vital impulse of the flowers. Now after breakfast, however, my state of mind has become rather unhappy, due to the extremely sore straits I'm in. Seeking a

---

64. Ibid., 17:92b.

way to understand and solve the situation, I discover the only thing I can do is strengthen my moral character. Success and failure are not things over which I have control.

**155.** My walk alone among the hills today was quite enjoyable. The vital impulse of things was richly displayed. Every now and again, I would go up to the top of the ridge and look all around me. Overwhelmed with joy, I wished to write a poem entitled, "The Whole Expansive View from a Mountain Top."

**156.** What I should do when trying to manage difficulties is only to follow the words of Confucius: "Let his words be sincere and truthful, and his actions honorable and careful."[65]

**157.** Early this morning, how enjoyable it is to observe the vital impulse of things. The waning moon is still in the sky, the dew-drenched flowers fill my view. The subtle appeal of this scene is not something words can describe. On the pillar in my eastern studio, a scroll reads:

The flowers outside my window suit my inner feelings.
The books on my desk delight my moral mind.

**158.** To lodge my body in the realm of natural ease and non-competitiveness, to allow my mind to roam in the sphere of contentment and non-disturbance, every day to take the excellent words and fine behavior of the sages and worthies and be enriched by them—wouldn't all this constitute some progress!

**159.** "I do not complain against Heaven nor do I blame other people. I study things on the lower level but my understanding penetrates

---

65. *Analects* 15:6 (trans. by Legge, *The Chinese Classics*, vol. 1, p. 295). This is Confucius' answer to a student who asked how a person should conduct himself in the world.

to higher things."[66] Who but a sage would appreciate the meaning of these words of Confucius?

160. If a person is unaware of his defects, that is all right. If he is aware of them but not courageous enough to subdue them, then he causes his situation to worsen daily. How could this be all right? This failure to "make firm the will" was cautioned against by Mencius long ago.

161. "Neither forgetting nor helping to grow": recently I have come to know something of what this dictum from Mencius means. If Heaven would grant me some additional years, I still could make some progress. Success or failure, gain or loss, they are not for me to consider.

162. Sorrows and difficulties are good for one's practice of self-cultivation. This is what Mencius meant when he said, "we thrive from experiencing sorrow and calamity, and perish from comfort and joy."[67] Still, for those whose strength of learning is weak, there are few who are not exhausted by it all. Alas, if the wood used for making pillars and beams cannot stand up under wind, ice, or snow, how can it sustain the weight of the roof it was meant to support?

163. A real man[68] ought to stand out above all others in the world.

164. It's the twentieth day of the third month. After breakfast, I did some teaching. As last night's rainstorm was just clearing up, the vital impulse of things filled the whole scene. I found it all extremely delightful. I read the *Spring and Autumn Annals* until close to noon. The

---

66. Ibid., 14:37.

67. *Mencius* 6B:15 (trans. by Bloom, *Mencius* p. 143).

68. The Chinese is *nan-er* 男兒. Wu uses this term often in his poetry to indicate that the pursuit of sagehood is not a matter for sissies.

rain-freshened scenery being so pleasant, the day leisurely lingered on, while Heaven and earth seemed so expansive and distant. Still, my sick body has completely exhausted its vital energies. Unable to avoid the cold and hunger, I just try to do what I can with my allotment in life. I am moved to write two lines of poetry:

> I do the best I can with whatever is at hand, enjoying the time I have.
> Who says life, for the most part, is unsatisfactory?

165. Tonight on my pillow, I have been reflecting on my lack of success in rejuvenating my vital spirit[69] so that I can advance in my learning.

166. This evening, I have been sitting here thinking how fortunate I am whenever I can achieve even the least bit of peacefulness within myself and my household. Even though my poverty is extreme, I accept it as my lot in life and that's all. Confucius said, "A person who fails to understand Heaven's will for him lacks what it takes to be a noble person."[70]

167. This evening in my eastern studio facing the moon, where flowers and bamboo grow mixed together, I find the clear view quite lovely. I have been listening to my students recite their lessons, the sounds of which provide me pleasure. From time to time, I wander outside for a stroll. The shade of the trees in the clear evening has a genuine appeal of expansiveness.

168. Last night, as I was thinking about past times, the recollection of events over the years and months deeply saddened me. Today,

---

69. What I translate here as "vital spirit" is not *qi* but *jing-shen* 精神, which has more of a connotation of physical energy and vitality.

70. *Analects* 20:3.

considerations of time are again on my mind. Alas, I have not yet established my moral character, yet time races quickly by until now it is quite late.

## 1434 (42 years old)

169. A Confucian of old once said, "The Way and its principle are ordinarily and uneventfully displayed." How true these words are! Isn't the meaning of the words "ordinarily and uneventfully displayed" just this, that when too hasty, you fail; when too slow, you fail? Lately it has become more and more evident that it is like this. Hence, when I compare the present state of my mind with that of former days, I find it has gradually become more settled. However, what I find lamentable is that for more than a year now, I have had to set aside my books because of an eye ailment.

170. In managing important matters, I must exercise the greatest care!

171. Early this morning on my pillow, I was thinking how most aspects of my personal practice do not measure up to the sages and worthies. Up to now, I have been unable to manage self-control. So I wish to write in large characters the following four words in order to urge myself on: DON'T DARE BLAME OTHERS!

## 1435 (43 years old)

172. Because of an eye ailment, I haven't dared do much reading. For a while today, however, I recited some poems from the *Book of Odes*. I was strongly moved by the depth of meaning in them, though I dared not read for too long a time. Being thus limited, I found myself sighing in frustration for a long time.

173. Spending time looking over some old papers of mine from twenty-eight years ago, I find matters seem blurred as if in a dream. I am overwhelmed with painful recollections.

174. Today I was reading a letter of the Tang Confucian, Han Yu, to his friend Li Ao. In it he pours out his heart about being out of favor at court, unappreciated, and poor. I found myself greatly moved by it.

175. Today I was reading essays by Han Yu. Then I got tired and went to sleep. In my dreams, I confusedly thought I was back in the time of my youth. Overwhelmed with feelings of sadness, I awoke. How true that I cannot recover the powers of my past days, but still I must every day assume responsibility for the Way and its virtue.

176. Today, the first day of the fifth month, I read some more essays by Han Yu. The brightness of the sun fills the window screens, a clear breeze penetrates the house, flowers and grasses spill over and fill up the verandas—this secluded scenery is so lovely!

177. From time to time today, I go out for a stroll, resting in the shade of the trees, benefiting from the cool breezes there. How very enjoyable it is!

178. Today, the twenty-first day of the seventh month, I was facing the fields, lecturing and reciting. As evening approached, I wandered around beyond the fields with my walking cane. How very pleasant it all was!

179. Today I was reading Zhu Xi's *Collected Works* and found myself greatly affected by it.

180. Today, the twenty-ninth day of the twelfth month, I made the year-end sacrificial offerings to my ancestors. The whole day I have been much saddened that students of the Way are so few and those with strong commitment to sagehood even fewer. Great is my worry over the ways of the world!

# 1436 (44 years old)

181. Master Zhu Xi said, "Nourish the self in a leisurely but profound manner." How excellent are these words!

182. Today I was reading the *Records of the Words and Deeds of Eminent Officials of the Song Dynasty*. I gained much insight from the part where Yang Shih, in discussing the famous scholar Su Shi, said, "What the noble person cultivates is not allowing a rude and perverse disposition to develop in himself."[71] Alas, since my will is not master of my vital spirit, as Mencius advised, my moral practice keeps getting interrupted. How extremely difficult it is to become a sage or worthy!

183. For several days now, I have been reading selections from the *Written Legacy of the Cheng Brothers*, which I have found to be extremely valuable. I am led to reflect that the words of the two Master Chengs can truly be considered the transmission of the Way of the Sages. How is this? Because the manner in which they explain the Way and principle is neither too lofty nor too vulgar; neither too insistent nor too easy-going. Their words are as mild as those of the Master, Confucius. Reading them naturally makes a person's mind and vital spirit peaceful, and eliminates all the myriad ratiocinations of the mind.

184. When I got tired today I took a nap. When I awoke, I came and sat here in the eastern studio to read from Zhu Xi's *Collected Works*.

---

71. *Records of the Words and Deeds of Eminent Officials of the Song Dynasty* 9:9b.

The sky is bright, the day long; the bamboo trees are luxuriant, the clear view pleasant. I'm in a very happy mood.

185. Today I was examining the *Recorded Conversations of Zhu Xi*. Preoccupied with the Way as presented therein, I found myself unaware of the coming of old age, the declining of my vital energy, and the frequency of my illnesses.

186. To nourish and care for the mind and also not allow it to be overwhelmed by external things are two things both apropos to the daily exertion of moral endeavor.

187. During a dream in the middle of last night, I found myself deeply vexed that I've as yet made no progress in my learning and I'm now old with no accomplishments. Weeping bitterly, I awoke.

188. Today I was out roaming among the banks and slopes until I reached the bottom of a ravine. I sat there for a long time, facing the sun, finding it extremely pleasant. Examining and scrutinizing my body and mind, I was fortunate to find some slight progress has been made.

189. Today I took a leisurely stroll outside the village. With a copy of the *Written Legacy of the Cheng Brothers* in hand, I slowly walked from Houfang Gully past Datung Spring. Gazing at the mountains and enjoying the stream, I returned by way of the gorge. I rested there for a long while. Using a stone for a pillow and the grass for a mat, I fell asleep. The warm sun dried my clothing, the bubbling stream cleansed my ears. It all had the nice result of making me feel that I too had been participating in the spring bathing rites celebrated in the *Analects*.[72]

_____

72. See note to entry 29 above.

190. Tonight on my pillow, upon examining myself, I found I have made some improvement. So I want to write these four sayings down in large characters to paste on the walls of my east-west studio:

"TOO MUCH TALK HARMS THE WAY!"

"GOOD PEOPLE HAVE FEW WORDS. HASTY PEOPLE HAVE MANY WORDS."[73]

"HAVE NO DEPRAVED THOUGHTS!"

Shao Yong's *CHANT OF FOUR WRONGS.*
The ear listens to nothing reckless,
The eyes look at nothing that is wrong.
The mouth speaks nothing that is reckless.
The mind considers nothing that is wrong.[74]

191. Last night on my pillow, I was thinking how lately I have made no progress in my learning and moral character. I tossed and turned, unable to find rest. It was only with the crowing of the cock this morning that I fell asleep.

192. When I read where Zhu Xi said he did not make any significant progress after he was sixty, I felt lost and beside myself.[75] Alas, the days and months pass away and I cannot recapture them.

193. Today I was looking over the *Records of the Words and Deeds of the Song Confucian Masters.* Alarmed, I found myself greatly moved inside. More and more I am inspired to move ahead, so much so that I've become unaware of the decline of my vital energies and how exhausted I am from my illnesses.

---

73. "Appended Remarks," *Book of Changes,* Part B, *juan* 9.

74. *Songs of Slapping an Old Gourd by the Yi River* 16:84a.

75. Wu was 44 at the time by Western reckoning.

194. It is the eleventh month of the year. I have been passing the nights with only a single-layered quilt. The cold has been extreme and my stomach full of pains. I added a summer curtain for an extra layer. Nevertheless, all the while I've remained free of the least bit of resentment toward my poverty.

195. Today I took a leisurely stroll outside the gate then returned. Master Cheng Hao said, "Happiness consists only in being at peace inside." To be sure, these are wise words!

196. Lately my body and mind have been rather tranquil. This would seem to mark one further step of advancement in my learning and moral cultivation.

197. I spent some time today looking over some old papers of mine. Unexpectedly I came across something I had written about the Song scholar Hu Anguo. In it, I expressed admiration for the way his fame had spread throughout the world, how he had obtained high positions in government, and how he had carried out in practice whatever he learned. After reading this, I was overcome with painful feelings that I had set him up as a model back then but never succeeded in accomplishing what he did.

198. Tonight on my pillow, I was giving careful thought to the fact that I must make progress from this moment on and dare not cut myself off from Heaven. In success or failure, gain or loss, I must follow Heaven's will. Even if I die of starvation in a ditch, I must not forsake my moral character.

199. Recently it has happened frequently that I have awakened from my dreams around the fourth or fifth watch (between 1:00 and 5:00 a.m.) and found myself vigorously scrutinizing my body and mind, and thoroughly examining the principle of things.

200. There is a saying by Cheng Yi, "There are events in the world which might cause joy or provoke anger. If a person reacts with more than what is called for, then what a waste of effort!"[76] How true these words are!

201. A wise man of old said, "The Imperial carriage competes in speed with the ox cart; the phoenix competes for food with the kite owl. Precious jade worth cities and broken pottery tiles clash against each other; the noble person vies in strength with the mean and petty person. Not only is the latter incapable of overcoming the former, he also should not be allowed to."

# (There are no entries for 1437–1448.)

# 1449 (57 years old)

202. On the night of the seventeenth day of the first month, I dreamed that a piece of jade produced orchid-like blossoms that filled the whole ground.

# 1450 (No entries for this year.)

# 1451 (59 years old)

203. What I depend upon is Heaven; what I trust in is its will for me.

204. On the night of the second day of the eighth month, I dreamed that there was a complete eclipse of the sun. When I, Yubi, breathed

---

76. *Written Legacy* 18:22a.

fire into it from the side, it flamed up immediately, its full brilliance thereupon restored.

## 1452 (60 years old)

205. Early this morning, the fourth day of the month, I have been copying over some old papers of mine. The morning sun is right at my window. With a background of autumn flowers, bright sunshine, a gentle breeze, and the shade of trees, my thoughts become open and expanded.

## 1453 (61 years old)

206. As Cheng Yi said, "If one cultivates himself, he will attain a sense of his oneness."[77]

207. Today by the pond, I was reading two or three passages from the *Compilation of Exemplary Biographies to Alert the Self*, which I found extremely valuable. More and more I understand why a person must take becoming a sage or worthy as his personal responsibility.

208. I have made some slight progress in my study of the *Book of Changes*. However, I regret that my vital energies are declining and that I have not much time left in my life. The only thing to do is exert effort according to my given abilities, thereby completing the remaining years of my life in this way.

209. Myriad are the sizes and shapes of mountains. It is up to the beholder to grasp them in his own way. Myriad are the shapes and forms of literature. It is up to the writer to find the one most suitable for himself.

---

77. Ibid., 15:1a.

## 1454 (62 years old)

210. Reading even a small bit of an official memorial to the emperor makes a person tremble in fear. Alas, honest criticism cannot be disregarded by anyone!

211. Today I have been thinking how to reach the principle of being at ease in all circumstances. As long as there is any breath remaining, a person must not tolerate the least bit of negligence with respect to his effort of the will. How can I use the excuse of old age to feel wearied by events!

212. For several days now, I have been thinking how I've passed the days of my life as a fake.[78]

213. Today I talked with my students for a long time, generally encouraging them to care for and cultivate the root of their true selves, not allowing the germination of even the tiniest sprout of concern for selfish gain.

## 1455 (63 years old)

214. Late in my life, I have come to understand how truly beneficial for reading and guidance are the various histories. I only regret that there is not much time left in my life to devote to them.

215. I received a letter from Mr. Wu Heng of Jiangxi province, telling me that my former student, Cheng Yong, has received an order from the prefect, the Honorable Mr. Wang, to go borrow a copy of Zhu Xi's *Classified Conversations* from the former chancellor of the National

---

78. Literally, "as an empty frame."

University, Hu Yan. He is to make a copy of it, then have it printed so as to spread this outstanding learning for posterity's benefit. I was overwhelmed with joy at hearing this, but regretted that I probably won't live to see the completion of this grand undertaking.

216. Today by the eastern window, I have been personally engaged with my brush and ink slab. I take pleasure in the saying, "When a person's learning has reached the point where he does not blame others, that is the perfection of learning."[79]

217. Having finished my bath, I sit by the eastern window personally engaged with my brush and ink slab. The breeze passing through the bamboo trees wafts over my desk, while the shade of the trees surrounds me.

218. Reading formal impeachments of government officials makes a person tremble in fear. I give some to the students to copy.

219. Before noon today, I was tending my garden. In accordance with the principle of poverty and low estate, of course, I dare not shrink from hard work.

220. Today, I wandered alone to the far side of the stream for so many steps, and then returned. There was no one to accompany me.

221. The height of humaneness is the ultimate of righteousness.

---

79. Zhang Zai, "Correcting Youthful Ignorance," (*Zhengmeng*) in *Complete Works of Zhang Zai* (*Zhangzi quanshu*) 2:25b.

222. Observing the goodness and evil of others leaves a person with nothing but to turn inward and reflect upon them in himself.


# 1456 (64 years old)

223. This is the first day of the second month. Last night, I had a dream that I was watching the rising of floodwaters with three other people. We had intended to go together to visit Master Zhu Xi, but the tides prevented us. Overwhelmed with sighs of lament, I awoke. I then composed the following poem:

> Though myriads of autumns separate us, we share deep feelings between us.
> Unable to part, I do not understand the state of mind I'm in.
> The golden cock suddenly announces the dawn at the spring window.
> With regret, my injured spirit gives out a cry of sorrow.


224. I came across this passage from the *Book of History* that I find helpful: "The good person, in the pursuit of goodness, finds that there isn't enough time in life. The bad person, in the pursuit of what is not good, likewise finds there isn't enough time."[80]


225. To try to gain utilitarian advantage is to lose it; to forego utilitarian advantage is to gain it.


226. "Awakening from a leisurely nap by the window, my mood is just as if I had been enfeoffed or awarded money." As for this line by Shao Yong, there is no need to phrase it this way. Master Zhu Xi's expressing it as "the nourishing of the self in a leisurely but profound manner" is better.

---

80. "Great Declaration," part B, *Book of History* (trans. by James Legge, *The Chinese Classics*, vol. 3, p. 290).

227. Fu Mei sent some noodles to me.[81] The poor scholar is one who has undergone the discipline of mastering himself in order to fulfill the claims of righteousness.

226. I must deal with the multiple aspects of life by having no selfish mind of my own.

# 1457 (65 years old)

229. The Three Bonds[82] and the Five Constant Virtues[83] represent the primal forces of Heaven and earth. This holds true for the family as well as for each individual person.

230. Zhu Xi said, "For every day that one is still alive, that day he must undertake his particular responsibilities."

231. While randomly picking flowers at the far end of the stream today, I became nostalgic about old friends and thought of two lines:

By chance, I am at the place once visited and enjoyed with old friends.
We picked flowers at the bend of the stream and delighted in the spring waters.

232. Whether in activity or quiescence, in speech or in silence, there is nothing outside the sphere of a person's moral effort.

---

81. This line is garbled. I read the first two characters as a person's name because otherwise it reads "In giving soup or sending noodles. . . ."

82. The Three Bonds include the relationships between ruler and subject, parent and child, and husband and wife.

83. The Five Constant Virtues are humaneness, righteousness, propriety, wisdom, and faithfulness.

233. Roaming on the far side of the stream today, I picked some flowers. The late spring weather was such that I was filled with pure joy.

234. After taking a look at the flooded fields today, I returned home late. Along the way, there was a heavy downpour of rain. Then the rain stopped and the moon appeared. My clothes were soaking wet, but such a thing is inevitable when one's lot in life is one of poverty and lowly estate.

235. To do quiet sitting when one is all alone is not so difficult. What is really difficult is living in the wider world, responding to its needs.

236. Whenever I try to rush matters, they end up spoiled.

237. Cheng Yi said, "Not to continue studying is to grow old and feeble."[84]

238. On the night of the twenty-fifth day of the fifth month, I dreamed that Confucius' grandson paid me a visit, saying, "I've come here commissioned by Confucius." The two of us were moved to tears; then I awoke. Even now, I can still distinctively remember his features.

239. Master Hu Anguo said, "In responding to the affairs of life, one should be as floating clouds and flowing waters, at ease with whatever one encounters."[85] He is most certainly right.

240. While resting today, I was reading passages from *Exemplary Biographies to Alert the Self*. In alarm, I scrutinized my own behavior. I must be stricter with myself in efforts at self-control.

---

84. *Written Legacy* 7:3a.
85. Quoted in *Classified Conversations of Zhu Xi* 102:7a (p. 4101).

241. Do not injure a sincere heart with vain hopes nor harm one's primal spirit with too much formality.

242. I spent this evening sitting by the gatehouse, watching the moon shining on the *wu-tong* trees and enjoying the clear breeze softly blowing this way.

243. A person must understand that all human life has already been settled. What end does it serve to waste your energies trying to plan everything to be like you want?

244. It is good planning when the intentions of Heaven are in accord with the times and circumstances. It is a good arrangement when human feelings are content with their lot.

245. Just consider this night when the wind is howling and the weather is freezing cold! Who is the man at the door with his steadied stance, secure amid all the chaos?

246. On the night of the tenth day of the twelfth month, I dreamed that a clear breeze swayed the tall stately trees of the myriad households.[86]

# 1458 (No entries. Year he went to Beijing for an audience with the Emperor.)

# 1459 (No entries for this year.)

---

86. "Clear breeze" is often used in poetry to refer to the upright pure gentleman.

# 1460 (68 years old)

247. A person should not be too calculating about any matter. Each person's life has its own fixed lot. In conducting himself, one cannot but "be watchful over himself while alone."

248. Reading some historical writings over the past several days, I have increasingly come to understand that self-recollection is one of the most important things in my moral practice.

249. As Confucius said, "A wise man lets neither men nor words go to waste."[87]

250. Putting in order my Life's Journal today, I find painful recollections assail me as I do.

251. A person must respect himself!

252. Confucius said, "I do not complain against Heaven or blame people. I study things on the lower level but my understanding penetrates to higher things."[88] I must treasure this saying for the rest of my life.

253. I had a dream in which someone told me, "A person who sets limits for himself will make no progress in developing his moral character." He furthermore said, "One who is aware of his own imperfections is capable of receiving important responsibilities and reaching great heights."

---

87. *Analects* 15:8. The sentences preceding this terse remark are: "To fail to speak to a man who is capable of benefiting is to let a man go to waste. To speak to a man who is incapable of benefiting is to let one's words go to waste. A wise man lets neither men nor words go to waste." (Trans. by D. C. Lau, *Confucius, the Analects*, p. 133).
88. Ibid., 14:37.

254. Every day I must practice doing what is right. Good or bad fortune, fame or disgrace are not things I can calculate. Rather I must follow what Heaven has ordained for me.

255. After eating today, I took a leisurely rest by the eastern window, feeling like one of the worthies of high antiquity.

256. I dreamed that I was chanting a poem that went:

Again I tell you, do not cut the trees in front of the eaves of my
  house,
Rather, listen to the Red Apricot Song in my lofty hall.

257. I had another dream that went:

"Loftily he rests amidst the white clouds in his high tower."

# 1461 (69 years old)

258. After eating today, I was tired so I took a nap. I dreamed that Master Zhu Xi and his son graced me with a visit.

259. Most people are alike in wanting to rush toward the powerful and famous. The noble person is alone in preferring to honor the virtuous.

260. I dreamed these lines of poetry:

Generally we understand the meaning of the east wind,
It is just springtime with crows and magpies along the bridge.

261. Leisurely resting by the window today, in the shade of trees in the clear daylight, I wonder how Heaven and earth can be so expansive and far-reaching.

262. Today I took an outing to Houfang Gully where I climbed to the top of a hill and sat on a massive rock. Everything around me gave me great pleasure. I would like to build a pavilion right here called "A View of Flourishing Nature Pavilion" to save me the trouble of climbing up and down. Evening time, when I finally left to return home, I noticed the sliver of a new moon shining above me.

263. Today I have been leisurely resting in my new studio. As the late day sun shines brightly through the window, I find I'm in a good state of mind. Because the "Way and its principle are ordinarily and uneventfully displayed," I should not be too purposive about things.

264. If another person treats me with deceit and stinginess, I shall try to treat him with fairness and openness.

# 1462 (70 years old)

265. This morning I was reading Journal entries from last year and the year before. When I grew weary I took a nap. Lying on my pillow, I carefully considered how the strength of my learning is limited to just this measly bit. My vital energies grow more enfeebled and weary with each day. Whether I look up or down, I find I am disappointed that I've wasted so much of my life in this world.

266. The *Book of Odes* says, "We should be apprehensive and careful as if we were on the verge of a deep gulf, as if we were treading on thin ice."[89] Only now that I am seventy-two years old do I understand the meaning of this. Truly, to emulate the worthies is not an easy thing to do.

267. This evening, quietly resting in my chamber, I had some profound insight to the meaning of Zhou Dunyi's phrase, "one is vacuous

---

89. *Book of Odes*, ode no. 195 (Legge, *The She King, or the Book of Poetry*, p. 333).

while tranquil, and straightforward while in action."[90] However, to exert effort during times of activity is not especially easy to do.

268. Master Cheng Hao said, "Most of those in the five relationships have somewhat failed to fulfill their functions."[91] How excellent are these words!

269. I was reading where Zhang Zai said, "When a person's learning has reached the point where he does not blame others, that is the perfection of learning."[92] It reminded me of something Confucius had said: "I have heard such words, but I have not seen such a person who has realized them."[93]

270. Today I was reading the *Diagrams to the Yi Rituals* and also examining old entries in my Journal. When I grew weary, I took a nap. I recalled that Master Cheng died when he was seventy.[94] This humble self of mine is seventy-two. What am I to do? What am I to do?

# 1463 (71 years old)

271. Last evening on my pillow, I was engaged in quiet reflection. I resolved that I would spend the rest of my life engaged in learning to be a sage and nothing else.

---

90. "Learning to be a Sage," chapter 20 in *Penetrating the Book of Changes*, (*Tongshu*) 4b (trans. by Chan, *Source Book in Chinese Philosophy*, p. 473).

91. *Written Legacy* 1:2a. The passage as a whole reads: "There is no creature in the world that does not possess sufficient principle. I have always thought that rulers and ministers, fathers and sons, brothers, husbands and wives have somewhat failed to fulfill their functions" (trans. by Chan, *Reflections on Things at Hand*, p. 17).

92. Quoted in entry 216 above.

93. *Analects* 16:11.

94. This is puzzling here. Cheng Hao died at fifty-four and Cheng Yi at seventy-five. He must be referring to the latter, but if so, Wu still has a few years to catch up with him.

272. I have been reading several passages from the *Written Legacy* as the light of the late afternoon sun brightens the room. My absorption in the words of Master Cheng Hao is as if I had been drinking strong wine and, without realizing it, had become intoxicated.

## 1464 (72 years old)

273. I took a slow walk inside the walls of my fields today, checking up on the new rice sprouts. Sitting on a footpath with my mind tranquil, I greatly enjoyed the spirit of spring everywhere visible.

274. Observing the principle of things in the midst of tranquility, a person is able to grasp it everywhere.

## 1465 (73 years old)

275. Today I went back and read over the entries in my Journal from 1425 and 1426. Doing so evoked a great deal of emotion in me.

276. Today I was looking over the past several years of my Journal. As for the myriad affairs that affect my life, I must not go about fault-finding, for that would only be to trouble my mind needlessly. I should be as Cheng Hao described the sage, "broad and extremely impartial, and respond spontaneously to all things as they come."[95] To be extremely impartial is humaneness; responding spontaneously is righteousness.

277. Early this morning sitting by the window, I recited to myself, "If I wish to achieve excellent merits, I must come up with some worthwhile plans." This wasn't just a dream that I suddenly found myself spontaneously

---

95. *Collected Works of Cheng Hao* 3:1a–b (trans. by Chan, *Source Book in Chinese Philosophy*, p. 525). This is quoted again below in entry 310.

reciting like this. Wasn't this a case of ghosts and spirits[96] sending me a warning? I must write these words in large characters on my wall as well as each day seek to make some progress.

## 1466 (74 years old)

278. When one has serious doubts about a matter at hand, look at the way the person handled the situation. That was Master Shao Yong's teaching.

279. There is a passage in the *Written Legacy* of the Cheng brothers that says, "A person must examine himself as to how he really is, and pay no heed to frivolous public opinion. When the will is preoccupied with frivolous opinion, then the mind is not present within and a person cannot respond to sudden, unexpected happenings."[97]

## 1467 (75 years old)

280. Whenever I pore over the words of the sages and worthies, my mind spontaneously becomes intoxicated, and without realizing it, my hands and feet move in joyful response.

281. Early this morning on my pillow, I was reciting passages from the *Book of Changes*. Later I read over last year's entries in my Journal which aroused deep feelings of alarm.[98] I dare not fail to take becoming a sage or worthy as my personal responsibility. Each day I must rouse myself to action so that I will not fail in my duties to my friends.

---

96. The terms for ghosts and spirits is *gui-shen* 鬼神.

97. *Written Legacy* 7:2a.

98. There are only two entries from that year in all the extant editions. There must have been more, raising the question whether they were lost or edited out.

282. This evening I was reading Zhu Xi's *Classified Conversations* and could hardly bear to put it down. However, because of the infirmities of old age, I dare not read for too long at one time.

283. As for what *Practicing the Mean* speaks of, "the virtuous nature" and "constant inquiry and study,"[99] I dare not be remiss in the least bit with respect to either. I only regret the fact that there is not much time left in my life.

284. In learning to be a sage, there is no other way than seeking within myself. As for good or bad fortune, fame or disgrace, I try to follow Heaven in any case.

285. The noble person tends to his own situation in life. How could he take what comes from the outside world as true honor or disgrace?

286. The Way of Heaven is to bless the good and bring evil to the bad. The noble person, however, still must diligently observe the honored teaching of the sages and worthies of old, "to rest in ease while waiting for the will of Heaven,"[100] and that is all.

287. Last night in my dreams, I recited the following lines: "How can I preserve and nourish the oneness of my mind?" Wasn't it the ghosts and spirits who taught me this?

288. This afternoon I have been reading the *Collected Works of Lu Zhi*, as well as the *Written Legacy of the Cheng Brothers,* and the *Book of Changes*. Every time I am in intimate contact with the words of the sages and worthies like this, my mind experiences its fundamental oneness.

---

99. *Practicing the Mean* section 27.
100. Ibid., section 14.

Although I am better able to make myself somewhat settled and calm, I cannot afford to let up in my efforts for even a moment.

289. Today when I got tired, I took a nap. A few lines came to me, namely, "Day after day, to nourish myself in a leisurely but profound manner, and whenever I start to waver, to be careful not to be enslaved by selfishness."

290. When examining some old papers of mine, I unexpectedly came across a letter from an old friend, Mr. Lo Dechang. It concerned some difficulties I was having associated with government grain tax matters. Alas! "If a person is to be mature in his efforts, he must pass through this discipline through hardship."

291. To achieve the type of presence befitting a sage or worthy, I cannot fail to exert myself for even a moment.

## 1468 (76 years old)

292. Today I was looking over a letter, a copy of which I have just put up on the wall of my room. It was written to my father by my now deceased friend, Kong E, when he was inspector censor of Jiangxi province:

> Sometime ago, I had a talk with your son, Yubi, for several hours. In searching out his inner state of mind, I discovered that he was the type of person, described by Mencius, who could not be bent or moved by force or might, poverty or riches. While at the present moment he is beset with difficulties, at a later time, he certainly will achieve something great. So don't worry about him.

Reading this produced a jolt of alarm since I haven't achieved anything great. So I copied it in order to caution myself against laziness. Kong was later assigned as Assistant Administration Commissioner in Honan province. When I was in Beijing in 1458, I heard that he had been dead for a good many years.

293. Everywhere I find myself, I can only sigh at the difficulty of learning to become a sage!

294. How lovely is the vital impulse of things evident after a rainfall! Taking this self of mine and letting it go amidst the myriad things in the universe, I look upon all things as the same, "deriving great pleasure in both the great and the small."[101]

295. Day and night, I am continually aware of the goodness of the sagely person. Yet a person of ordinary endowment like myself finds it difficult to strive for.

296. Relaxing in my pavilion today, I watched the vegetables being harvested. I rested there for a long while, observing my state of mind in the midst of tranquility. This is the method of nourishing and caring for the nature.

297. Master Cheng said, "Everything between Heaven and earth can be said to stand alone."[102]

298. Relaxing in my pavilion today, I was poring over with pleasure several passages from Zhu Xi's *Classified Conversations*. I found myself overwhelmed with joy from doing so.

299. Master Zhu Xi said, "The Way declines with each day."

---

101. *Written Legacy* 15:7b. Quoted again in entry 301 below.
102. Ibid., 2A:9a.

300. All day today, I have been thinking how I must spend the remaining years of my life persevering in my efforts to learn to be a sage, trying to subdue all within me that is unbefitting a sage.

301. This evening, while relaxing in my chamber, I have been thinking about what Master Zhu Xi said, "Merely being at leisure is not true happiness." This led me to understand what Master Cheng Hao meant when he said, "A person really has no obstacles between Heaven and earth. To find joy in both the great and the small is true happiness." I must exert myself! Yes, I must exert myself!

302. Once Master Cheng Yi overheard a student of his, Zhang Yi, scolding a servant. Cheng said to him, "Why don't you do what Mencius said, 'stimulate your mind and strengthen your nature'?"[103] Master Zhu Xi said, "Anybody holding a baby that isn't crying can seem like an expert with children." He also said, "To deal with favorable situations is not as good as constantly having to deal with adverse situations. Only when 'the mind is stimulated and the nature strengthened' can one hope to succeed."

303. This afternoon I was resting in my pavilion. In the midst of tranquility, I felt a great sense of inner peace.

304. This afternoon I have been reading from my Journal. On such a nice bright day as today, I raise my thoughts to the principle of things.

---

103. Zhang Yi was a disciple of the Cheng brothers. This instance is included in the chapter on "Correcting Mistakes" in *Reflections on Things at Hand*. "Stimulate your mind . . ." is from *Mencius* 6B:15 ("When Heaven intends to confer a great responsibility upon a person, it first visits his mind and will with suffering, toils his sinews and bones, subjects his body to hunger, exposes him to poverty, and confounds his projects. Through this, his mind is stimulated, his nature strengthened, and his inadequacies repaired. . . . From this we know that we thrive from experiencing sorrow and calamity, and perish from comfort and joy." (Trans. by Bloom, *Mencius*, p. 143.)

305. Today I was looking over several books and found myself quite moved by what I read. However, since my vital energy is in short supply, I dare not read for too long. How I lament the wasted days of my youth!

306. There was a recent event in another locale that showed how contemptible were the prevalent mores there. Alas, I realized the need to strengthen my own moral character so I won't be influenced by this. I must be on my guard! I must be on my guard!

307. Today I was reading Zhu Xi's *Collected Works*. I grew weary so I went and lay down for a while. Looking up, I reflected on ultimate principle. When I found myself in accord with it, without realizing it, I began tapping the mat in joyful approval.

308. Today I copied over a page from my writings about being separated by hundreds of years from Zhu Xi, but still feeling how much we shared similar sentiments and how I didn't fully understand my state of mind.[104]

# 1469 (77 years old, last year of his life)

309. Today I have been reading Zhu Xi's *Collected Works*. Being in intimate contact with the Master's teachings allows a person to transcend the ordinary world and eliminate his numerous worries. I venture to wonder what it took at that time to have been one of his disciples.

310. I often feel oppressed by household business. Still, I must carry on, acting according to principle, remembering what Cheng Hao said: "The constant principle of the sage is that his feelings are in accord with all creation, and yet he has no feelings of his own."

---

104. See above entry 223 from the year 1456, twelve years earlier.

**311.** Today when I got tired, I went and lay down. Looking up, I began thinking about past and present dynasties: their order and disorder, their successes and failures. I also thought about famous families: their flourishing and declining, their successes and failures. It all made me shiver in fright.

**312.** There is no time or place not meant for the exertion of my moral effort!

**313.** Today I took a stroll for a while outside the main gate. There I found the blossoms of the peach and plum trees in full brilliance. The sun resplendent and the breeze so warm and genial, I recalled a line from the *Book of Changes*, "Thus the kings of old, and in harmony with the times, fostered and nourished all beings."[105]

**314.** What greater fortune is there than every day to be in intimate contact with the excellent counsels of the sages and worthies! I only regret that I have been so late in reading them.

**315.** Early this morning, I was resting in my Pavilion of the Self-at-Ease (*Zide-ting* 自得亭). Personally occupied with my brush and ink slab, I paused to watch the scene before me, a light mist hanging over the village, a pond of swimming fish, and the vital impulse of the vegetables growing. I found all this worth taking great delight in.

**316.** In carrying out my duties, I must be as effective as a heavy crossbow. In disciplining myself, I must become as pure as highly refined metal.

**317.** When a person hates annoyances in his old age, this is not behaving according to principle. I must remember that for every day I am alive, that day I must undertake my responsibilities.

---

105. Hexagram 25 "Innocence" (trans. by R. Wilhelm, *The I Ching or Book of Changes*, vol. 1, p. 108).

318. Time quickly passes by, yet I seem to only be regressing instead of making progress in my learning and moral cultivation. I wonder, would the person of firm resolve be demoralized by this or not?

319. Today, I was poring over with pleasure the *Written Legacy*, but, alas, wasn't clear about my own direction with respect to the teachings of the two Chengs. How do I know what constituted the merits of these men? These sages were always kind in their criticisms of others. This helped me understand that their intent was only to rectify the situation, not to expose the faults of others.

320. Today I was looking over some old papers of mine written way back in the days when I lived in Wufeng, having just returned home from the capital. I found that all too many painful recollections are bound up in these.

321. Last night I was reflecting on the various experiences of my life and only fell asleep at the fifth watch (between 3:00 and 5:00 a.m.). The sage never forgets the world around him. Confucius said, "How fixed is his resolve. There is nothing difficult to him."[106]

322. Today I was poring over the *Book of Changes*. In silence, I tried to seek out its meaning and found myself overwhelmed with great joy. I only regret that there is not much time left in my life for further study of it.

324. After getting dressed this morning, I have been occupying myself with my books in the eastern studio. The sun shining through the bamboo brightens the whole room. I find myself thinking back to the time when I first returned to my native village in 1411. I had a poster on one of the pillars at my house in Shiquan that read, "If I wish to reach the realm of the great worthies, I must proceed from the results of 'studying things

---

106. *Analects* 14:42.

on the lower level.'" Looking back, I realize that that was almost sixty years ago. Alas! When will I ever reach that realm of the great worthies?

**325.** I try to keep in mind Cheng Hao's saying, "Whenever one feels bored and wearied by some matter, it shows a lack of sincerity."[107]

**326.** Today I thought over these two quotes. "They speak of the most confused diversities without arousing aversion. They speak of what is most in dynamic change without causing confusion."[108] One should be "broad and extremely impartial and respond spontaneously to things as they come."[109]

**327.** When I got tired today, I went and lay down to care for my illness. I found myself thinking about my own past experiences and the honored teachings of the sages and worthies. When I got up, the day had already grown late.[110]

**328.** Although the myriad changes in the universe are numerous and bewildering, there is a definite principle with respect to responding to each of them.

---

107. *Written Legacy* 5:2a.

108. "Appended Remarks," *Book of Changes* (trans. R. Wilhelm, *The I Ching or Book of Changes*, p. 327 modified).

109. *Written Legacy* 3:1a–b.

110. In the 1590 and *Siku* editions, this entry is part of the following one. I follow the 1526 edition that takes them as separate entries.

# Letters and Miscellaneous from Wu Yubi's *Collected Works*

═══════════════════════════════════

*When Chinese communicate with each other, whether in speech or letters, they often engage in what is known as ke-qi hua 客氣話, "polite talk." It involves conventions such as adopting a humble tone, putting oneself down, and couching what one wants to say in indirect ways. The speaker adopts a level of formality befitting the status of the recipient. The more superior the recipient is, the higher the level of formality. Since one's father was regarded as a superior, Wu Yubi adopts a very formal tone in his letters to him. He also does so with his brother-in-law Sun Yuerang. At another place on the spectrum of formality, communications among friends, a level of informality can be found, as in the letters Wu writes his friend Hu Jiushao. Most of the other letters included here are somewhere in between. For names of texts mentioned, refer to the Glossary of Book Titles. Only names of well-known figures are identified.*

*Of the forty letters in his* Collected Works, *I have selected fifteen. They have been selected for their insights into Wu's philosophy of education or his personal efforts at self-cultivation. Most come from the years 1421 to 1425. I have numbered them from one to fifteen to make referring to them in other parts of the book easier. The number at the end of each piece indicates its location in his* Collected Works.

## (1) Letter to My Esteemed Father 1421

On the twenty-eighth day of the third month, I saw Qiu Yanyong and learned that you had returned to your official position in the capital and that the whole family was doing well. I was overwhelmed with joy to hear this. At first, I was only thinking about Grandmother (the Master's maternal grandmother), that she would be returning home here this spring. However, according to Qiu Yanyong, no date has been set for her return.

Consequently, the following day of the twenty-ninth, I obtained a travel permit and set out to visit you.

Day and night I have been bitterly upbraiding myself about what has happened between us. I remember how when I was young and still immature, you were far away at the National University in Nanjing. It was only when I was twelve years old[1] that Uncle took me to the capital to be with you. But you and I, father and son, didn't recognize each other at first. During the time I lived in the capital, you once told me at night in bed, "In the past, while I was away from home, I often thought of you, but not being able to see you, I was moved to shed many tears. Now that you are here with me, you must exert your efforts to advance in your learning, striving to become a mature and accomplished person." At the time, I did not yet realize how apropos these words were.

When I got to be eighteen and nineteen, even though I was fairly good at my studies, still, since I was overly self-confident and pushy, I would boast to myself that to match the achievements of the ancients was not all that difficult. I would frequently slight the men of the past and carry out my affairs carelessly and disrespectfully. Even though you would severely take me to task over and over again, yet in the end my unbridled mind would not be corrected.

When I was twenty-one, I returned home to the country. As I gained some experience in human affairs, I gradually realized that achieving the results of "practicing with vigor"[2] was not easy and that "Heaven's confounding a person's undertaking"[3] always goes to the extreme. At the same time, beset by various illnesses, I was confused and did not know which road to follow. How could I have hoped to please you? But even though we were physically separated by the distance of a thousand miles, still a night would not go by that my soul was not by your side. I would often grieve late at night that not even death could erase my guilt.

Last year, in the sixth month, I came to wait upon you, hoping to get one glimpse of your face. I wished to report in full what had been

---

1. Ten years old by Western reckoning.

2. *Practicing the Mean,* section 20. "To practice with vigor is to be close to realizing humaneness."

3. Alluding to *Mencius* 6B:15.2, the whole passage of which is quoted above in the note to Journal entry no. 302. Here I opt for Legge's translation (*The Chinese Classics*, vol. 2, p. 344) "it confounds his undertaking" over Bloom's "confounds his projects."

happening these past ten years since I had left the capital for home, thinking I would rouse myself to action from that time on. But my offenses were so great that your mind remained unchanged and you refused to see me. Filled with great sorrow, I returned home. Is there any place in the world where one can be without a father? Truly I was like "a poor man who has no real home to which to return."[4]

(For some unknown reason, last year his father, Guai, refused to see the Master. The Master bore his blame and accepted his guilt, wailing as he knelt from dawn to dusk. Even though he did so for a number of days in a row, his father still didn't receive him. In the winter of this year, the Master again went for a visit. This time Guai was moved by the sincerity of the Master's filial piety, and father and son became as close as in the past.)

This year after hearing the news from Qiu, I again wished to go pay you a visit and escort Grandmother home. My low spirits, however, caused me to vacillate. I wished to go ahead yet also to stay back. How could this unfilial son of yours be worthy of pity? To go would only add to your sorrow. Since my underlying desire was to please you, if, on the contrary, I only added to the burden of your sorrows, how could I be considered to have the heart of a human son?

Hence when the boat arrived at Hukou, I dared neither disembark in order to get a boat to Nanjing nor return home. Rather, I continued on westward as far as Hukuang. From Hukou to Hukuang is about a month's ride. Along the way, I dared not discuss my family background with anyone I met on board, fearing that to do so would implicate your virtue. But now the time has come for the crops to be harvested, so I am taking a boat to return home. I have unexpectedly run into a friend from Sichuan on board who is on his way to Nanjing, so I am taking the opportunity respectfully to send you this letter to give a report of myself.

Since the beginning of this year, I have been reading the Four Books a great deal, not letting up for even a moment. I have some sense that my whole self—body and mind—has benefited from this in its own rough way. In my efforts at sharing the lot of the sages and worthies, I have made a good beginning. Only now do I realize why Heaven inflicted poverty and sickness on me and why you scolded and admonished me for my behavior. What a great blessing for me! Alas, although I still have much time ahead

---

4. *Mencius* 5A:1 speaking of the sage ruler Shun. "But because he was not in harmony with his parents, Shun was like a poor man with no home to return to." (Trans. by Bloom, *Mencius*, p. 98.)

of me to advance in my moral character, I am concerned that your own days are limited. I only wish that you would comfort yourself well, thinking of our ancestors. Many blessings upon you! Many blessings upon you!

Respectfully submitted by your son, Yubi, on the fourth day of the sixth month aboard ship at Wuchang (Hubei province) (8:13a–14b)

## (2) Letter to Xu Xiren, Assistant Director in Local Schools[5] (1421)

I have heard that, of the most excellent things in the world, there is nothing to compare with the Way of Sagehood. Because the Way is brilliant, it is easy to perceive; because it is simple, it is easy to practice. The reason, however, that few in the world succeed in following it is because they do not study how. If we trace the reason for this, we find there are two types of people. The first type is the simple, ordinary person, ignorant and dull, who does not devote himself to learning. The other type is one who studies the Way yet finds himself inadequate for the task because he is not sincere enough. Because he is not sincere enough, when he is confronted with external events, he experiences conflict within himself between moral principle and selfish desires. When he seeks to follow principle, he finds himself entangled in desires; when he seeks to follow his desires, he realizes that there are indeed things which he will not lower himself to do. Inner vexation and depression ensue. When even one of his thoughts is in error, he is aware of the distance separating him from the Way of Sagehood and the depth of his descent into bad habits. Doesn't this not only lead to the diminishment of what little goodness he already has achieved and eventually to even losing that? How can he fulfill what he seeks? Even though he is considered one who studies the Way, he is just the same as the first type of person who does not pursue learning.

For more than ten years, I have been guilty of this fault, finding myself filled with depression day and night to an extreme degree. Ever since the spring of this year, however, I have completely immersed myself in the *Great Learning,* the *Analects, Mencius,* and *Practicing the Mean.* One day, in a kind of an awakening, I found I had a few rough insights into these works. Thereupon I heaved a deep sigh and told myself that the Way of

---

5. Teacher of Wu in his youth and a friend in adulthood.

Sagehood is, after all, easy to understand and, after all, easy to practice. Ever since then, I have learned ways to avoid the daily depression and how loftily to enjoy the outer manifestations of things. Because I have stepped up my efforts in following the Way, I have a much more personal appreciation for what I've learned.

Thereupon I sighed again and said, "The mundane world indeed forsakes me, but I try my best to help myself. The mundane world indeed laughs at me, but I try my best to enjoy myself. In intimate association with the sages and worthies, why should I care about these others?"

For many years, I undeservedly have received kindnesses from you. The ancients placed much value on friends "helping to encourage goodness"[6] so how could I be selfish and not share with you what I have learned? Now I know well that you understand what constitutes the excellence of the Way of Sagehood, because I've been in your presence when you've expressed admiration for another person's good behavior. You have also confessed to me your sense of personal insufficiency. How could this be any different from my own problem with low spirits? Please realize that it isn't impossible for you to be released from your distress and for you to enter the realm of happiness. You just must trust that the capacity for doing so lies within yourself and that the methods for activating it are all in the writings of the sages and worthies. So how could you not strive to exert your efforts in this regard?

Recently I did some traveling. On my way back I caught a cold, which has made it difficult for me to get around and relate all this to you in person. I hope you won't begrudge me the honor of writing me every now and then. I would be most fortunate if you would. (8:14b–16a)

## (3) Letter to Zhang Shiyan, Assistant Director in Local Schools[7] (1421)

Recently, while looking through some old papers of mine, I came across several scrolls of poetry we had exchanged in the past. I was once again moved by the friendship I have shared with you, my old friend. This led me to recall how last year, when I went to the capital to visit my father, you

---

6. Allusion to *Analects* 12:24, which speaks about friends helping to support each other in their moral efforts. The Chinese is *fu-ren* (輔仁).

7. Another former teacher and friend.

kindly gave me some words of advice about how I should take the great sages Yao, Shun, the Duke of Zhou, and Confucius, as my models and expressed your hope that I would reach to such a high state.

Alas, this is something only a great worthy can hope to achieve. How could such a small, unimportant person as I dare to have such wild hopes? Yet, I have observed that the ancients embodied the Way and its virtue in their own persons, and their achievements have illuminated the Way for thousands of years. This was all because they did not underestimate their capacities but preserved the mind in its full purity. Your words of advice to me were for the sake of enlarging my capacity and purifying my mind. How marvelous are the results of friends "helping to encourage goodness"!

The ultimate in sagehood was reached by Yao, Shun, the Duke of Zhou, and Confucius, and nothing further can be added. Yet even they did not rest content with their original capacities, nor did they allow themselves any rest with respect to the cultivation of their minds.

They in turn were followed by heroic men who bravely stood out above their contemporaries. These figures aspired to have the same capacity as these four sages and to make the mind of the sages their own. In all their thoughts and actions, they kept the various sages continually before their eyes as models. When they looked at them with respect to moral character and found themselves not yet adequate, or when they looked at them in terms of achievement and found their own not yet great enough, they would exert their efforts tirelessly, refusing to be satisfied with their present capacities. How could they have settled for what was limited? How could they have allowed their minds to be less than fully focused on the Way? They did not allow their capacities to remain limited or their minds impure. As a result, in the end they were able to accomplish something.

If we take the next group down, there are those who aspired to be like these great worthies who had come before them, strongly exerting their efforts in moral conduct. In all their undertakings, there was nothing they did not succeed in: indeed, in each thing they proved effective.

Now if a person aspires to become a sage, even if he does not make it all the way, he will not fail to become a great worthy. If a person aspires to become a great worthy, even if he does not make it all the way, he will not fail to become an ordinary worthy.[8] Now, when people of the world

---

8. Alluding to Zhou Dunyi's comment, "The sage aspires to be Heaven, the worthy aspires to be a sage, and the noble person aspires to be a worthy" (*Penetrating the Book of Changes*, chapter 10).

look at these outstanding figures of the past, they just say that their success was due to their Heavenly endowment and not something they achieved through their own efforts. Whenever anyone mentions the ancients, they put them aside as being outside their range of consideration. But whenever people mention their own contemporaries, they say, "I am better than he is," or, "I am the same as he is," or "Even though he is better than I, it is not by very much."

Even if there is one in a hundred who sees his own limitations, he resignedly regards the ancients as too difficult to follow and readily contents himself with easy accomplishments in minor skills. He doesn't try to expand his capacity but allows his mind to become mixed and adulterated. Any insignificant accomplishment makes him proud and overbearing, as he regards his responsibilities to human society as going no further than these. Alas, isn't this what distinguishes the ancients from men of the present? Even though I feel I hardly deserve your high aspirations for me, still I dare not fail to take this worldly way of thinking as something against which to caution myself, and to maintain my determination to dedicate myself completely to the great worthies of the past.

I am now thirty-one years old. When I was six, I entered primary school. At seven, I was learning couplets; at sixteen, I studied poetry.[9] At eighteen, I was studying for the official examinations. When I turned nineteen, I got hold of the *Record of the Origins of the School of the Two Chengs* and read about the doings of the various Song masters, Zhou Dunyi, the Cheng brothers, Zhang Zai, and Shao Yong, with respect to taking up or declining office. Generally speaking, I knew then the excellence of studying to become a sage or worthy, and that sagehood was what my mind longed for. Thereupon, I completely burned up all my examination papers and totally set my mind on studying to be like these Masters Zhou, Cheng, Zhang, and Shao. I studied this for several years and then noticed that my behavior began to differ from my contemporaries. For some, my ways were too much of the past and inappropriate for the present. For others, they were impracticable and inapplicable to the conduct of affairs. Some called them eccentric, others called them strange, the ridicule and criticism both reaching an extreme.

Even though I have never dared completely forget my original ambition, still, at the same time, I have had to make some concessions to go

---

9. Literally, the *shi* 詩 and *fu* 賦 modes.

along with the times. Yet the deeper the tendency to follow along with the times, the more lax my original ambition has become. At the same time, one illness or affliction has led to another, my living situation has been miserable and joyless, and I have been confused and at a loss as to what to do. Troubled by my present situation and longing for the past, with the morning wind and the evening moon, I become overwhelmed with sorrow.

Since the beginning of spring this year, however, I have been focusing solely on the *Great Learning,* the *Analects, Mencius,* and *Practicing the Mean,* feeling that I have gained some insights from doing so. My former ailments have somewhat abated, and my vital spirit has somewhat improved. Only after meditating on this back and forth, day and night, have I come to realize that the Way of the sages and worthies is not solely of the past and inappropriate to the present, that truly it is not impractical and inapplicable to the conduct of affairs, that really it is neither eccentric nor strange, as my critics have charged. The setbacks and antagonisms of the past ten years were due to the fact that I neither clearly understood nor vigorously practiced it. The criticisms that I received then were not totally unjustified. But now, relying on the spiritual intelligence of Heaven, on the blessings of my ancestors, and on the teachings of my father, older brothers, teachers, and friends, I have obtained some guidance to help me go forward. How fortunate I am!

However, time is passing by. The youth and prime of my life will never come again. I am remorseful for all the time that has been lost. I take it, sir, that with your perspicacity, you understand what I mean here. One of the reasons I deign to bother you further now is to let you know that I sincerely believe that your son, Chen, is quite a talented youth. I hope that you will do a good job of guiding him along the Way so that, at a later period in his life, he will not have the kinds of regrets about wasted time as I now have. If you weren't such an old friend of mine, I wouldn't dare trouble you about this. If your son were not so capable of learning, I wouldn't try to encourage him like this. It is for you to decide and settle this.

Some other students of mine such as Fu and Lou have benefited from the progress they've made in their studies. They are worthy of affection and respect. You, too, should exert yourself, yes, exert yourself.

I recently returned from a trip and caught a cold. I cannot travel very far, so there is no way to see you. But I would count it a blessing if you would continue writing me with your helpful instruction. (8:16a–18b)

## (4) Letter to Fu Bingyi[10] (1421)

For several months now I have been reading only the Four Books. What I have gotten out of the reading is somewhat different from the time we last parted. Returning home from a recent trip, I paid another visit to your Yiqiu studio, but you were at your school teaching and had not yet returned home. But I saw your older brother Shiwang and learned that my letters from Xunyang had all arrived.

The last time we did meet, I was honored by your seeing me off at the bank of the river. At that time you told me that you felt you must begin afresh and study harder from then on. I wonder what the results of your resolve have been since we parted. What were your reactions after you received my letters and heard that I had returned home? If you only want to make a living like a common man, then you can say "that's enough." But if you wish to advance a step higher to become the type of good human being who honors his ancestors, makes his family great, and has something to hand down to his descendants, it would be fitting that you accompany your son to the mountains here where we can meet together. I live in a remote place, removed from everyday affairs. Every day with two or three students, I engage in the practices of book reading and plumbing principle, delighting in the Way of Yao and Shun—that is all. I dare make no claims of anything beyond this. (8:18b–19a)

## (5) Letter to Fu Bingyi

How has your progress of "daily renewal" been since we parted? I've spent the first half of this first month of the year, poring over the *Analects* of Confucius from beginning to end. On the evening of the fifteenth, I recited all of the *Great Learning* as well as Zhu Xi's *Answers to Questions on the Great Learning*. My whole self—body and mind—seem to have made some progress from this. If a person could continue applying effort like this, why should he worry about whether there are any advantages for him in it? Only if one is on and off with his efforts will he fail in the end.

Yesterday, while reading Zhen Dexiu's *Extended Meaning of the Great Learning*, I contemplated his descriptions of the sage kings Yao and Shun,

---

10. A close friend.

and the flourishing of the Three Dynasties.[11] That the rulers were truly rulers and the ministers truly ministers at that time was the result of their being rooted in the basic items of self-cultivation presented in the *Great Learning*, namely, the investigation of things, the extension of knowledge, making the will sincere, the rectification of the self, and the cultivation of the mind. In contrast, even during the heights of good government reached by the Han and Tang dynasties,[12] when the desire of some rulers to follow the Way at times was quite sincere and the guidance of their ministers at times was quite outstanding, still they were not clear enough about the Way of the *Great Learning*. They only reached the heights of the Han and Tang and that is all. Thus it is all wrong for a person to be engaged in learning and not be rooted in the teachings of the *Great Learning*.

As for you, what in fact are you doing about your own commitment in these matters? The day before yesterday, your son, on the point of his departure from here, said that he might come back to see me in the mountains in the fourth month. This is now just the first month and he wants to wait until the fourth. He is lazy and not working to establish himself. What's to be done about him? Moreover, from his use of the word "might," his laziness is even more apparent. Alas, it is clear that he is incapable of being taught! Will you follow in his same tracks as this overturned cart?

Last night I was again reading the *Extended Meaning of the Great Learning*, examining excerpts Zhen included from the classics and histories dealing with fraternal relationships. I saw that in these matters, friends should be close and not distant, generous and not harsh with each other. I found this to the point and profound. Reading this certainly made me fear-stricken with my hairs on end. I wish I could have read it together with your brother, Shiwang, and you so we could encourage each other in our pursuits. (8:19a–20a)

---

11. Three Dynasties refers to the Xia, Shang, and Zhou (c.2205–256 BCE).

12. These were regarded as China's most powerful dynasties. But Neo-Confucians of the Cheng-Zhu school criticized them for not following Confucian teachings about benevolent government, relying as they did on too much physical force to rule.

## (6) Letter to Hu Jiushao[13] (1421)

After we parted, I wrote you two letters that I trust you received. I took a trip to the city for a little over ten days, staying temporarily at the home of the Battalion Commander Niu, which was very pleasant. Someone had returned from the capital and told me that my father had returned home in the first month to resume his official post, and also, that everybody in the family, young and old, were doing well. This news added to my happiness.

Still, for the last half a month, this feeble body of mine has been plagued with boils. It has been painful, but I have tried to accept it as my lot in life. From morning to evening, I have been devoting a lot of time to reading *Practicing the Mean*, and seem to have derived some small benefit from it. What I've learned is that a person should take the upright and illuminating learning of the sages and worthies as his fundamental basis. Then when external things impinge on the self, one has the means with which to illuminate them. The mind remains totally present and not lost. Once the mind is lost, is it not like the wandering of water and the drifting of the wind in that no one can get hold of it? What I fear is this losing it and nothing else. What I hope for is having it present and nothing else. Anxious that I won't reach it and dispirited as if I had already lost it, I am unaware of the passing of time, from the evening changing to dawn and dawn receiving the night. I've written several poems that give vent to my feelings, but I'll have to wait to share those when I have more time.

I'm curious what you, my friend, in the time you have left over from your responsibilities of taking care of your parents and managing family affairs, have gained from the efforts you have put into the Four Books. You can't ever have your youth and prime of life back again. So, exert yourself! Exert yourself! The heroic great man[14] must not fall into the ways of the world. This will be all for now. (8:20a–21a)

---

13. A student of Wu Yubi and one of his closest friends.
14. In Chinese, *da zhang fu* 大丈夫. Allusion to *Mencius* 3B:2.

# (7) Reply to a Letter from Hu Jiushao (1421)

On the twelfth of this month,[15] you and I stayed up talking until midnight. The next day, the lingering joy was still special to me. It was just as a former worthy said, "In learning one needs to have discussion before one comes to understand the Way. And the friendship derived from teachers and friends is the way to get this." "Because the sages knew that the most benefit comes from friends, therefore they rejoiced when friends came to see them."[16] Even though a person might frequently repeat these words, it is only when he has personally experienced them that he knows the full taste of these words of the sages.

On the evening of the fourteenth, I was enjoying the nearly full moon and waiting for you, but you never came. On the evening of the fifteenth, a couple of local fellows, among them Student Zong from Fengcheng and Student Wang from nearby Dongpo, joined me. We sat under the moon, strumming the lute and singing poetry while we drank. We were extremely happy, yet your being absent again caused me deep concern. Afterward, I still heard no news of you at all and feared that you had gotten sick. Today, I received your letter and learned that, just as I had suspected, you had been ill. You now must do a good job of nourishing your mind in order to nurse yourself back into good health.

In your letter, you said, "I've lost my grip on things and my actions go contrary to my intentions." Is this really a problem unique to yourself? This is just the kind of thing I have been constantly suffering from. You are only now becoming aware of this problem. The trouble with most people is that they are ignorant of their problems. At the very moment when a person has even a little bit of insight into his faults, that is the time to vigorously exert effort.

Your younger brother, Ziyong, wants to come to study with me. That is very good to hear. How dare I not follow your instructions to take him on as a student? However, he must have firmly made up his mind to learn.

The messenger is in a hurry to get back to you, so I will stop here for now. (8:21a–b)

---

15. With the lunar calendar, the fifteenth of the month was always the time of the full moon.

16. Zhang Zai, "Discourse on the *Analects*," *Complete Works of Zhang Zai* 14:4b.

## (8) Letter to Fu Bingyi (1421)

A person cannot but follow the Way because the Way has never been something that could not be followed. If a person applies himself to the Way for just a moment, he will have one moment's worth of results; if he applies himself for a day, he will have one day's worth of results. If he can accumulate these results over a long period of time, his disposition naturally will be transformed.

Recently, we were able to talk together for several days. I observed that you certainly cannot be compared to the stupid, dull kind of person who is unaware of things. If you are capable of devoting your energies to this self-cultivation, so that at a later time I can get some help from you and your sons, there would be no greater good fortune for me.

Once there was an old man who went to see Master Zhou Dunyi. He voiced his admiration of the Way yet pitied himself that he was already too old. Master Zhou advised him, "There is no harm in being old. If only you follow my teachings, then you can hope to have some results to show for it." Looking at it from this point of view, people's trouble is merely that they do nothing. Even though I dare not hope to be even a fraction of what Master Zhou was as a teacher, yet you are younger than this old man speaking to Zhou. So you cannot but exert yourself! (8:21b–22a)

## (9) Short Note to Hu Jiushao (1421)

After parting from you recently, I have been deeply pondering how mediocre my life is. I have been just passing the days, mixed in with the crowd, unaware of any righteous principles. I have failed to make the most of my Heavenly bestowed endowment. In what way do I differ from the common herd? Time moves on. How can I prolong my youthful vigor? I am overcome with signs of regret.

For several days, I have been reading four commentaries on the *Spring and Autumn Annals* and am almost through with them. Yesterday I reread the "Zuo" and "Guliang" commentaries and the text itself. By evening, I had read one complete section, gaining a rough sense of its meaning.

Something else, my poor wife is extremely ill. I must trouble you, my worthy friend, to come and accompany me to Zhonghu to consult a doctor. I would be most appreciative if you would. (8:23a)

## (10) Letter to Hu Bian[17]

Last night I met Student Suo on the road. We talked for a long time. It was midnight before we parted. The general sense of our conversation was quite good. He told me that since the last time he saw me, he has been able to stick to his schedule of his reading for a considerable period of time. Gradually his studies have enabled him to get a grip on his whole self—body and mind. How worthy of respect he is! He went on to say that he has been trying to be more economical in household affairs, and this has helped him better concentrate on the application of his mind to his studies. Recently he considered buying a new house and having a decorative pond dug, but thought better of it. Thinking about this, I feel he is really worthy of respect. During our talk, the great enthusiasm he has in his commitment was evident. I wonder whether you can match him and progress as he has. There is even hope for the lazy! (8:24b)

## (11) Letter to a Friend 1422

I understand that you received the letter I wrote you last year from Xiaogu. The fact that you did not take my clumsy words as foolish, and that you have abstained from alcohol to progress in your studies, shows that you are a person who rejoices to hear about your faults and courageously tries to correct them in your practice. How worthy of joy and respect you are!

Recently I ran into Wu Derang, who told me you had suddenly fallen ill from exhaustion. This is the result of reading books to a harmful excess. The best thing for you is to do a good job of getting yourself back to good health. I myself, in the past, when I was inexperienced and green, was so eager to get ahead that I would over and over exhaust my energies in reading books. I would recite them aloud in a great loud voice, dissipating my vital energies[18] until I reached the extreme of causing great harm to myself. During the time I was living in the capital, I became seriously ill and no longer dared to read books in such a loud voice. After moving back to the country, however, it happened once that, after having expounded on the *Great Learning* at a friend's house for several days, I exhausted my vital

---

17. As I cannot find out anything about him, I assume he was a local student of Wu's.
18. Literally, "primal energies," used to mean strength, vigor (*yuan-qi* 元氣).

spirit[19] and the old illness recurred. Ever since then, I have been careful not to over expend my vital spirit. Each time I engage in reading, I try only to do as much as my energies allow me. If I become even the least bit tired, then I stop. It is only cultivation of the mind that should not be interrupted, not reading.

As for the basis of learning, one must try for daily progress and monthly advance with a free and easy, unconstrained manner. Then and only then can one sustain his efforts over a long period of time. If one is in a hurry and presses for quick results, then he will only cause himself pain and end up in failure.

On the whole, the essentials of what the sages and worthies transmitted are all contained in the one word "reverence" (*jing* 敬). If a person can put his attire in order, make his speech and actions correct and dignified, and conduct himself with a sense of propriety, then his mind naturally will be collected. Even if he does not read books, he still will gradually make progress in his self-cultivation. All the same, it is an even better thing if he can read books and understand principle in order to better nourish and care for the mind.

However, if this mind is constantly enslaved by external things, the body has nothing with which to restrain it, and then one's passions are given full rein. Then, even if one invests great pain and worry day and night into his practice of reading books, I'm afraid he will have no way of escaping from confusion. What benefit ultimately is there for the body and mind if a person is only able to expound on some hackneyed words on paper? It merely wears out his vitality and causes him to pass the years in vain. How extremely regrettable!

I share this little bit of insight I have gained from my own past exertion of efforts. Please bear with me in doing so. (8:25a–26a)

## (12) Letters to My Esteemed Father

### (a) 1423

In the spare time from my work in the fields, I dare not dispense with my program of reading books. Still, while I am aware of some gradual progress

---

19. Here Wu uses the term *jing-shen* 精神 to refer to a kind of physical vitality. The pursuit of sagehood cannot be done without the energies of good physical health.

in my studies, I also feel my moral character has become harder to cultivate. This village is a secluded place, and I haven't the benefit of help from
teachers and friends. At the same time, because I have been bothered by
various ailments and have had no one to whom I can entrust household
responsibilities, I have been unable to make any significant progress in my
self-cultivation efforts. Yet time passes by. I'm ending up falling into the
status of a mean and petty person, with no reason for even the slightest
hope of ever reaching the realm of the sages and worthies. Time and again,
I heave a deep sigh that there is no place where I can hide in shame.

As for my younger brothers, the best thing for you to do is to require
them to work hard. I anxiously hope that you will be good at nurturing them, enabling them to have abilities in areas where they have none,
to have a sense of balance in areas where it is lacking. How fortunate,
how fortunate for them! As for the books they should read, it is only the
*Elementary Learning* and the Four Books that are the most crucial. After
that they should read the plain texts of the various classics, without their
commentaries. Since other writings in philosophy and history should not,
on any account, be read in a light, superficial manner, they must follow the
reading of these more basic texts.

My few insights have all come from the *Elementary Learning,* the Four
Books, the *Digest of the Recorded Conversations of Zhu Xi, Reflections on Things
at Hand,* and the *Records of the Words and Deeds of Eminent Officials of the
Song Dynasty.* (At this time, the Master had not yet seen the *Written Legacy of
the Cheng Brothers* or the *Classified Conversations of Zhu Xi.*)[20] With respect to
these several books, if a person hasn't any deep understanding of them, then
other books will easily ruin his processes of thought. The harm from this is
not insignificant. This is why you have continually tried to provide me with
instruction. Only now have I come to appreciate this, and I fear my exertion
of effort is too late. I am overcome with sighs of regret! (8:26a–b)

## (b) 1423–Tenth Month

In my leisure time from working the fields, I have been delighting in Zhu
Xi's *Collected Commentaries on the Analects.* Whenever I get to parts that I
understand, immediately and without realizing it my hands and feet move
in joyful response. Ever since the eighth month, I have been aware of having made considerable strides in my advancement. Each day I scrutinize

---

20. This is an editor's note found in the original Chinese text.

and personally examine what Mencius called the "four beginnings," and have discovered the means by which to conduct myself, manage the household, and deal with other people. And in each of these, it seems I have something to hold on to and follow. What I dislike is having to study alone in this lonely and rustic place without teachers or friends to explain and clarify matters for me.

Sun Yuerang[21] told me of your idea to send my three younger brothers back home here to the country. Truly this is a far-reaching plan that has actually been a deep wish and pure hope of this, your unfilial son. Not only is life in the country simple, honest, and frugal so that a person can advance in his learning and moral character, but also it allows a person early on to learn the toils and hardships of a farmer's life so that at a later time he will not fall in with the reckless and lazy. I have no doubt but that you will decide in favor of this. I pray that you will send them right away.

As for the various writings you promised to give me, that is, your collection of books, handwritten personal papers from the past, and letters from relatives and friends, I'm looking forward to receiving them. If you could send them back with Yuerang and Zhicheng on their return, that would be wonderful. (8:26b–27a)

## (c) 1425–Seventh Month (intercalary)

Lately, I have been deeply apprehensive about my inability to make any significant advancement in my learning. Looking above, I have disgraced my ancestors; here and now, I have dishonored you, my father, and my teachers. Grieving over this day and night, I have had no time to manage my daily routine.

I'd like to ask you to please be sure to send me back the copy of the *Collected Works of Zhu Xi*. Lately I have felt even more how profound and appropriate are the sayings of Master Zhu. Still, my own efforts at cultivation have not reached his standards. (8:27a–b)

## (d) 1425–Twelfth Month

On the eighth day of the eleventh month, I was visiting the youngest son of a fellow villager, Huang Zixiao. He had just returned from the capital

---

21. Wu's brother-in-law, married to his eldest sister.

with news that you are enjoying many blessings and that the whole household is well. My sad countenance changed upon hearing the news, and I became overwhelmed with joy. I also heard that you would be returning home next spring for the sacrificing and sweeping of the family graves during the Qingming Festival. The prospect of our whole family reassembling is cause for great joy. What greater good fortune could there be!

As for me, I have been just living in the country, following a constant routine. The autumn crop is doing fairly well. My only resentment is that I have been encumbered by illnesses. As for my books, I have neglected them; as for my body and mind, I have become lazy and remiss. I don't even dare put myself in the category of a human being. The years and months gallop by, while my physical vigor declines with each day. What has happened today to the determined, rousing will of my youth? Confucius said, "When a man at forty is disliked by others, he will always be so." Isn't it just as he says! When my younger brothers were here, they didn't at first take to their studies. I sincerely hope they will not follow in the tracks of an overturned cart like me, their older brother.

Speaking of my younger brothers, colleagues and friends returning from the capital speak with deep concern that they have grown used to the wealth and high living of the capital, and that they will find their return here difficult. As I silently reflect on it, I don't find it surprising that they should react thus, having been born and raised in the midst of plenty and then having to change their residence and its comforts. I humbly hope that you will be good at teaching them so that they can eliminate their old habits. If they return to the country here with its simple life, gradually get more involved in the farming, and gradually improve themselves from their daily associations with colleagues and friends of the village, then their advancements and achievements truly will be immeasurable. From what our ancestors accumulated in good deeds, it is only fitting that my brothers be able to accomplish this. At least, this is what I deeply long for day and night. (8:27b–28a)

## (13) Letter to Hu Jiushao 1426

Since we last parted, I have been beset with several ailments that have been quite painful. Still, I have tried to accept them as part of my lot. I've put new efforts into my studies and moral practice, and for consecutive days

I've found that some progress has been made. Recently I received your gift of a copy of *Master Zhu's Works on the Management of Human Affairs and Providing a Standard for Literature*. Every day I read it with great reverence. My response to it is just like a mountain stream swelling forth, followed by a sudden and heavy rainstorm. The threads of my thoughts are too many to express well in writing. Also, because you have yet to establish the kind of foundation that only long efforts in moral cultivation bring, it is difficult for me to pour out everything to you at once.

The main essentials for entering the gate of the Way are just to put aside all other books and concentrate solely on the Four Books and the writings of the Cheng brothers, Zhou Dunyi, Zhang Zai, and Zhu Xi.[22] Read these thoroughly in a set order, "neither forgetting nor helping to grow," and "being easygoing but thoroughly absorbing what you learn."[23] If you therein accumulate efforts over a long period of time, you will naturally accomplish something. But this is not something you can force. The taste of this is truly difficult to appreciate. It is exactly what Master Zhu Xi meant when he said, "Although plain looking, it is really rich." How fortunate that I have suddenly reached this realm by reading this book! What great joy! What great joy!

In your letter, you stated that, compared with the last few years, you have been better at overcoming your faults. This is extremely good news. Still, do not be too severe in the application of your mind to these things. As Mencius said, "He who advances with precipitation will retire with speed."[24] Truly, these are not empty words! Since your vitality is in short supply and your body is weak, you should double your efforts to nourish and care for yourself. I hope you will be all right! (8:28a–29a)

## (14) Reply to a Letter from Sun Yuerang[25]

I can't believe that a year has passed since we parted on the hilltop. Though separated, we share deep feelings of longing and remembrance. As for my efforts at moral cultivation since last winter, I can't say that those efforts

---

22. Literally, the Masters of Yi, Lo, Guan, and Min.

23. *Written Legacy* 15:2a.

24. *Mencius* 7A:44 (trans. by Legge, *The Chinese Classics*, vol. 2, p. 475).

25. Wu's brother-in-law.

at learning have not been painstaking. In my daily affairs, I can't say they have not been productive.[26] Still, my sickly body is in declining health and I am tied up with household matters. I have no way of making any kind of significant improvement, yet time continues to pass by. Looking up at the ancients, I find the distance that separates us to be beyond calculation. This is what pains my heart from morning to night.

This fall, I unexpectedly received a letter from you. From it I realized that you have not been remiss in your determination to advance in your moral character. I was overwhelmed with joy! I reread your letter by the window of my study so as to console my feelings of longing and to rouse my own self to action. At the end of your letter, you requested that I send you some advice. Since you have kindly chosen not to look down on me, how can I remain silent?

Now, you have already said yourself what I would say to you. Your letter stated, "I have put all my energies into the Four Books." All I can say is that this is not a waste of your energies but rather the way to get to the root of all learning. Even though I might wish to say anything beyond what these texts say, what would it be for? Not only is this true of me, but even if one of the sages and worthies came back to life to teach, how could he go beyond what is contained in these books? Since parting from you, my own moral practice has concentrated on these books and nothing else.

In your letter you also asked, "Even though I am able for a while to understand the words on paper, in the end what benefit does it have for my body and mind?" These words of yours raise an important issue which is precisely what you should reflect upon. Now the problem for people is that they don't know how to turn inward and seek within themselves. For them, books are just books, the self is just the self, and there is no connection between the two. When the books that a person reads only benefit his mouth and ears, then it is all a great failure. Since you now are aware that books have not been benefiting your body and mind, you should move in the direction of finding such benefit. You should focus your mind on this, sincerely believe in this, strongly hold on to this, and deeply long for this. When reading, don't calculate your results based on the number of times you read a book. Polish yourself for months and years, but do not be eager for results. As Cheng Yi advised, "Be leisurely and at ease, thoroughly

---

26. Wu uses a double negative here to be polite and not sound like he is bragging. He is really saying that he has taken painstaking efforts and these have been productive.

absorbing what you learn," in the midst of it all. Then benefits from your "daily renewal" program will naturally arise. Don't expect it to be thus and it will be thus. (8:29a–30a)

## (15) Letter to Sun Yuerang (1429)

I remember back when I first returned home from mourning the death of our father.[27] Because some matters had not yet been resolved, my sense of guilt was deep. I didn't feel at ease anywhere, and a hundred other worries piled up on me. I was unable to fulfill in the least bit the duties of etiquette due to my older sister and you. Even though those who understood the situation have not borne me a grudge, still how great has been the sense of remorse I have felt inside!

The day you came to the local magistrate's office was just when I was harvesting rice in nearby Huangbo. When I looked out into the distance and saw the dust you had raised in leaving, I was overcome with feelings of shame. For a while now I have had the wish to go east to visit you and to unburden myself of all that I have kept inside. Exhausted from bearing my burdens, I haven't been able to find even a little bit of relief, and so this wish of mine to visit has not been an easy one to fulfill. Still, even in sending you greetings in letters, I have been remiss. I know I am at fault, yes, I know I am at fault.

All this while you have continued to send me gifts. While gratefully receiving them, I only feel even more ashamed and uneasy. My younger brother, Yunian, tells me that you have been conscientious in the performance of your job. How worthy of joy and respect you are! I remember once when we were talking together on the road to Huangbo, you told me of your resolve to read the Four Books and Five Classics over and over again in a set order. How has that been going?

In the twelfth lunar month of last year, I moved to the village of Xiaopo. Because everything is so new and unfinished, there have been lots of

---

27. Wu Pu, his father, died in Nanjing in late 1426. According to Wu Pu's biography, Wu and his siblings did not have money to give Wu Pu a proper burial and had to depend on their fathers' colleagues to help them. Perhaps this was part of the guilt and shame about which Wu speaks in this letter. Sun Yuerang, as mentioned before, is Wu's brother-in-law, the husband of Wu's oldest sister.

difficulties and hardships. Still, I can only manage according to my given abilities. But I find that my physical vigor is further declining, and that I haven't advanced much in my studies and moral character. I have nothing with which to wash away even a fraction of my guilt as an unfilial son and uncaring brother, heavily burdened as I am by the expectations of father, brothers, teachers, and friends. Day and night, alarmed by it all, I have no place to hide myself in shame.

This new year, there have been some students in the village who have come to study with me. But each day, with my many ailments, I can only make a small amount of substantive progress with them. This has been a source of additional shame for me. Brother-in-law Xu Daying recently paid me a visit. What's more, he has a mind to move here, which would be a wonderful thing indeed.

While your son is still attending you, how fitting for you to teach him with diligence. Have him thoroughly read the *Elementary Learning*, the plain texts of the Four Books and Five Classics. Have him nourish his moral nature, not allowing him to become lax and remiss in his efforts. Your own curriculum, too, should not depart from these essentials. As for the *Elementary Learning*, a person cannot but take pains to apply his efforts to mastering it. Proceed chapter by chapter, passage by passage, carefully digest it and allowing it to enter your mind. You will then come to understand that the meaning of the sages' teachings clearly appears beyond the actual words used. In this way, you will be able to make some progress.

In my humble opinion, I have always thought that the management of affairs by later generations has not been up to par with the ancients because people have failed to take the *Elementary Learning* as their basis. Once you have thoroughly mastered it, then apply your efforts to the Four Books and Five Classics. Recite them until they are committed to memory, causing the words to come out of your mouth as if they were your own. Then your own sense of their meaning will be special to you. The ancients said, "In reading a thousand pieces of writing, the meaning will naturally emerge." How true!

After you have mastered the plain texts of the Four Books and Five Classics, then you can read their various commentaries, and after that go on to the philosophical and history writings. If a person, intent on penetrating the essence of these writings, doesn't follow this order but reads them in a careless, random way, he will fail in the end. He will have wasted his vital energies and passed the years in vain. What a great pity that would be! In my own life, I have found myself mired in this fault. My regrets come too late!

With your youth and your ability, you should by all means hasten each day to push ahead with your moral efforts. Do not disgrace those who gave you birth. In recent years, I had a certain student who was completely lazy, enslaved by motives of profit and desire, unable to control himself. The source of his problem was just that his past efforts with the *Elementary Learning* were slapdash, his reading of books in general was haphazard, and he had never established a firm foundation to his learning. Therefore, it was easy for external things to agitate and disturb him. Take this as a warning! Take this as a warning!

What sorts of book collections do you have in the various counties of Huizhou where you are stationed? If you would be so kind as to tell me each and every title, I would be so grateful. As there is no way for us to get together any time soon, I only hope you will love and cherish yourself. This will be all for now. (8:30a–31b)

## "Encouraging Learning," an Essay Presented to Yang Dequan

The reason human beings are different from birds and beasts is that they are replete with the four beginnings of humaneness, righteousness, a sense of propriety, and wisdom. Once these beginnings are obscured, then a person loses the substance that makes him human and he becomes no different from the birds and beasts. But even among animals, bees and ants have some sense of the ruler-subject relationship, tigers and dogs have some sense of the duty to repay their ancestors, and ospreys have some sense of the complementary roles of married couples. So even though they are animals, they all embody one of the four beginnings. In contrast, a human being who drowns his mind in selfish considerations of profit and desire and remains unsettled and obstinate, is not even as good as these animals.

One who wishes to distinguish himself from an animal will indeed say to himself, "When I turn inward and seek my mind, I will certainly find there humaneness, righteousness, a sense of propriety, wisdom, and nothing else. If I wish to substantiate these four in my own person and yet dispense with the writings of the sages and worthies, then there will be no place where I can direct my efforts."

Yang Dequan of Fengcheng (Jiangxi province) was a university student returning home to pay his respects to his parents. As we happened to be on the same boat, we talked to each other for several days. He enthusiastically set his resolve on cultivating himself like this. He was worried, however, that once he arrived home, he would be confused by worldly affairs and his bad habits wouldn't be easy to overcome. He solicited my advice for some ways to advance in self-cultivation as well as ways for him to maintain a sense of alertness.

This is what I told him. In the affairs of the world, there exist only two poles: the common good or private interests, moral principle or selfish desire, rectitude or profit. Their power constantly alternates between the two. When the former (the common good, moral principle, and rectitude) is strong, then the latter (private interests, selfish desire, and profit) is weak; when the latter is strong, the former is weak. Once the strong and weak have been distinguished, the benefit or harm from some affair will be made clear. If one understands this, he will not be upset when the latter's power is strong but will pay attention to how he is going to accumulate and increase the strength of his own position.

Go home, and clean and sweep out a room. Set up some maxims of the ancient sages and worthies on your desk. In your free time from serving your parents, enter your chamber, straighten your clothing, and sit in a serious and proper manner. Thoroughly read and digest the writings of the sages and worthies, examining their application for yourself. Whether active or quiescent, whether talking or silent, always seek what is worthy of the sages and worthies, and get rid of whatever is not worthy. If you accumulate your efforts over a period of time, then the power of your tasting the Way and emulating the worthies will daily strengthen, and the power of your old habits and past defects will daily weaken. Don't worry that you will not reach the gate of the ancients.

Whenever you get together with your relatives and friends, loyally admonish them and skillfully lead them on. Since every person has a mind that holds to moral principles and is fond of virtue, I can foresee all of you enthusiastically working together to make advancements in this. How can you then be upset about being confused about affairs? Exert yourself, yes, exert yourself, and be not remiss. (8:41b–43a)

## Standards for Learning (1430)

**Item:** It is necessary for all to follow a fixed order. Begin by thoroughly reading the *Elementary Learning* and the plain texts of the Four Books, committing each of them to memory. After that, read the plain texts of the Five Classics. Become so well versed in them that you can recite them from memory. Do all this with a view to gradually gain entrance into the Way. For your efforts to be effective, you must work hard at this for months and years. How anyone can think he can plant a tree in the morning and enjoy its shade that very evening is something I don't understand!

**Item:** The goal of study is to learn to become sages and worthies. In the classroom, it is absolutely necessary to engage in discussing and clarifying matters such as the principles of righteousness, self-cultivation, and solicitude in action. If anyone wishes to wade and hunt through books only to benefit his mouth and ears, and to be skillful in poetry and couplets for superficial showing off, then that is something I don't understand.

**Item:** When the ancients engaged in book learning, all of them committed their whole selves to it and didn't waste time in other activities. In this way, they vigorously undertook their moral practice. In three to five years, they were able to establish a firm foundation and advance to higher matters. Now, if a person sometimes works hard and sometimes slacks off, with one hot spell to every ten cold spells, then even if he were to read books for a hundred years, I can't see how he would succeed. (8:43a–b)

## "Colophon" to the *Record of the Origins of the School of the Two Chengs*

In the winter of 1409, the Honorable Li Nengbai, who was the Assistant Sub-Prefect to Suzhou Prefecture (Zhejiang province), sent my late father this collection of biographies. I pored over it by lamplight, humbly examining the single thread of the true transmission of the Way. Without realizing it, my mind became intoxicated. I was especially moved by the story of how Master Cheng Hao curbed his love of hunting.[28] Now in the past,

---

28. The passage Wu read was this: "Once I said that I no longer loved to hunt. My teacher Zhou Dunyi said, 'Why lightly say so? The desire is merely suppressed and not

before reading this, I had said that those sages and worthies who bore the responsibility for the continuation of the Way were all specially endowed by Heaven, that sagehood was not something that could be reached by ordinary efforts. Consequently, I had set aside sagehood as something outside my range and had given up on myself.

When I got to the point of examining the matter in light of this text, I realized that even Master Cheng made mistakes and that even he relied on learning to correct them. At that very moment, I was inspired to rouse myself to action and ventured to set my hopes in this direction. Thereupon I completely burned all my old examination papers and vowed not to stop my moral efforts until I had reached the level of the sages and worthies.

The winter of 1411, after I had returned to my native place in the country, our residence in the capital caught on fire. I thought for sure this book must have been among those reduced to ashes. Since then, I have continually wished for the opportunity to read it over again but have been unable to get hold of a copy. In the spring of this year, while going through the books left by my late father housed in our ancestral home in Liantang, I was delighted to discover this text was still intact. Consequently, I have with great reverence brought it back with me to my humble abode in Xiaopo.

Every day I respectfully read and savor its flavor in order to satisfy my lifelong wish of becoming a sage. Ah, that I, Yubi, altered my course away from the path of error even a small bit really did begin with the reading of this book. From this, one can see how great was the generosity of Master Zhu Xi in compiling this collection of biographies so that later generations can benefit by it. And as for the Honorable Li's deep gift of encouragement, how dare I ever forget it! (12:1a–b)

---

aroused. Once stimulated, it will be as active as before.' Twelve years later, when I saw someone hunt, I realized that in fact I had not given up the desire for hunting." This is then followed by the parenthetical remark: "(Master Mingdao loved to hunt when he was sixteen and seventeen. Twelve years later, when he returned home toward the end of the year and saw some people hunting in the country, he was delighted, without realizing it)." In the *Record of the Origins of the School of the Two Chengs* 1:4a–b; also included in the "Correcting Mistakes" chapter of *Reflections on Things at Hand*. (Trans. by Chan, *Reflections*, p. 163.)

# Textual Variations in the
# Different Editions of the Text

## Journal

Entry no. 26: The 1526 edition has *hu* 忽 "remiss," instead of *wang* 忘, "forgetting," rendering the translation, "I cannot allow for even a moment of being remiss." I follow the *Siku*'s reading of *wang*, forgetting.

Entry no. 28: The 1526 edition has *zi* 恣 "reckless," instead of *wang*, forgetting, in the *Siku* edition.

Entry no. 30: Here the 1590 and *Siku* editions have an obvious textual error. They have *Zisi* 子思 the name of the author of *Practicing the Mean*, instead of *jiusi* 九思 the nine matters. I follow the 1526 edition here.

Entry no. 32: The *Siku* edition reads *ting-jian* 庭 間, "in the courtyard" or veranda, while the 1526 and 1590 editions have *cheng-jian* 塍間, "on a path between the fields." I follow the latter reading, in line with Wu's inclinations to be out of doors. There is no overriding reason why the other reading cannot be used.

Entry no. 56: I follow the 1526 and 1590 editions that read 欲責人須思吾能, instead of the *Siku* edition that reads 欲責須思吾吾能, "If I wish to criticize, I must think about myself, whether I am capable of it."

Entry no. 273 The *Siku* edition has the character *sheng* 生, to be born or to produce, while the 1526 edition has *zuo* 坐, to sit. I follow the latter reading.

## Letters and Miscellaneous

Letter 1: I follow the 1526 edition reading of *chang* 嘗 "once," instead of the *Siku* edition that has *chang* 常 "often."

Letter 2: I follow the 1526 reading here instead of the *Siku* edition that has 惡在能有足哉, "How could he have any sense of satisfaction with himself?"

# Comments on the Journal

As for the Journal, the two Chinese characters that I translate as "journal" literally mean "daily record" (日錄), although it was not kept on a daily basis. The mid-sixteenth-century scholar Zhang Gun praised Wu Yubi's journal, calling it "a personal history. All that he recorded were his own affairs. This is unlike people who flippantly make sweeping statements as they append their own ideas to well-known theories or append well-known theories to their own ideas."[1] In keeping a journal, Wu was not self-consciously attempting to present an account of his life just for its own sake. Rather he had the larger goal of contributing to his program of self-cultivation, as part of his pursuit of sagehood.

An earlier name for it was the Record of Daily Renewal, the idea of "daily renewal" coming from the *Great Learning* text: "If you can one day renew yourself, do so from day to day. Yes, let there be daily renewal."[2] Lou Liang, a prominent Ming dynasty Neo-Confucian who studied with Wu and who himself kept a journal, described Wu's Journal as something "in which he recorded the accomplishments of his 'daily renewal' program and expressed all that he had learned for himself."[3] As a teacher, Wu encouraged his students to keep records of their own personal behavior as part of their daily programs of self-cultivation:

> When you return home, you are to each remember the teachings
>     with which I have provided you.
> With the practice of keeping your own private record,
> Renew yourself day after day.[4]

---

1. Quoted in Huang Zongxi, *Case Studies of Ming Confucians* 1:1b.

2. *Great Learning*, chapter 2.

3. Lou Liang, *Biographical Account of Wu Yubi* 10:12b. Lou's journal no longer exists; all of his writings were destroyed.

4. *Collected Works of Wu Yubi* 2:46b (hereafter CW; unless otherwise noted, all references are to this collection).

# A Closer Look at the Journal

As we have seen, Wu's lifetime pursuit of the goal of sagehood was anything but steady and smooth, but rather went in fits and starts. Nor were his accounts in the Journal consistently detailed and systematically maintained. The entries vary greatly in number and length from year to year. The subject matter ranges from personal expression of intense emotion and quotations from the classics to moralizing on human behavior. The very last entry in the Journal reads, "Although the myriad changes in the universe are numerous and bewildering, there is a definite principle with respect to responding to each of them" (11:42a, no. 328). So too, in approaching the many kinds of entries in the Journal, the reader must keep in mind that they all in some way, directly or indirectly, relate to the central theme of Wu's pursuit of sagehood.

Given this great variety in the content of the entries, discussion of the Journal will be organized around three basic polarities. The first is that between what Wu perceives as the obstacles to his goal and what he feels are the sources of support in overcoming these obstacles. The second polarity is that found in his program of self-cultivation between disciplining and restraining the self on the one hand, and nurturing and expanding it on the other. The last one is that which he finds in his constant self-evaluations about his successes and failures in his undertaking. It is in the interplay of these polarities, and how they cause the tone of the Journal to alternate between light and darkness, that the contours of his life and interior self are brought out, giving the reader some sense of a three-dimensional human person. To be sure, the entries are not nearly as psychologically detailed as a modern reader would expect to find in a journal. But still, Wu's personality clearly emerges from the overall work, unlike what we find with many other writings by Confucian scholars.

## Obstacles and Supports

The Journal begins significantly with accounts of his two dreams about Confucius and Zhu Xi, the two principal figures of the Confucian and Neo-Confucian traditions, respectively. These two set the standard as models of sagehood for him and illustrate Wu's sense that these two served as active presences in his life to guide him. Then he gets right down to more personal matters of his own conduct. The entries in the early years are dominated by a rather dark tone, by his greater sense of the obstacles in the way of reaching his goal of sagehood. Because of the preponderance of this type of entry, our discussion begins here, with a focus on the polarities of what he considers the obstacles and supports in his endeavor. As for the obstacles, Wu sees them as coming from three sources: the difficult external or material circumstances of his life, the imperfections of the people around him, and his own wayward disposition.

### Obstacles in Wu's Endeavors

Among the features of his life situation with which Wu expresses dissatisfaction are his limited financial resources and his poor health, especially as these impinge on the responsibilities of managing a household. As for his poverty, Wu laments:

> Near evening time today, I went to a neighbor's storehouse to borrow some grain. I remembered then that I had not yet repaid my former debts. This new debt will only add to what I already owe. Oh, what should I do about this life of mine? (11:15a, no. 72)

As with other expressions of his poverty, he mentions having to put aside his books to go plant vegetables, enduring a leaky house during a heavy rainstorm, and lacking oil for his study lamp at night. Poverty contributed to the greater difficulty of managing his household, forcing him to worry about making ends meet in times of poor harvests and hard times:

> The late-year crop of rice has turned out to be a poor harvest. This evening on my pillow, I've been thinking what sore straits I'm in with respect to household necessities and how I cannot concentrate on my reading. (11:20b, no. 116)

Wu bemoans not just his lack of financial resources but also his physical disabilities, in that he suffered from general poor health and a series of unspecified illnesses:

> On my pillow tonight, I recalled the days when I lived in the capital and could study day and night without interruption, yet never got sick. But for these past ten years or more, various illnesses have followed one after the other, so that I have hardly been able to make

the same kind of progress as in those days. I am overcome with deep regrets, though there is nothing I can do about it. All this while, I have been poor and without the medicine to take proper care of myself. (11:17b, no. 23)

He typically speaks only in a general way of being sick without specifying the nature of his illness, though he does at times mention boils, rheumatism, and eye ailments. His condition was serious enough that he was forced in 1453 to make a major trip to Nanjing for medical care.

Wu's reaction to these limitations is not one of ready acceptance. More often, it is one of anger and resentment:

In the midst of poverty and distressed circumstances, I find matters keep coming on me one after another. At the same time, I am suffering from painful boils. I can't help from time to time getting angry and frustrated by it all. (11:2b, no. 9)

His resentment stems from feeling impeded in his attempts at self-cultivation. These circumstances interrupt his reading schedule and destroy his inner equilibrium. He feels he is being kept away from his pursuit of sagehood by irksome distractions with which he should not have to bother:

Sick, exhausted, and tied up with household worries, I find I cannot give my full attention to the sacred writings of the sages and worthies. Inwardly, I feel mean and deceitful, lacking in the means by which to extend my knowledge. Outwardly, my manner has become more and more volatile and rude, with no energy for personal application of effort. (11:5b–6a, no. 18)

At times, he responds not in anger but in confusion and despair:

In handling an important matter recently, I was unable to do the best I could and so have been extremely dispirited in thought. At the same time, I have been suffering from chills, the tremors from which at times are strong enough to overwhelm me. As a result, my program of reading has been interrupted. Muddled and dazed all day, I am strongly moved to wonder by what means I can enter the realm of the sages and worthies. (11:15b, no. 74)

In his frustration, Wu declares in a poem, "Difficulties I am willing to accept as part of life, / But I never thought they would be as extreme as this" (11:25a, no. 153), and wonders, "perhaps the ancients were not as poor as we are today" (11:12a, no. 57).

Wu has difficulty accepting not just the limitations imposed by his external situation but also by the imperfections of the people around him. He describes himself as prone to lose his temper, as impatient with the faults of others, and as being self-righteously critical of others:

> Lately, in handling a certain matter with a neighbor, I have tried to be forbearing with him but haven't succeeded in my attempts. Today I was at the end of my patience, and since he still didn't understand the matter, I couldn't help telling him off. This losing my temper over unimportant matters is something which I later regret. (11:1b–2a, no. 4)

Wu's frustration with the limitations of his life situation and the shortcomings of the people around him is compounded by those of his own self, especially, he says, his tendencies to be stingy, lax, and prone to anger: "this stupid self of mine is plagued by an inability to control and eliminate the obstinacy of my natural temperament . . . when the least little thing does not accord with my wishes, I lose my temper" (11:3a, no. 10). He also admonishes himself for "lacking a magnanimous spirit" in handling household matters (11:6b, no. 20). As for his laxity in moral efforts, he reports: "For the past ten days, I have been neglecting my studies and moral cultivation" (11:18b, no. 101).

Disheartened by these various obstacles to achieving his goal of sagehood, Wu, nevertheless, owing no doubt to his headstrong nature, refuses to be ultimately overcome and defeated by them. He continues to struggle. Gradually what emerges for him is a more mature and refined notion of what sagehood is really about and how it has to be lived out in the context of his own particular situation.

One of the principal problems Wu has to face is the immaturity of his notions about the sage's state of inner composure. He feels that to be a sage he must develop a state of mind that is tranquil and calm without the least bit of inner disturbance. As soon as any one of the basic human emotions disturbs this equilibrium it means he has gone astray from the Way and let himself be overwhelmed by external things. He struggles constantly to achieve inner equilibrium and reports occasional successes. However, success is more often than not followed by another failure, causing further discouragement on his part:

> I began to suspect I was one of the stupid ones who could never in the least bit emulate the sages and worthies, and that there was nothing to prevent me from ending up as what Confucius described as a "mean and petty person." (11:4b, no. 13)

A big part of the problem stemmed from his stoical sense of this equilibrium. In one entry, he declares that one should neither enjoy what is pleasurable nor dislike what is not. In my translation, I have qualified this stoicism with the phrase "too much." Wu is suspicious of positive feelings of enjoyment and negative feelings of dislike because they disturb his sense of inner equilibrium:

> Both enjoying and disliking things too much cause a disturbance of inner equilibrium that should not be upset. The mind of the sage or worthy is like still water. Whether situations are favorable or adverse, he deals with both using principle and nothing else. How could he let what comes from the outside determine his inner sorrow or joy? (11:6b, no. 19)

Though Wu can articulate for himself this ideal of sagely detachment, which clearly has its basis in Neo-Confucian views on human feelings, still his resolution to mend his ways at the end of this entry seems forced. He does not seem fully convinced of its truth or confident of realizing it. "Alas!" he cries, "How can I succeed in reaching this state?"

The longest entry in the Journal (no. 13), in contrast, chronicles a particularly arduous but fairly successful struggle over this matter of achieving inner equilibrium. Compared to the entry just discussed, his resolution at the end of this one seems more genuinely felt.[5] The reader senses a real

---

5. In my attempt to put some order into the content of the Journal, the reader will note that I do not follow a straightforward chronology. I am superimposing a structure of my own that I hope is helpful to the reader. For example, this entry (no. 13) precedes the one just discussed (no. 19) in its placement in the Journal. What this tells us, I think, is that his progress was anything but linear. One instance of a breakthrough did not guarantee that backsliding would not occur.

release of tension, a breakthrough in understanding and an expansion of feeling. In this entry, Wu begins by describing the considerable improvement he has made since the beginning of the year (1425) in his attempts to maintain his composure when faced with adverse situations. Though still moved by events, especially difficult ones, on the whole he feels himself able to deal with much of the resulting agitation, not allowing himself to be overwhelmed by either his emotions or the situation. Suddenly, however, he finds himself confronted with a situation he could not get a grip on: "on the twentieth of this month, I found myself in another adverse situation, the inner agitation from which I could not rid myself. My mind became more and more discontented" (11:4b, no. 13).

Struggling with this discontent, Wu comes to perceive the faulty basis of the equilibrium he was seeking and at times thought he had obtained. In his immaturity, he says, he sought an inner peace wherein everything went according to his wishes, leaving him unencumbered by the all-too-human realities around him. It was as if, having dedicated himself to the lofty pursuit of sagehood, he could expect things to conform to his good intentions, that he would not be held back by mundane matters such as having a sick child or annoying neighbors. But such equilibrium, achieved only at times when he had things just as he wished, could be nothing but brittle and easily shattered. And once his composure was shattered, Wu's tendency, as we have seen him admit, was readily to give way to anger or self-pity:

> This [discontent] was because my usual practice was only one of negatively restraining myself and not one of positive nurture. I still lacked the intention of completely eradicating the root of the problem. Only after having reflected back and forth on it did I realize that my recent problem derived from wanting to have my mind and vital spirit at peace, yet at the same time, hating all those external things that go contrary to my wishes and that spoil my inner equilibrium. But this is wrong. (11:4b–5a, no. 13)

The reason for this approach being wrong, he comes to realize, is that it failed to take into account the complexity and diversity of the world around him, as well as the deeper basis upon which all beings, including himself, are grounded. His inner equilibrium had to be founded on something larger than his own wishes and his own limited conceptions of sagehood. It had to be based on something more flexible, enduring, and inclusive, something that would enable him to deal with the multiplicity of life in truly sagely fashion. This, he realizes is the role of principle, the underlying truth and unity of the total order of things in which the myriad things have their being. Wu comes to understand that when rooted in principle, the core of his being, he is able to know how to respond to and manage his situation, since principle illumines and directs the mind to the proper responses. Looking at matters from the point of view of principle, in its unity and diversity, he begins to see that rather than antagonism between things, there is mutual resonance and shared identity. Thus, he need not fight his life situation or even himself. Principle serves the integrating function between himself and the multiplicity of the larger order of things. Moreover, principle functions right at the heart of his particular situation and must be discovered therein, not in some idealistic world apart from his own. The purpose of inner composure in this context, then, is not to achieve some escapist type of peace of mind, but to participate deeply in the life around one:

> All things in the world are unalike. How can I hate those things that are contrary to my tastes? The correct thing for me to do, in the midst of the universal diversity of life, is to carefully examine the principle of each thing in order to respond properly to each of them. Upon realizing this, I felt a great unburdening inside. (11:5a, no. 13)

Human feelings are not to be left out, upstaged, or repressed, but are to be respected and given their due expression amidst this open-ended source, principle. The self is to be enhanced, not diminished, in self-cultivation. By focusing on the fundamental resonance between himself and things based on principle, Wu sees that he could achieve better results in his efforts at cultivation by emphasizing the nurturing aspect and not strict discipline alone. This, he is sure, will be a more pleasant and natural way, as well as lead to a more enduring type of composure, one that can sustain itself during periods of both calm and agitation:

> Now the practice of negatively restraining and not positively acting is a rigid and painful approach, whereas using principle to deal with each situation is a flexible and smooth one. Thus, I thought, it is not that I have never before experienced the state of my mind and vital spirit being at peace, but that I have never experienced it

uninterrupted for eight to nine days like this. Furthermore, those were times in the past when the household was calm, with not much going on. (11:5a, no. 13)

Wu ends this extended reflection with firm resolutions about his conduct and the type of practice he hopes will help him achieve his goals, writing them down in a notebook:

"My goal is to progress to the point of 'mastering myself and returning to the rites' by means of the practices of reading books and plumbing principle, as well as by devoting myself to the cultivation of reverence and empathy." Whether I succeed right away or it takes a long time, I dare not know. (11:5a–b, no. 13)

Reading books and plumbing principle are among the principal practices for self-cultivation in the Cheng-Zhu tradition. As for reverence, this involves a deep seriousness about the whole sagely venture and a profound respect for the deeper resources within the self. The quality of empathy would demand of Wu that he not live in his own idealized world but develop sensitivity and a sense of fellow-feeling with others in the wider world.

Related to the realization that his peace of mind must be rooted in principle, the ground of his being, was a growing understanding of the will of Heaven in his life. He sees that it is not enough stoically to put up with the distractions and frustrations in one's life, but that one must comprehend what particular meanings these things have for him. Principle is not something abstract, static, and impersonal but related to Heaven and its will for him, the unfolding of his life purpose.

The notion of the will or mandate of Heaven (*tian-ming* 天命) here must be understood in the Confucian sense that Heaven has placed each person in a specific context within which to work out his or her sagehood.[6] Context involves the resources and limitations in a person's life over which he does not have control, such as wealth or poverty, short or long life, fame or obscurity, and good or bad fortune. Aware that "Each person's life has its own fixed lot" (11:34b, no. 247), Wu reminds himself about Confucius'

---

6. In *Analects* 2:2, Confucius mentions that he only fully understood Heaven's will for him when he reached the age of fifty.

words that a person "who fails to understand Heaven's will for him lacks what it takes to be a noble person."[7] What is required of a person is that he seeks to discern Heaven's will for himself and then follow it though without any resentment. Wu thus resolves to be like the sages and worthies who "followed Heaven's will in all cases with respect to good and bad fortune, without the least bit of inner disturbance" (11:6a, no. 19).

As arbiter or custodian of his fate, Heaven is not some remote, impersonal force for Wu. He quotes the Han Confucian Dong Zhongshu, who said, "In human actions, the extremes of good and evil in a person's behavior penetrate, interact with, and mutually respond to Heaven and earth." Wu's response to these words is, "Alas, how awesome is the boundary point where Heaven and humans meet!" (11:16a, no. 77). This is so awesome for Wu that he maintains a special respect and reverence of this cosmic force ("What I depend upon is Heaven; what I trust in is its will for me" [11:31a, no. 203]), and is fearful of being cut off from it ("If there is even the tiniest bit of the Way that I have not exhausted, then I have cut myself off from Heaven" [11:19b, no. 108]). He expresses faith in the ultimate justice of Heaven: "The Way of Heaven is to bless the good and bring evil to the bad" (11:38a, no. 286).

In trying to discern his own fate, Wu decides that it is one of poverty and low estate, as well as one of sorrow and difficulty, taking these categories from section 14 of *Practicing the Mean,* which he frequently quotes. His pursuit of sagehood must be done within this specific context and not in some other, more ideal state:

> Every day I work hard at my farming. This is my personal lot in life, so why be resentful about it? As the *Practicing the Mean* says, "In a position of poverty and low estate, the noble person does what is proper in such a position." (11:11a, no. 52)

Given the various limitations in his life, Wu comes to realize that there is one thing over which he does have control—his moral character: "then slowly I began to realize that the only thing to which I could apply my efforts is my moral character. Outside of this, I know of nothing else. So what is that which I seek for myself? I seek only to strengthen this moral character of mine" (11:3b, no. 11). A person's greatness is ultimately

---

7. *Analects* 20:3, quoted in CW 11:27a, no. 166.

determined not by his external status or achievements in life but by the quality of his moral character.

Unlike the external circumstances of one's life situation, one's moral character is open-ended, with unlimited capacity and infinite possibilities. Wu reminds himself that, with respect to his moral character, he must "take the capacity of Heaven and earth as my capacity and the moral character of the sages as my moral character" (11:15a, no. 73). In an entry shortly after this, he sighs, "Alas, he who has not reached the way of Heaven and has not reached sagehood cannot be called a 'complete person'" (11:15b, no. 75). Thus, though one must confront and reconcile oneself to the limitations of one's life situation, one cannot compromise oneself when it comes to the call to sagehood, the call to fully develop one's human capacities. There, any limitations are of one's own making.

What Heaven ultimately expects of a person is that he does the best he can with what resources he has with respect to his particular life situation. Thus, Wu continually encourages himself to proceed with his learning and self-cultivation, not by the standards of men of the past or contemporary friends, but according to his own portion (fen 分), with all that entails regarding his abilities and limitations:

> Last evening, on account of being simultaneously bothered by poverty and illness, I couldn't concentrate on my reading and couldn't help feeling restless inside. After deep reflection, I realized that what is required is to direct my moral efforts right at this very problem spot, make myself composed inside, and, in every situation, to progress in my learning according to my given abilities. Then all will be as it should be. (11:23b, no. 138)

While Wu comes to accept the importance of discerning and following Heaven's will in his life, he remains awed by the difficulty of actually doing so. He enjoins himself over and over again to follow Heaven's will without any consideration of personal advantage: "Whether fate brings success or failure, short or long life, I will follow Heaven in any case. I will behave according to my sense of righteousness and that is all" (11:24b, no. 147). This sentiment is expressed with such frequency throughout the Journal, that it could not have been something that he was easily inclined toward or quickly able to master, but rather was something about which he had to constantly remind himself.

With similar frequency, Wu exclaims about the difficulty of learning to become a sage: "thinking about the hardships I've experienced in my life, I found myself more and more lamenting the fact that learning the way of the ancients is not easy" (11:19b, no. 106). In this, however, Wu is reminded by Zhu Xi that "If it were easy to do, there would be innumerable sages and worthies in the world at any one time." Wu's own comment to this is, "Alas, only one who has actually exerted himself in this regard knows how difficult it is!" (11:2a, no. 7).

Though Wu often complains, tries to resist his fate, and take the easy way out, he gradually learns that hardship and difficulties have in fact contributed to his personal development and have their own positive value. He quotes the *History of the Later Han* to the effect that, "If you have not had to cut through twisted roots and gnarled branches, you don't really know how to distinguish a sharp tool."[8] Hardships test a person's mettle and strengthen his abilities. Wu realizes that they challenge him to go beyond a mediocre way of life, forcing him to examine himself more thoroughly and to search more deeply for resources within himself:

> Today I realized that I have actually benefited somewhat from my poverty and difficulties. It seems people who have never exerted effort in circumstances of poverty and difficulty find that in the end, they don't succeed and they end up weak and timid. (11:17a, no. 84)

While Wu, after much reflection, comes to acknowledge that he is not to complain against Heaven for his fate and the limitations of his life situation, he still has to come to terms with the problem of "blaming other people," that is, losing his temper over the shortcomings of others. The insights he arrives at include both a sense of his own hypocrisy in criticizing others when he himself is not faultless, and a sense of the need for patience and understanding with the imperfections of others, especially in his role as teacher with his students.

As for the first aspect, Wu takes himself to task:

> Since I have no time left over from strenuously examining myself day and night for my faults, how can I find the time to engage in the practice of checking into the faults of other people? If a person

---

8. *History of the Later Han* 88:21b, quoted in 11:2b, no. 9.

criticizes others in great detail, he will be careless in managing himself. (11:2b, no. 8)

To expect change in others before one has changed oneself is not only a total waste of one's efforts but even more a mark of selfishness and a lack of understanding of others. One morning, feeling remorse for his critical nature, Wu composed this saying to advise himself: "The point is not that other people are hard to change, but truly that my own moral character is not up to par" (11:21a, no. 120).

He comes to realize that he lacks the Confucian virtue of empathy in judging others and cites as one of the admirable merits of the Cheng brothers their capacity always to be kind in their criticism of others: "their intent was only to rectify the situation, not to expose the faults of others" (11:41a, no. 319). That is, they were careful not to make a point of their own virtue at the expense of others with more obvious failings, thus showing a concern for the "face" of others. Besides lacking empathy, Wu's impatient attitude reflects an unrealistic view of what behavioral change entails. His Journal testifies to the fact that to change one's self takes time, and that one cannot expect to make progress straightaway without any relapse. He makes resolutions to be stricter with himself about criticizing others ("If I would judge myself in the same spirit as I judge others, I could fulfill the Way" [11:11b, no. 56]), as well as to be more generous in his treatment of others no matter what ("If another person treats me with deceit and stinginess, I shall try to treat him with fairness and openness" [11:36a, no. 264]).

Associated with this propensity to criticize others is a sense of loneliness on Wu's part, a sense that he lacks sagely friends to help him advance in the Way: "Above I have no teacher, below I have no friends. As for my program of self-cultivation, I have grown more lax with it. How can I bear this life of mine?" (11:18b, no. 97). He often ends an entry with the plea, "where can I find a good friend to help me realize this ambition of mine to reach sagehood?" (11:18b, no. 101. See also nos. 63 and 98). He longs for friends with outstanding abilities and insights so that he can benefit from their goodness. Just as he is sure he could be a much better person if he had better health and a less limited financial situation, he also feels that he could be a better person if he had more sagely friends around him, as would have been the case, he supposes, if he were living in the time of Confucius, the Cheng brothers, or Zhu Xi. This frustration about his lack of sagely companions in time gives way to a better understanding of the noted Song Neo-Confucian Li Tong's achievement of sagehood: "it was not that Master Li had the benefit of associates who were all sages and worthies," but rather that he was like "'Tang the Completer,' who 'did not demand perfection in others but scrutinized himself as if he still had not reached it himself'" (11:3a–b, no. 10).

Aware that he cannot blame either Heaven or other people, Wu is left with himself and his particular disposition to make his way in his pursuit of sagehood: "In learning to be a sage, there is no other way than seeking within myself" (11:37b, no. 284). That is to say, one must search within to overcome one's wayward disposition and make sagehood blossom from within one's being.

### Supports in Wu's Endeavors: The Sages

Though Wu feels ultimately responsible for the success of his goal, he is not totally alone in the enterprise without any external supports in coping with its challenges. In this next section, we shall find his life to be far less bleak than the previous section may suggest. If there is much sorrow and difficulty expressed in the Journal, there is also plenty of joy and pleasure. We now take up these more hopeful aspects that encouraged Wu in dealing with life's darker moments. His inspiration comes primarily from three sources: the sages (of both the classical period and the Song), his dreams, and the natural world. All three contribute to his sense of an expanded self—they are the things he celebrates, enjoys, and feels enriched by.

For Wu, sages are those men who have perfectly realized in their own lives the way of Heaven, heroically maintaining the transmission of the Confucian Way. In the Journal, he describes the excellence of the sages in these terms: they listened to the will of Heaven in all cases without any inner disturbance; they did not let what happened in the external world determine their sense of their own worth; they dealt with each situation in accordance with principle; and they were consistent in all this throughout their lives from youth to old age. Wu is convinced that the one way to be a complete person and to have a life free from defect is to follow the learning of the sages, and he resolves to be guided each day by their teachings. He aims to rid himself of anything unworthy of the sages and to cultivate all that is worthy. In his development, as the years go on, Wu declares that, "More and more I understand why a person must take becoming a sage or worthy as his personal responsibility" (11:31b, no. 207), and he reaffirms his resolve to spend the remaining years of his life thus occupied.

Wu's most direct and intimate encounter with the sages is through books, either the sages' writings or accounts of their lives by others. He thus finds himself strongly attached to his books and to his program of reading. Therein he loses himself in a kind of all-consuming absorption and experiences the fundamental oneness of his being. It is his attachment to the works of the sages as a means of staying close to them in spirit that makes him so reluctant to be separated from his books and so resentful of interruptions in his reading schedule. Elsewhere in his *Collected Works*, he wrote: "Each time I savor the words of the sages and worthies, I regret that I was not born in their time, could not stand at their gates among their disciples, and in one leap reach their realm" (10:14b).

In a 1421 letter, Wu wrote that "The ultimate in sagehood was reached by Yao, Shun, the Duke of Zhou, and Confucius, and nothing further can be added" (8:16b, Letter 3). Elsewhere, in a poem entitled "At Night Cherishing Thoughts of the Ancients" (2:6b–7a), he divided the sages into three categories: the sage kings of antiquity (Yao and Shun), the sage teachers of the classical period (Confucius and Mencius), and the masters of the Song period. Though Wu had the utmost regard for all of these, it is to this third group that he displays his greatest personal devotion.

Wu shows his devotion to the Song masters not just by reading their books but also by visiting their shrines, harmonizing with the rhymes of their poetry, and meditating on their portraits. Once, while visiting a shrine dedicated to the Song Neo-Confucian Masters Zhou Dunyi and Zhu Xi, he wrote a poem to express his deep admiration for them that ends:

> I only regret I have no way to hasten to the edge of their mat for instruction.
> In this holy shrine, I bow deeply as I reverently make my approach.
> (1:24a)

Several poems later, Wu speaks of contemplating the portraits of the major Song figures he has come across in his reading. In this poem he describes the greatness of these Song men in having restored the Way of Confucius and Mencius, making it shine brightly like the sun and moon for all to see. But he also laments his own inferior achievements by comparison. Meditating on their pictures helps to assuage his longing for them:

By means of their pictures, I try to probe their minds.
More and more this serves to mold my careless nature.
Not as good as they are, I am still fearful of failing them.
Who knows how distressed this mind of mine is?
On occasion, I undertake to sketch their pictures;
At all times, I persevere in reverently bearing their trust. (1:25a)

The Song masters are more compelling models for Wu because they are closer in time than the other sages, and they accomplished their sagehood in everyday situations that seem not all that different from his own. There are also more detailed accounts of their lives available to him. In addition to his more intellectual and philosophical works, Zhu Xi compiled a number of books for pedagogical use, including collections of biographies to put before students models that could be imitated. These writings include the last chapter of *Reflections on Things at Hand,* entitled "On the Dispositions of the Sages and Worthies," the *Record of the Origins of the School of the Two Chengs,* and the *Records of the Words and Deeds of Eminent Officials of the Song Dynasty.* Wu, in the course of his reading schedule, includes all of these, as well as another less-known work, *Compilation of Exemplary Biographies to Alert the Self.*[9] We have already seen in the discussion of Wu's life how he attributed his initial conversion experience to reading the *Record of the Origins of the School of the Two Chengs* and being inspired by the living reality of sagehood in the lives of the figures portrayed there. We shall also see how his attraction to the Song masters had more to do with the personal qualities they exhibited than with their abstract, intellectual ideas.

Wu was not attracted to all of the Song masters in the same way and with the same intensity. Certain figures he singled out for special devotion as models with which he felt a deep affinity. He was drawn to each figure for a different reason. The three principal ones are Cheng Hao (1032–1085), Shao Yong (1011–1077), and Zhu Xi (1130–1200).

Starting with Cheng Hao, we have already discussed how Wu attributed part of his conversion experience to the personal example of Cheng, who had struggled with and overcome his love for hunting. He also admired him for heroically assuming responsibility for the transmission of the Way after it had fallen into oblivion for a thousand years after Mencius:

---

9. See Glossary of Book Titles for information on these texts.

Only the Master carried on the line that had been transmitted for a thousand years. Each time I recite his poetry, read his writings, or imagine his features as a person, I regret that I was not born during his time. (9:7b)

Cheng had become a worthy in his own lifetime, not from superhuman efforts but in the very humanness of his being, making mistakes at times but correcting them through learning, as when he overcame his enjoyment of hunting. Wu always referred to him by his sobriquet Master Mingdao, or one who enlightens the Way. Wu took great delight in reciting out loud the *Biographical Account of Cheng Hao,* written by Cheng's older brother, Cheng Yi. The effect of chanting this, by Wu's own account, was always highly emotional:

This evening I was reciting the *Biographical Account of Cheng Hao* and found myself immensely affected by it. Whenever I came to a place that resonated with me, without realizing it, my hands and feet moved in joyful response. (11:23a, no. 136)

According to Wu's student Lou Liang, the appeal of Cheng Hao for Wu had to do largely with Cheng's mild and easy manner, one that Wu wished he had instead of his own intense and volatile nature. Besides his affable manner, Wu admired Cheng's sense of self-possession and self-contentment. In a poem written in 1450, Wu wrote that he named his newly built pavilion "The Pavilion of the Self-At-Ease," inspired by Cheng's poem "Autumn Days." The first half of Cheng's poem goes:

With leisure, everything is relaxed.
When I awake, the sun shining through the eastern window is
    already red.
All things viewed in tranquility are at ease with themselves (*zide*)
The delightful spirit of the four seasons I share with all.[10]

For the classical Confucians, the meaning of the term *zide* (自得) is more specifically the ease that comes from "appropriation of the Way

---

10. Translated by Chan in "Neo-Confucian Philosophical Poems," *Renditions* 4 (1975), p. 11.

for oneself," as in Mencius' words that "The noble person delves into it [learning], deeply according to the Way, wishing to get it in himself."[11] Once one finds the Way for oneself inside oneself, then self-contentment and self-possession emerge, naturally and spontaneously, and one realizes a sense of oneness with all creation. As Wu's own sense of self-contentment and self-possession increased with age, he found himself frequently quoting lines from Cheng Hao about the matter of sagely composure: "The constant principle of the sage is that his feelings are in accord with all creation, and yet he has no feelings of his own," and one should be "broad and extremely impartial and respond spontaneously to things as they come."[12]

Cheng Hao thus inspired Wu with his personal qualities of affability and mildness, of self-possession and contentment, ease and joyfulness, and spontaneity amid composure. As we shall see shortly, Wu also derived his important idea of the "vital impulse of things" (*sheng-yi*) from Cheng.

Wu's poetic, nature-loving side found a great affinity with the Song thinker and poet, Shao Yong. In studies of Chinese thought, Shao is usually associated with his theories of numerology and commentaries on the *Book of Changes*. But for Wu, Shao's appeal was his strong appreciation for the intimate relationship between human spontaneities and those of the natural world. In an early entry in the Journal, after describing his own sense of peacefulness in the context of a natural setting, he remarks that:

> This experience verifies what Master Shao Yong meant in a poem:

> > One only notices the bright day when the mind is tranquil.
> > One only appreciates the blue sky when the eyes are clear.
> > (11:3b–4a, no. 12)

This sense of affinity of the human and natural realms is best expressed in the poetic mode, and Shao is regarded as one of the outstanding Song Neo-Confucian poets in this respect.[13] Wu is fond of quoting Shao's poems in the Journal, and of writing poems following Shao's rhyme schemes in his

---

11. *Mencius* 4B:14 (trans. by Bloom, *Mencius*, p. 88).

12. Both quotes are from Cheng Hao's "On Calming the Nature," in *Collected Works of Cheng Hao* 3:1a–b (trans. by Chan, *Source Book in Chinese Philosophy*, p. 525). The first quotation is cited in entry no. 310, the second in no. 326.

13. Chan, "Neo-Confucian Philosophical Poems," *Renditions* 4 (1975), p. 8.

collection of poems. In one such poem, Wu writes about teaching Shao's poetry to his students, describing the effect Shao's poems had on him thus:

> Having finished chanting these wonderful poems, I forget my
>     troubles amidst all this joy,
> I also fail to notice how the months and years of my fleeting life are
>     mounting up. (4:40a)

Along with this poetic sense of joy, Wu appreciates Shao's conviction that many of the fundamental pleasures of life are free and thus cannot be denied to a person, even one who is poor. Enjoying nature and taking naps are among the best of these:

> Today while resting, I read some of the poetry of Shao Yong. Subsequently, I fell into a deep sleep. When I awoke, my state of mind was quite excellent, just as Shao himself described in a poem, "no less than had I been enfeoffed or awarded money." Even though I am extremely impoverished, that is my fate. But it cannot destroy this present happiness. (11:24a, no. 143)

Elsewhere Wu quotes Shao that "Even though I am poor, it does not affect the lofty peace I enjoy each day" (11:24b, no. 146). For both Shao and Wu, like Confucius' disciple Yan Hui, there is the Confucian sense of being poor yet delighting in the Way.

One cannot help but observe that both Shao Yong and Wu have the same character, *kang* (康), in the sobriquets they chose. Although in modern Chinese *kang* is used in the sense of good health and vigor, in classical literature it has more to do with a sense of peacefulness, tranquility, and harmony. Wu never mentions anywhere why he chose his particular sobriquet, Kangzhai ("Studio of Tranquility" 康斋), but given his attraction to Shao Yong whose sobriquet was Kangjie ("Tranquil and Pure" 康節), it is likely that he had Shao in mind when he chose it.

Of all these Song Neo-Confucians, however, no one stands out more than Zhu Xi as an object of devotion for Wu. He puts Zhu in a wholly different class from all the others, as the following poem of Wu's illustrates:

> The former philosophers had noble characters, all of whom I
>     respect;
> But Master Zhu of Kaoting especially engages my attention.

He is like the ocean in its vastness that swallows up all other bodies
    of water;
Like Mounts Tai and Hua whose lofty heights dwarf the myriad
    other mountain peaks. (1:34b–35a)

In 1179–1180, Zhu Xi spent time in northern Jiangxi province as an
education official in Nanchang and worked to restore and expand the
White Deer Grotto Academy there. This was a place that Wu tried to visit
on his trips to Nanjing. He most often referred to Zhu by his sobriquet,
Master Huian (晦奄先生). One indication of Wu's special regard for Zhu
can be seen in the fact that Zhu is the only non-classical figure who visits
Wu in his dreams. These dreams about Zhu reflect Wu's intense feelings
for him. As discussed earlier, the second entry in the Journal records Wu
waiting in attendance upon Zhu Xi and displaying his deep reverence and
admiration for him. In 1456, he had a very moving dream in which he,
along with three friends, tried to visit Zhu but were prevented from doing
so by floodwaters. Wu found the anguish hard to bear, and in his sadness
he composed this poem to express his feelings:

Though myriad of autumns separate us, we share deep feelings
    between us.
Unable to part, I do not understand the state of mind I'm in.
The golden cock suddenly announces the dawn at the spring
    window.
With regret, my injured spirit gives out a cry of sorrow. (11:33a,
    no. 223)

Later, in a dream recorded in 1461, Zhu and his son honored Wu with a
visit. The next year, 1462, Wu made a pilgrimage to Zhu's birthplace in
Fujian province. That one of Zhu's descendants came out to greet him during his visit was a great source of honor and pleasure to him. In all of his
various travels, Wu would note if Zhu Xi had ever traveled or lived in the
same area, taking pleasure whenever he sensed that their paths had crossed,
even though it was hundreds of years later.

For Wu, Zhu was the master teacher, and thus, "Ordinarily I am never
without Master Zhu's instructions on my belt" (7:12b–13a). The force
of Zhu's writings was powerfully transformative for him: "Today I have
been reading Zhu Xi's *Collected Works*. Being in intimate contact with the

Master's teachings allows a person to transcend the ordinary world and eliminate his numerous worries" (11:40a, no 309).

It is not surprising that Zhu's philosophical works would predominate in Wu's reading program, such as Zhu's *Collected Works* and his *Classified Conversations*, but what is striking is the role Zhu's poetry played in Wu's relationship with the sage. Many of Wu's poems mention reading Zhu's poetry and composing his own poems following Zhu's rhyme scheme (1:34b–35a, 2:12a, and 2:16a–b). In one poem, he speaks of the cooling effect of reading Zhu's poetry in the hot summer (2:14a). In the Journal, he describes one occasion of teaching his students a collection of Zhu's poems: "The emotion in my voice rose and fell in cadence with the poems' rhythms. We were all immensely affected by them" (11:23b, no. 139).

Although one might easily comprehend Wu's attraction to Cheng Hao and Shao Yong with their warmer and more genial personalities, his particular emotional response to Zhu Xi is likely to be somewhat mystifying. The stereotypes of Zhu in contemporary scholarship are far from the type of person associated with objects of warm devotion. Acknowledged as a brilliant scholar and a skillful architect of the Neo-Confucian tradition, Zhu has often been characterized as pedantic, stuffy, aloof, and humorless. Whether these characteristics are indeed accurate or not, what is of interest is how Wu perceived him so differently. He saw Zhu as a helpful, sympathetic presence who could meet some of his deepest spiritual and emotional needs. He dreams about him; he writes poetry "with" him. One might go as far as to speculate that Zhu replaced Wu's father as the chief source of authority in his life, as the chief object of his loyalty and devotion.

The dynamics at work in Wu's relationship with all of these models might be seen as a resonance with personal, human qualities that transcend time and place. Wu's reverence for these models is such that he feels he is able to enter into their presence, participate as it were in their being, and have new energies evoked within himself. To him, these figures do not represent strict standards outside himself with respect to which he must suppress his own individuality in order to become like them. Rather, he sees them as sources of access to his own greater participation in the larger order of things. To be sure, his relationship to the sages is not a simple matter. While a powerful sense of the presences of these sage models in his life provides him with inspiration and encouragement in his own attempts to achieve sagehood, at the same time, it also contributes to a feeling of disgruntlement with his own situation and a sense of nostalgia for the past. Frustration arises from his wanting to participate more fully in their sagely inner circle yet being unable to do so, cut off from them as he is in time.

### Sources of Support: Dreams

Besides the inspiration that comes from the models of the sages that have gone before him, Wu derived great support from his dreams, which play a prominent role in his life. The phenomenon of using dreams as a guide to one's behavior is not something new or unusual in the Confucian tradition. In the *Analects,* a disconcerted Confucius was moved to cry, "How extreme is my decline. For such a long time, I have not seen the Duke of Zhou in my dreams."[14] In the Ming dynasty, dreams took on more widespread importance. According to Ming scholar Lienche Tu Fang, "the Ming people seem to have been over concerned with dreams. They recorded their own dreams and those of others and wrote stories about dreams. Dreams were told and retold. Even in recounting a dream which may sound like utter nonsense, there is little indication of embarrassment."[15]

As for the centrality of dreams in Wu's life, we have evidence in the way the Journal itself begins with accounts of three dreams, two of which have been mentioned, and also how Wu dreamed about his father frequently before and after their reconciliation. In his poetry, Wu has occasion to mention numerous dreams, mostly of relatives and friends, either living or dead. In the present discussion, however, we are more interested in dreams that relate to his program of self-cultivation, those dreams that inspire, direct, and support him in his efforts. What he calls dreams is an odd mixture, and I have tried to classify them into three groups: those involving the sages; those involving symbolic images or lines of poetry; and those with cautionary warnings or advice. Although these dreams tend to be inspiring and "bright" in tone, he also records some rather "dark" dreams that leave him in tears upon waking.

As for the first category, those involving the sages, these are the most famous of all Wu's dreams. These are the dreams that have drawn the attention of writers about Wu. According to the editors of the *Catalogue of the Imperial Manuscript Library,* Wu had such devotion to the sages that

---

14. *Analects* 7:5.

15. "Ming Dreams," *The Tsing Hua Journal of Chinese Studies,* New Series X, no. 1 (June 1973), p. 55.

it translated itself into these images in his dreams: "This can only be said
to happen as a result of extreme admiration, such that a person's mind
could produce images related to principle."[16] Confucius and Zhu Xi are
the principal sages that visit him, most often to offer him advice and show
their concern for him. The Journal, as mentioned earlier, begins with the
recording of two dreams about these men.

The first is of Confucius and the founder of the Zhou, King Wen,
paying a visit to Wu's father's residence in Nanjing. Wu wishes to ask for
their guidance, but before he can do so Confucius provides some non-
verbal advice by picking up and leafing through King Wen's genealogy. In
the Confucian tradition, King Wen and his ancestors are considered sage
rulers who have articulated the Way for all who come after. Wu can do no
better than to follow in their footsteps. Immediately following this entry,
Wu records a dream of appearing in Zhu Xi's presence, an appearance he
finds awe-inspiring. He is moved to wait upon him with a great show of
reverence.

The Journal continues with other dreams involving these two sages,
including Wu's aforementioned thwarted attempt to visit Zhu (1456), a
visit by Confucius' grandson (1457), and a visit by Zhu Xi and his son
(1461). In the dream of Confucius' grandson, we can see the depth of the
emotional effect these dreams had on Wu. The grandson arrived, announc-
ing to Wu, "I have come here commissioned by Confucius." Then Wu
notes, "The two of us were moved to tears; then I awoke. Even now, I
can still distinctively remember his features" (11:34a, no. 238). Four years
later, in 1461, the year before he was to visit the birthplace of Zhu Xi, he
dreamed that Zhu and his son paid him a visit: "After eating today, I was
tired so took a nap. I dreamed that Master Zhu Xi and his son graced me
with a visit" (11:35b, no. 258). This was the last of his recorded dreams
about the sages.

One of the most fascinating dreams in the Journal is not one of his own
but rather one of his wife's, although Wu takes it as if it were his own. In
this dream, while Wu was away from home erecting a new house for the
family, his wife dreamed that Confucius showed up with three disciples.
One of the disciples came in and asked for Wu. When his wife told him
that Wu was away at the time, she was told by the disciple to give Wu the
message that Confucius had come to teach him how to advance in his

---

16. *Catalogue of the Imperial Manuscript Library (Siku quanshu zongmu)* 170:12b.

learning. When Wu returned home and heard his wife's dream, his reaction was intensely emotional:

> When I heard my wife recount this, I was at once alarmed and apprehensive, excited and overjoyed. In gratitude, I got up repeatedly to pay my respects to Heaven and earth. I felt shivers go up and down by spine on account of this.

The aforementioned editors of the *Catalogue of the Imperial Manuscript Library*, with a degree of skepticism about Wu's dreams in general, comment, "Wasn't this a case of his wife teasing him and his not even being aware of it?"[17] But Wu took it seriously, regarding the dream as if it were his own, seeing that it was a sign for him to exert himself more: "From now on, how dare I not make my mind and vital spirit calm, and fully concentrate on my learning and moral character? How dare I be stingy with my energies, worn-out and inferior though they may be?" (11:19a–b, no. 103).

Among these dreams of the sages, Confucius and Zhu Xi stand out as the primary figures. In a real sense, they are the archetypal figures of the Confucian and Neo-Confucian traditions, respectively. Dreams related to Confucius seem to have in common a concern on the part of Confucius to provide Wu with instruction, either directly himself or indirectly through some emissary (Wu's wife or Confucius' grandson). The dreams related to Zhu Xi seem more personal. Wu is either waiting on him, or trying to visit him, or is visited by him. What is striking in all these dreams is Wu's faith in them as reflecting the active concern on the part of these sages to provide guidance to those aspiring to follow the Way in their lives.

The second group of dreams, that of symbolic images or lines of poetry, has in it some fascinating but enigmatic dreams. They are described so briefly, without any elaboration or explanation, that we can only speculate as to their meaning. These dreams all come in the later years of Wu's life, from 1449 to 1461.

The first of these, described in the only entry for the year 1449, is a dream in which "a piece of jade produced orchid-like blossoms which filled the whole ground" (11:31a, no. 202). Jade is a precious stone, prized for its beauty, purity, and durability. Could it be a symbol of the Way flourishing in the world, producing virtuous sages like orchids? This dream is

---

17. Ibid., 170:12b.

followed two entries later, in 1451, by a dream with even more dramatic content: "On the night of the second day of the eighth month, I dreamed that there was a complete eclipse of the sun. When I, Yubi, breathed fire into it from the side, it flamed up immediately, its full brilliance thereupon restored" (11:31a, no. 204). Here the sun, like the jade, can be seen to refer to the Way, which, Wu was aware, declines with each day and could be totally eclipsed as it was for the period of a thousand years from Mencius to Cheng Hao when its transmission was not carried on. Wu seems to be pointing to his sense of responsibility to restore the Way to its previous brilliance and power, just as he does in the dream to restore the sun to its full brightness.

Two extremely puzzling dreams include both an image and a line of poetry. First the dream with an image: "I dreamed that a clear breeze swayed the tall stately trees of the myriad households" (11:34b, no. 246). And second, the dream in which Wu is chanting lines of poetry: "Again I tell you, do not cut the trees in front of the eaves of my house, / Rather, listen to the Red Apricot Song in my lofty hall" (11:35b, no. 256).

The third group consists of dreams of advice given to Wu, either by ghosts or spirits or by unidentified sources. For the Neo-Confucians, ghosts and spirits are regarded not as spooky things but spirit forces in the universe. Once Wu dreamed that he was reciting the line, "How can I preserve and nourish the oneness of my mind?" When he awoke, he commented, "Wasn't it the ghosts and spirits who taught me this?" (11:38a, no. 287). But some of the advice that comes to him in dreams is not attributed to any one thing directly: "I dreamt that I was advised that 'a person who limits himself makes no progress in his moral character'" (11:35a, no. 253). These dreams echo on a general level the admonitions and reminders he already has been giving himself. No doubt there is more of an impact when Wu senses that forces beyond him, like ghosts and spirits, are concerned to alert him in matters of moral conduct than merely his own conscience.

What is interesting about Wu's dreams is the whole matter of Wu recording them, his taking note of these nocturnal happenings and regarding them as means of support and guidance in his undertaking to achieve sagehood. The range of Wu's dreams themselves suggest an imagination that is not narrowly or dryly moralistic but rather one that is more poetic or even mystical. Wu's primary concern is with the Way: he sees the Way as dynamically functioning even in his dream life. Ghosts and spirits are forces in the universe that do not exactly belong to either the human or the natural world but overlap both. These powers, too, serve the purpose

of the Way by offering explicit though generalized advice to followers of
the Way.

### Sources of Support: The Natural World

At least as sustaining for Wu as the sage models and dreams is the whole
natural world, if not more so. "Contemplating the flowers and trees around
me today, I feel one in spirit with them" (11:9a, no. 36). Some of Wu's
more exalted and tranquil moments in the whole Journal are when he is on
his way to and from his fields or on some outing in the neighborhood, in
direct contact with nature. In approaching Wu's appreciation for the natural
world, it is helpful to keep in mind that Jiangxi province where Wu lived is
part of the fertile and scenic south-central part of China, where waterways
and mountains abound, and where the climate remains temperate most of
the year—where nature presents a benign image.

As for Wu's contact with nature through his farming, it prompted com-
plaints from him, especially in his early years as a farmer, when it interfered
with his program of study. But it also inspired in him a sense of joy on
the occasions when it made him aware of the connectedness of all things.
"Today, I was harvesting the rice fields around Qingshi Bridge. On my way
to and from the village, I felt a tremendous sense of joy with all that was
around me" (11:20b, no. 115).

Although we do not know for sure the extent of Wu's direct involvement in farm work, it was probably not inconsiderable, especially in his
earlier years when his financial situation was so limited. He saw his profes-
sion as both a farmer and a teacher. What is of interest here are the links he
saw between the two professions, and between the natural world and the
moral principles of the Way. Farming was not just a way to make a living,
but a way to participate in the creative processes of the world. We shall go
into this in more detail in the section on Wu as a moral teacher.

Besides farming, Wu had contact with the natural world through frequent outings in the surrounding areas. His poetry and Journal are filled
with descriptions of the beautiful local scenery and of the great delight he
takes in it. The dominant tone on these outings is one of leisure and ease,
as well as joyful exuberance: "Roaming on the far side of the stream today,
I picked some flowers. The late spring weather was such that I was filled
with pure joy" (11:29b, no. 233).

Though often alone in his ramblings, Wu also delights in the company
of his students and his children (and later, his grandchildren) on these

outings. He also takes great pleasure when he is joined by special friends to enjoy the scenery with wine and poetry. In one entry, he recalls these special pleasures:

> While randomly picking flowers at the fare edge of the stream today, I became nostalgic about old friends and thought of two lines:
>
>> By chance, I am at the place once visited and enjoyed with old friends.
>> We picked flowers at the bend of the stream and delighted in the spring waters. (11:33b, no. 231)

Wu's appreciation of the natural world does not conflict with his intense devotion to the sages of the tradition and his program of reading books. Indeed, Wu experiences an extra special pleasure when he is able to be in intimate contact with the world of the sages and the world of nature at the same time, as when he is able to engage in his studies outdoors. At these times, he becomes aware of the integration or coherence of these two worlds, between what he is reading and the spirit of life in the natural world. Both share in the essential creativity of the universe, sustaining and furthering life in their respective ways:

> Today, I have been sitting outside my gate, my table covered with diagrams and books. Surrounded by my students, I take advantage of the shade of the trees and enjoy the cool breeze. The vital impulse of the manifold things fills my view. The beautiful mountain stands as guest and host. Contemplating this glorious view, I experience a great sense of expansiveness. (11:20a, no. 109)

Even when he cannot be outdoors, Wu tries to do such work as reading, writing up his lessons, practicing calligraphy, or composing by his window, so that he can be fully aware of and in contact with the larger natural scene beyond.

The most striking thing in the entries dealing with Wu's relationship with the natural world is the complete absence of any sense of constraint or dark brooding. There is none of the depression, frustration, or heavy tone of his "inside" life. Instead, a sense of openness, brightness, spontaneity, and lightness prevail. The contrast between Wu's life in and out of doors at times is so striking, especially in the early parts of the Journal, that one is tempted to advise him to stay out of doors as much as he can. Nature seems to exert a transformative influence on him. He himself is not unaware of how the natural world affects him—how it calms him down so that he can realize the depths of tranquility, and how it loosens the inner constrictions so he can experience the expansiveness of the larger cosmic order:

> Today I was out inspecting my fields. On account of an ailment from boils, I lay down on the grass for a leisurely rest. The extreme tranquility I felt there on the path between the fields was as if there were no human world. (11:8b, no. 33)

In nature, the goals that Wu struggles to achieve in his self-cultivation program—purity, openness of mind, tranquility, freedom, and a sense of expansiveness—all seem to come about of themselves, directly and spontaneously. While his nature imagery displays no profound originality, nevertheless, it reflects a deep appreciation for the beneficent aspects of the natural world which contribute to his transformation. He is thus sensitive to the way the sun and the wind, trees and rocks, water and mountains, flowers and birds—indeed, all of nature—each in its own way of functioning, works for his benefit, warming and brightening, soothing and calming, cooling and cleansing, opening and broadening him.

In doing so, the various forces of nature serve to place Wu in a larger context than his own narrow and limited self, and give him a sense of participation in the greater workings of the universe. In this larger context, harmony rather than competitiveness and friction among parts prevail. Each thing has its particular purpose and work, and all function together in the smooth operation of the Way. Later in the Journal, Wu speaks of coming to understand Cheng Hao's saying: "A person really has no obstacles between Heaven and earth. To find joy in both the great and the small is true happiness" (quoted in 11:39a–b, no. 301). Once a person rids himself of petty, divisive selfishness, he realizes that there are no obstacles between himself and others. Once aware of this, a person is able to realize his expanded self that fills the whole universe and to take pleasure rather than offense at the multiplicity of things.

The underlying principle evident in the natural world that links Wu to the larger order of things is that of *sheng-yi* 生意, "the vital impulse of things," or as one scholar prefers, "spirit of life." This vital impulse is related more specifically to the spirit of growth in plant life:

> Early this morning, how enjoyable it is to observe the vital impulse of things. The waning moon is still in the sky, the dew-drenched flowers fill my view. The subtle appeal of this scene is not something words can describe. (11:25b, no. 157)

Wu got this concept of *sheng-yi* from Cheng Hao, the Song master who, as we have seen, was one of Wu's great heroes. According to Cheng, "The most impressive aspect of things is their spirit of life. This is what is meant by origination being the chief quality of goodness. This is *jen*."[18] Zhu Xi later glossed this passage as: "In the growth of all things and in the operation of the mandate of Heaven, from beginning to end, principle is always present; however it is particularly easy to see when things begin to grow and its purity has not been diffused."[19]

The concept of *sheng-yi* is thus bound up with ideas of creativity and moments of origination when principle is most pure and vital. These moments, more than any others, point to the fundamental nature of a thing, as well as to its direction of growth. The fundamental nature of the universe, according to the *Book of Changes*, is to produce life again and again, and not only to give life but also sustain it. The natural world, where plant life abounds, is a rich source for reflecting this fundamental creative intentionality or impulse of the cosmic order. This appreciation for the creative impulse of life is not merely an aesthetic one, in the sense of a person being a passive spectator of the beauties of nature. Rather there is an

---

18. *Written Legacy of the Cheng Brothers* 11:3b (trans. by Chan, *Source Book in Chinese Philosophy,* p. 539. (*Jen* is the Wade-Giles romanization of *ren* 仁, humaneness.) Cheng Hao also used the term *chun-yi* 春意, "impulses of spring," to express this: "'Change means production and reproduction.' This is how Heaven becomes the Way. To Heaven, the Way is merely to give life. What follows from this principle of life-giving is good. Goodness involves the idea of origination (*yuan* 元), for origination is the chief quality of goodness. All things have the impulses of spring (spirit of growth) and this is goodness resulting from the principle of life." *Written Legacy* 2a:12b (trans. by Chan, *Source Book in Chinese Philosophy,* p. 532).

19. *Classified Conversations of Zhu Xi* 95:19a–b (trans. by Chan, *Reflections on Things at Hand,* p. 21).

awareness of how the human directly participates in these natural dynamics, of how the human and natural orders share in one total life process. Wu feels himself drawn to the vitality of nature not as an aesthete but as a participant who is refreshed, purified, and energized by it.

The equating of the creativity of the natural world with that of the larger Way reflects the ultimate creative nature of the Way to which humans aspire to participate. While not a dominant aspect of Song Neo-Confucianism (but not an insignificant one either), this insight has often been overlooked in studies of the tradition. The best representatives of this orientation are Cheng Hao and Shao Yong, both of whom exerted a special influence on Wu, as we have seen. In an article on Neo-Confucian poetry, the scholar Wing-tsit Chan has noted:

> No Neo-Confucian philosopher has expressed this feeling in poetry better than Shao Yong. . . . The feeling of ease, serenity, and harmony with Nature is equally strong in Cheng Hao . . . To him, Principle is not merely an abstract concept but a living reality found in the wind and flowers.[20]

Chan goes on to describe how for both Shao and Cheng, if the Way indeed prevails in the world, it reveals itself everywhere, in everything. The distinctions between the realms of Heaven, earth, and the human lose their sharpness from the perspective of the Way. The crucial thing is that, as Chan writes, "All things merge into one and are at ease, and joy is shared by all."[21] This sense of joy and ease suggests an appreciation for the more intuitive and mystical aspects of the Way which underlie its more rational and moral aspects. It is not surprising that Shao and Cheng thus turned to poetry to express these aspects of the Way, and that an integral part of their thought found expression in the poetic mode.

With Wu, too, there is a great attraction to the poetic mode for expressing his thoughts and feelings, as can be deduced from the fact that seven out of the twelve *juan*[22] in his *Collected Works* are collections of his poetry. His joy in writing poetry can be seen from this entry in the Journal:

---

20. Chan, "Neo-Confucian Philosophical Poems," pp. 8, 11.

21. Ibid., p. 11.

22. Chinese texts are divided into *juan* (卷), usually translated as fascicle. It is somewhat (but not entirely) like a chapter.

Today, the twenty-eighth day of the second month, is such a beautiful, clear day. I have been composing poetry in my outer southern studio. The sunlight reflecting through the mountain mist shines on the flowers and trees, while birds flutter up and down in song. What a joyful mood I'm in! (11:8a, no. 29)

His student Lou Liang described Wu's poetry as "rooted in his nature and feelings, and having its origin in righteousness and principle. It is easy-going yet vigorous throughout, with the lively spirit of High Tang poetry."[23] The editor of Wu's *Collected Works with Appended Sources* commented on his poetry as follows: "Whenever there was something he understood, right away, it took form in a poem. What is more, all his poems came from the genuineness of his nature and feelings. Once he put the brush to paper, he did not have the problem of having to revise it."[24]

Though Wu cannot be said to have been a great poet, still, several of his poems were included in such anthologies as the *Compilation of Ming Poetry* (明詩紀事) and the *Record of Ming Poetry* (明詩綜).[25] The eminent twentieth-century scholar of Neo-Confucianism, Qian Mu,[26] placed Wu beside Shao Yong and Chen Xianzhang as the foremost Neo-Confucian poets, singling out Wu for including the agricultural aspects of nature in his poetry, not just nature as seen in landscapes. Qian cites this couplet as best representing the spirit of Wu's poetry:

As placid as the autumn waters is the taste of poverty;
As peaceful as the spring winds is the result of tranquility. (11:37b, no. 16)

## Disciplining and Nourishing (Weeding and Watering)

Having thus examined the first polarity, of the sources of difficulty and support for Wu in his quest for sagehood, we turn now to the second set of

---

23. *Biographical Account of Wu Yubi* 10:12b.

24. Wu Tai, *Collected Works of Master Wu Yubi, with Appended Sources* (hereafter referred to as "Appended Sources," CW), 22b–23a.

25. Wu has three poems in the former (23:1a), and two poems in the latter (part 2, 12:4b).

26. Qian Mu, "Study of the Currents of Thought in the Early Ming Chu Hsi School," in *Collection of Discussions of the History of Chinese Scholarship and Thought*, vol. 7, p. 1.

polarities, between disciplining and nurturing himself in his daily program of self-cultivation. Here he is preoccupied with making progress in his *xuede* (學德), or learning and moral character. At one point in the Journal he remarks that, "As for what *Practicing the Mean* speaks of, 'the virtuous nature' and 'constant inquiry and study,' I dare not be remiss in the least bit with respect to either" (11:37b, no. 283). He is alluding to section 27 of *Practicing the Mean*, which is about "honoring the moral nature and following the path of inquiry and study," taken to be the two sides of a coin in Neo-Confucian self-cultivation. I have taken *xuede* to be Wu's shorthand for this dual concern, *xue* (學), for following the path of inquiry and study, and *de* (德), for honoring the virtuous nature.

Wu does not aim to be original in his program of cultivation but largely follows the general approach advocated by the Cheng-Zhu tradition, which essentially is a combination of book-reading and self-reflective practices. The polarity here is the interplay of efforts at self-discipline with those of self-nurturing. His book learning and his meditation both functioned to help him reach a balance between restraining the negative aspects and expanding the positive aspects of the self.

The reading of books constituted an essential part of moral effort in the Cheng-Zhu tradition. To advance in virtue, a person first had to know and understand the principle involved in various situations, for, it was believed, one who knew principle would naturally and joyously follow it. One had to be clear in his mind about what the truth of the situation was in order to act properly therein. Though all humans have an innate sense of principle and goodness, they have need of outside points of reference to evoke and develop this innate sense. The investigation of things was aimed at doing this.

In the Cheng-Zhu tradition, the different ways one could investigate the principle of things included reading books, evaluating people and events of the past and present, and handling affairs. But of all these, "For the extension of knowledge, nothing is more important than reading."[27] In this activity of reading books, the emphasis was not on the quantity but on the quality, being able to grasp the essentials of what was read. Asked about the methods of study, Cheng Yi advised, "One must explore and get the real taste of the words of the Sage, remember them, and then exert

---

27. This is Song thinker Yeh Cai's description of the contents of chapter 3 of *Reflections on Things at Hand* (Chan, *Reflections on Things at Hand,* p. 88).

effort to put them in practice."[28] In doing so, one should be transformed as a result of his reading. "If after having studied it, one is still the same person as before, he has not really studied it."[29]

As one who sees himself in the mainstream of the Cheng-Zhu tradition, Wu Yubi approaches his reading in the spirit of Cheng Yi's words. Reading books is a great joy for him in that it brings him into contact with the sages of the past, whom he sees as guiding and supporting him with their words and example. Reading serves the crucial function of collecting his mind in the process of self-cultivation:

> The mind is a lively thing. If I am not thorough in my nourishing of it, then the mind cannot help but be shaken and moved by things. Only by constantly settling it down by reading books will the mind not be overwhelmed by external things. (11:18a, no. 92)

Elsewhere he describes the effect of reading on him in these terms: "Every time I am in intimate contact with the words of the sages and worthies like this, my mind experiences its fundamental oneness" (11:38a, no. 288).

Because reading helps to collect the mind and effect its oneness, Wu readily turns to it to help him deal with a variety of situations. One of the most important uses, especially in the earlier parts of the Journal, is in coping with distressful situations:

> In the midst of poverty and distressed circumstances, I find matters keep coming on me one after another. At the same time, I am suffering from painful boils. I can't help from time to time getting angry and frustrated by it all. At times like these, I slowly try to order my attire and turn to my reading. Often then I immediately become aware of a loosening up within me. (11:2b, no. 9)

Reading is not a burdensome task for Wu, but something in which he takes great joy. "After putting household matters in order today, I read in my southern studio. There is great joy in this, and I am thereby able to gain insight into the original pure mind" (11:6b, no. 22). We find Wu not only

---

28. Ibid., p. 101.
29. Ibid., p. 100.

reading in his studio at home but also taking along a book or two with him to the fields or on an outing.

When we look at the books he read and his comments on them, we see that he did not approach books as a professional scholar engaged in research for its own sake. Rather his purpose with books had to do more with the moral and devotional, and he thus conducted his reading with intense emotional involvement. Wu rarely tells the reader specifically what he learns from the particular books he cites, but rather only describes his emotional response. These responses are not without significance in understanding his overall approach. As we have seen earlier, they range from feelings of great joy and even intoxication to those of alarm, fear, and apprehension, depending on the sense of resonance or discrepancy between his conduct and the ideals set forth in the books. The positive feelings come when he comprehends certain passages in a personal way from his own experiences, or when certain books provide helpful insights into the current situation with which he is grappling. The more negative responses of alarm and fear arise at those times when he is painfully aware of his lack of progress and his failure to realize the values and ideals illustrated in the reading.

The Four Books (which include the *Great Learning*, the *Analects*, *Mencius,* and *Practicing the Mean*) are the most frequently mentioned books in the Journal, followed closely by the writings of Zhu Xi and the Cheng brothers. To give a sense of the particular flavor they each had for Wu, I include some of his remarks about them. Of the Four Books, *Practicing the Mean* is the one that seemed to give him the most consolation and inspiration. It was this text on which Wu lectured when he was called to court in 1458. His devotion to this particular text is reflected in the frequent mention of his silently chanting it on his pillow at night or out in the fields during the day or evening:

> This evening, slowing walking through the fields, I was silently chanting passages from *Practicing the Mean*. I took my time, going over each word and phrase, chanting them with great feeling. Realized in my mind, verified by my experiences, this book has given me a good deal of insight. (11:10b, no. 49)

In 1430 Wu composed a poem about how one day, while chanting it on his pillow, he had a sudden insight into its meaning, after many years of studying it:

> Having read each line and section for several tens of years,
> I have always been vague in my overall understanding of it.
> This one morning, it seems I'm able to immerse myself in it in a
>     long and leisurely way.
> In appreciation, I applaud and heave a deep sigh of admiration for
>     Zisi, worthy descendent of our dear sage Confucius. (2:14a–b)

He elsewhere opined that Zisi wrote it "in order to discuss their [the sages] utmost achievements. He also wrote it to raise up the Way of Heaven and earth, that the sage might be their counterpart" (11:15b, no. 75). The most frequently cited passage of *Practicing the Mean* in the whole Journal is section 14, which Wu usually quotes in parts, not as a whole:

> The noble person acts according to his position in life and does not desire what is beyond it. In a position of wealth and honor, he does what is proper to a position of wealth and honor. In a position of poverty and low estate, he does what is proper to a position of poverty and low estate. . . . In a situation of sorrow and difficulties, he does what is proper in a situation of sorrow and difficulty. The noble person can find no situation in which he is not himself. When holding a superior position, he does not treat his inferiors with contempt. When holding a lowly position, he does not try to get in good with his superiors. He rectifies himself and seeks for nothing from others, so that he is not an object of criticism. Above he does not blame Heaven, and below his doesn't criticize others. Therefore the noble person is quiet and calm, waiting for the appointments of Heaven, while the mean and petty person walks in dangerous paths, looking for lucky occurrences.[30]

Dealing as this excerpt does with the challenge of realizing sagehood in terms of the limitations of a person's life, it both consoled and distressed Wu in difficult times. Accepting his lot in life, as we saw earlier, did not come easily for him.

As for the *Analects* of Confucius, a favorite passage is one which echoes the lines from *Practicing the Mean* just quoted: "I do not complain against

---

30. *Practicing the Mean* section 14 (modified translation of Legge, *The Chinese Classics*, vol. 1, pp. 395–96).

Heaven nor do I blame other people. I study things on the lower level but my understanding penetrates to higher things."[31] Wu's various comments after quoting this passage include: "Who but a sage would appreciate the meaning of these words of Confucius?" (11:26a, no. 159) and "I must treasure this saying for the rest of my life" (11:35a, no. 252). Aware of his tendency to be impatient with life and critical of others, Wu finds further guidance from the *Analects* in the idea of "mastering myself and returning to the rites,"[32] as well as being hard on himself and easy on others in terms of criticism.[33]

As a teacher, Wu hopes to learn from Confucius how "by orderly methods skillfully to lead others on" (11:17a, no. 85). Several times, he mentions occasions when he is teaching the *Analects* to his students and to his daughters. Upon these occasions, he finds himself being made aware of his own shortcomings with respect to the teachings and records his reactions to doing so as those of alarm and fear: "While teaching my daughters the *Analects* today, I was moved by the subtle and profound words of the Sage. Frightened, I found myself moved to step up my efforts" (11:18b, no. 101).

In some ways, Wu's appreciation for the *Mencius* was even more personal that for the *Analects*. He was reassured and heartened by Mencius' perspective on the role of suffering in one's life, especially for those persons committed to the Way. Mencius explains sorrows and difficulties as part of Heaven's way of preparing a person to assume important responsibilities: "When Heaven intends to confer a great responsibility upon a person, it first visits his mind and will with suffering, toils his sinews and bones, subjects his body to hunger, exposes him to poverty, and confounds his projects. Through this, his mind is stimulated, his nature strengthened, and his inadequacies repaired." Wu had occasion to allude to this quote in his famous letter to his father (Letter 1) when he acknowledged the constructive value of the difficulties of his life with respect to his moral development. He realized that difficulties are not just something sent by Heaven to those with special responsibilities, but rather they are a necessary part of life. Thus when he quotes the very last line of this *Mencius* passage, "From this we know that we thrive from experiencing sorrow and calamity, and

---

31. *Analects* 14:37.

32. Ibid., 12:1, quoted in entries no. 13 and 26.

33. Ibid., 15:14, paraphrased here but quoted in entry no. 56.

perish from comfort and joy,"[34] Wu adds, "Still, for those whose strength of learning is weak, there are few who are not exhausted by it all" (11:26b, no. 162).

Besides this perspective on difficulties, Mencius is also a source of important notions concerning the meditative aspects of self-cultivation, something we will be dealing with shortly. These include Mencius' comments about "neither forgetting nor helping to grow," "maintaining firm the will and doing no violence to one's vital energies," and "turning and seeking within." Of all the Four Books, the *Mencius* deals the most with internal reflection on the mind, emphasizing as it does the internal spontaneities and promptings of the self and their need to be cultivated and channeled. It is not altogether surprising, then, that we usually find Wu reading Mencius in the context of a peaceful, meditative setting:

> Today in my southern studio, I have been taking great delight in reading *Mencius*. My mind is clear, receptive, and bright, permeated by what Mencius described as the rejuvenating "effects of the calm air of the morning," unvexed by anything. Amidst the shade of the trees in the clear morning, a warm breeze languidly blows, while the far-off mountains and forests stand so still. (11:3b, no. 12)

The spirit of the *Mencius* seems to resonate with the natural world for Wu. In one entry, he records having to set aside his reading schedule to plant vegetables. Nevertheless, he manages to slip in some reading of Mencius, attached as he is to it.

This accounting of what Wu read and how he responded to his reading (and even the setting in which he described his reading) should give a clear indication of the particular approach he took to book learning. As we have already observed, he is not a professional scholar in his approach, but nor is he a simple-minded, anti-intellectual devotee who scorns learning or who keeps his reading to a minimum. He read not only the basic classical texts that are more explicitly moral in purpose, but also the histories, memorials, and poetry.

Along with reading books went self-reflection, conducted primarily in the form of the Neo-Confucian meditation practice called quiet-sitting.

---

34. *Mencius* 6B:15 (trans. by Bloom, *Mencius*, p. 143).

Cheng Hao, Wu's hero, had extolled the merits of this practice in these terms: "When there is nothing to put into practice, go and do quiet-sitting. For while doing quiet-sitting, we can cultivate our original mind and become calm to some degree. Although we are still not free from chasing after material things, when we come to an awakening, we can collect and concentrate our mind and then there will be a solution."[35] Quiet-sitting can be seen as a Confucianized version of Buddhist meditation. This practice involved contemplating the state of the self in tranquility before the feelings have emerged, as well as examining and scrutinizing the feelings after they have emerged in their active state. Based on these insights into the self, one then cultivated the self with a balance of nurturing its deeper spontaneities of goodness, as well as chipping away at the impediments that block their full expression. The virtue of reverence was seen as serving the crucial integrative function of these two reflective aspects of self-cultivation:

> A person must order his mind with principle so that it will be bright, pure, and always alert. Only then will all be right. This is the practice of using reverence to straighten the inner life. Alas, if there is no reverence, then there will be no straightening; if there is no straightening, then a person will stumble in confusion, and, as a result, all his affairs will fail. (11:16a, no. 78)

Here, reverence or seriousness is directed to care for the deep moral life of the individual person. It affirms the value of interiority and of the integration of the self with the larger order of things.

In the Journal, Wu rarely talks explicitly about the practice of quiet-sitting, although most of the entries in fact represent the written expression of his reflections. Many of these come while on his pillow, either at night (often quite late) or early in the morning. He describes his activity at these times variously as "carefully considering (细思)," "quietly reflecting upon (默思)," "deeply pondering (深思)," "slowing reflecting upon (徐思)," or simply "reflecting (思)":

---

35. Cheng Hao, quoted by Zhu Xi in *Classified Conversations of Zhu Xi* 96:12a–b. (Trans. by Chan, *Reflections on Things at Hand*, p. 151.)

> Tonight on my pillow, I have been reflecting on my lack of success in rejuvenating my vital spirit so that I can advance in my learning. (11:27a, no. 165)

Though most of his meditative activity takes place there on his pillow, the Journal also indicates that he continues this reflective activity when out of doors and engaged in his daily activities:

> This evening, I stood on a path between the fields, quietly reflecting on why I have not succeeded in becoming a noble person who has genuinely and purely realized his goals. (11:8a, no. 32)

As for the task of examining and scrutinizing the active, functional aspect of the self, this was associated with disciplining and bringing under control its negative aspects. He speaks of this task as one of "scouring and grinding" his faults or making the imbalances of his temperament disappear. To succeed, he must keep a strict watch over himself, rigorously scrutinizing himself to make sure he is perfectly restrained and not giving vent to expressions of selfishness.

Wu follows Mencius in his sense that the will (*zhi* 志) must be the leader of the psycho-physical aspect (*qi* 氣) of the self, and that the key to success lies in the exertion of this will to direct and bring the self to higher goals. In addition, Wu learns that this exertion of the will must be a constant thing, with no letting up for even a moment—what Mencius meant by "let there be no forgetting." One of the most common endings for Wu's reflections echoes this phrase, exhorting himself, "Exert myself, yes, exert myself, with no forgetting." For Wu this involves a continual fight against the inertia of the self, or the tendency to take the easy way and let things slide. He thus regards the task of examining and scrutinizing the self as serious business and tries to engage in it as much as possible, no matter what the time or the place:

> Today I was out roaming among the banks and slopes until I reached the bottom of a ravine. I sat there for a long time, facing the sun, finding it extremely pleasant. Examining and scrutinizing my body and mind, I was fortunate to find some slight progress has been made. (11:29a, no. 188)

Besides exhorting himself at the end of his reflections to exert himself and not forget, Wu makes numerous other resolutions for the purpose of disciplining and restraining himself. Some examples include:

> Cut out bad habits and "daily renew" myself! (11:18b, no. 99)

> On the one hand, I must manage the difficulties; on the other hand, I must still try to advance in my learning. (11:22b, no. 132)

One of the interesting characteristics about Wu and his resolutions is his strong impulse to write them down in large characters to hang on his wall as a constant reminder for his edification. Here are two illustrations:

### VIGOROUSLY TRY TO ELIMINATE LOSING MY TEMPER OVER PETTY MATTERS! FIRMLY MAINTAIN MY INTEGRITY EVEN IN POVERTY! (11:5b, no. 17)

### STUDY TO THE BEST OF MY OWN PARTICULAR ABILITIES! (11:14b, no. 69)

Wu demonstrates a finely tuned psychological awareness of his states of mind that are associated with his efforts at disciplining himself. He speaks of his reactions after having examined and scrutinized his behavior in terms of being "frightened," "fearful," "alarmed," "apprehensive," and "at a loss." He is "disappointed" and "distressed," as well as overcome by feelings of shame, sadness, and regret, all of which take the physical form of heavy sighs. In a rich vocabulary of psychological states, he uses words like *ti* 惕, *ju* 懼, *song* 悚, and *li* 慄, to express his sense of alarm or fear; words like *cang* 愴, *ce* 惻, and *chi* 悽 for his sense of being sick at heart and distressed, and words like *chang* 悵 and *yang* 怏 for his sense of dissatisfaction and disappointment with himself.

These emotional states must be seen in the context of Wu's sense of urgency about the pursuit of sagehood, his sense of struggle in overcoming the recalcitrant aspects of his self, and his sense of failure in his conduct. For Neo-Confucians, there are things about which one should be fearful and alarmed, things with which one must struggle. Cultivating the self requires a certain vigilance and a state of constant alertness, along with the proper respect, fear, and awe for the gift of life from Heaven. One must take this responsibility seriously and worry that one will not completely fulfill it, that one will fail to become a complete human being.

These emotions that Wu expresses are not all the same in intensity, but range from mild feelings of fear and awe to intense ones that immobilize him. These feelings either spark fresh resolve to do better or else depress him. We often find him caught in deep struggles with himself in this regard. This comes across most strongly in descriptions of his late-night reflections, of tossing and turning and being unable to sleep, or else waking from dreams in which he is overwhelmed by a sense of having made no progress at all. Anxiety, tightness, fatigue, and restlessness are all associated with these tortured ruminations of his.

These nocturnal struggles are not without positive outcomes at times. Wu describes a particularly difficult time of lying awake all night, trying to figure out how to manage the responsibilities of his household and personal cultivation:

> Since last night, the twelfth day of the seventh month, I have lain awake on my pillow considering what extremely sore straits I'm in with respect to my family's livelihood. I feel so incapable of dealing with the situation. Turning it over and over in my mind, I cannot come up with any solution. Now I find it's already well into the morning and still I haven't gotten up.

Because he does not give up, but continues to turn the matter over in his mind, something at last comes to him resulting in his nightlong struggle not having been completely in vain:

> Ruminating a while longer, I finally came up with something: namely, there is no other clever way out except to follow along with my given allotment in life, economize in my expenses, and be content in poverty—that is all. I vow that even though I "die from the cold or starvation," I won't dare change this basic resolve of mine.

With this, he is able to get started again after feeling immobilized in his efforts, and his emotional state changes: "Thereupon I got out of bed with a feeling of joy. I understand even more deeply the meaning of the passage, 'To be mature in your efforts, you must go through this discipline through hardship'" (11:23a, no. 133).

Wu recognized the need for self-discipline, but that could only be one aspect of his approach to cultivating himself. Discipline and restraint could not be ends in themselves. Rather, since "A person must respect himself," he cannot force himself into some mold, disciplining the life out of himself. Reverence entails an appreciation for the intrinsic value of the self and nourishing its natural goodness. To positively care for and nourish the self, a person must first attempt to get in touch with the deeper aspects of the mind by quieting it down and achieving a state of tranquility. This state of tranquility is important so that one can focus his attention on and observe the deeper nature, thereby obtaining a clear understanding of its fundamental principle:

> Relaxing in my pavilion today, I watched the vegetables being harvested. I rested there for a long while, observing my state of mind in the midst of tranquility. This is the method of nourishing and caring for the nature. (11:39a, no. 296)

The purpose of this gentle, silent, contemplative approach to the self is not to get fixated on some idealized and irrelevant principle, but rather, having observed the principle of one's nature, to know how to integrate and channel it into the conscious, functional aspect of the self. Then one is able to comprehend spontaneously the functioning of principle in the world as well and thus act accordingly: "Observing the principle of things in the midst of tranquility, a person is able to grasp it everywhere" (11:37a, no. 274).

Nourishing the self involves more than just observing the deeper nature, but also nurturing what Wu termed his vital force (*qi*) or his vital spirit (*jing-shen*). These two are related to the psycho-physical energies of the self that are needed to bring the goodness of the deeper nature into conscious functioning: "For several days now, I have succeeded very well in nourishing my vital spirit. I must continue this on a regular basis, allowing for no interruptions" (11:18a, no. 96). Wu learns from Mencius not just that one must assert the will as the leader of the psycho-physical energies of the self, but also that since these energies are vital to the fulfillment of the self, they must have no violence done to them or be suppressed in any way. And just as a person must be continually persistent and alert in his efforts ("no forgetting"), there must also be no compulsive or heavy-handed forcing of the self to develop and improve it at an unnatural rate, what Mencius meant by "let there be no helping to grow."

Wu is fond of quoting Zhu Xi's statement about the manner of cultivating the self, "to nourish the self in a leisurely but profound manner." In contrast to the mental states of fear and apprehension that we noticed accompanying Wu's more disciplined aspects of cultivation, those of leisure and ease come with the nourishing aspects. Leisure here connotes more than just not doing anything. It is rather a state of mind that is lofty, tranquil, and pure, one in which a person is at ease with himself and the world, without any barriers or obstacles. As he wrote in a couplet:

> In a state of deep tranquility, I am content with my lot wherever I am.
> In a state of peaceful relaxation, that is the time for reading books.
> (11:5b, no. 14)

In contrast to the sleepless nights and sense of struggle of which we spoke earlier, here there is a dominant sense of rest and relaxation, with numerous references to sleeping, napping, or lying down outside on the grass. The nourishing process takes account of the need for human refreshment and renewal that comes with rest:

> I got up from my nap today, my body feeling relaxed and my mind free and untrammeled. Content in poverty, delighting in the Way, what else need I seek? (11:7a, no. 24)

One will recall that Wu had a deep appreciation for Shao Yong's sense of leisure, especially with respect to his great joy in taking naps. Even someone in poverty can enjoy a good nap, feeling invigorated and enriched by it as if he were a rich person:

> When I awoke, my state of mind was quite excellent, just as Shao himself described in a poem, "no less than I had been enfeoffed or awarded money." Even though I am extremely impoverished, that is my fate. But it cannot destroy this present happiness. (11:24a, no. 143)

Wu draws not just upon Shao for this sense of leisure but also the famous fourth-century nature poet Tao Qian. Wu has one entry that reads,

"After eating today, I took a leisurely rest by the eastern window, feeling like one of the worthies of high antiquity" (11:35a, no. 255). This echoes a passage by Tao quoted in his biography in the *History of the Jin Dynasty:* "Taking a leisurely rest by the northern window, while a clear breeze wafts by, I call myself one of the worthies of high antiquity."[36]

The term that I have translated here as "leisurely rest" is *gao-mian* (高眠). It conveys the sense of a lofty and pure type of peace or rest. It does not imply a dull passivity, but rather a deep participation in the natural processes of the Way. There is the sense among such writers as Tao, Shao, and Wu that in primordial times, when the worthies of high antiquity lived, everyone enjoyed a life of ease and freedom from anxiety, not in a trivial but in a profound way. They seek to reach such a state in their own lives, such that they can feel a part of the ancients' world. Wu used the term *gao-mian* with more frequency as he got older, most often when speaking of his activity of meditation, "leisurely resting by the window." All sorts of insights came to him at these times.

The crucial element in the total effort at cultivating the self is a discerning sensitivity to the specific needs of the self at particular moments. This entails the awareness of the appropriate response to make: when to push harder, when to let up, when to water, and when to weed. Wu realizes the need for both aspects of cultivation, but he is not always clear which one the situation calls for. In his early years, his inclination is to come down hard, more on the side of discipline, afraid as he is of letting himself get out of hand. Over the course of the Journal, he develops a clearer sense of how to handle himself, though more often this is after much groping and learning from his mistakes. As he accumulates experience, he develops deeper insights into the workings of his self and can better respond to its needs. He learns, in the long run, that he responds better to gentler handling: "With a temperament that is mild and peaceful, I have the means with which to overcome the recalcitrant and narrow nature of my mind" (11:22a, no. 127). He learns too that personal change takes time: "it is impossible suddenly to make the imbalances of my physical nature and the defects in my learning disappear. I can only gradually diminish them" (11:9a, no. 38).

This sensitive discernment in dealing with the self becomes especially crucial at those moments when Wu is too confused and too overwhelmed

---

36. *History of the Jin Dynasty* 94:37a.

by events to go forward. Here he is guided by Zhu Xi's words: "If you cannot at last succeed, don't give up altogether but just let up for the time being." At such times of impasse, he has to have the sense not to keep pushing himself, but to try and do what he can to keep going for the moment, however little that may seem to be accomplishing. He must not weigh himself down with superhuman expectations in heroic fashion but abide in his situation until he can find the thread and pick it up again.

## Self-Evaluation of Successes and Failures

Thus far we have looked, first of all, at Wu's perception of the obstacles to and supports he has in his pursuit of sagehood, and second, his program of cultivation to achieve his goal, which involved reading books and engaging in quiet-sitting. But the power of the Journal does not lie in any one of these. Rather it resides in the larger picture of the personal growth and development of a human being over the gradually unfolding course of a lifetime. Since the main purpose of keeping the Journal for Wu was to master himself in order to achieve the full sageliness of his being, the ongoing question in the Journal was whether he is succeeding or failing in this undertaking. The question of his progress represents one of the principal topics of his reflective activity, although I have chosen to wait to discuss it here rather than in the earlier section on self-reflection. In this type of reflection, Wu is constantly weighing and gauging the type and degree of his personal growth or the lack of it.

Wu often saw signs of concrete progress that had been made in his efforts at self-mastery. He frequently reports progress in settling his mind, in handling difficulties, and in achieving greater control over his temper:

> A young boy lost one of my ducks and I got a bit angry. Still, compared to my reaction last year to losing a duck, the extent of my anger has been greatly reduced. (11:10a, no. 44)

As time goes on in his life, Wu describes how he is better able to accept his lot of poverty and be content with it. He cites examples of remaining unaffected and without resentment when having to endure cold winter nights without sufficient blankets or a leaky house during a heavy rainstorm. These claims of progress give Wu a great sense of joy and contribute to his personal confidence in his ability to realize his goal: "Today, I was discussing with a neighbor how I have begun to shoulder some heavy responsibilities and that I have felt somewhat happier with myself" (11:11a, no. 51).

But in contrast to this brighter side, whether because he judged himself too strictly or because he felt compelled to acknowledge his failures more than his successes, he more often reports that he has made no progress at all. His confession that "I have made no progress in my learning and moral character," ranks with his resolve to follow Heaven's will and his lament over the difficulty of learning to become a sage as the three most frequently uttered statements in the whole Journal. Together they serve as the main refrains of the work as a whole.

We need not take Wu completely at his word that he literally has made no progress at all. There are cases of his confessing no progress immediately after an entry in which he has announced some improvement in himself. We should take his statements rather in the sense of his having made no progress in his current stage of development or with a particular challenge that he has set for himself at the moment. Since one does not reach a point in one's quest for sagehood where one can stop for good but must continue it over a lifetime, Wu prods himself again and again to keep moving ahead, so that his moral efforts may keep pace with his natural growth processes.

If achievement in his conduct gave Wu a sense of pleasure and self-confidence, his sense of lack of progress troubled him greatly and undermined his self-esteem, especially in the earlier years. We have seen how often Wu could not sleep or would wake from dreams in tears because of his intense anxiety over his poor progress toward sagehood:

> I haven't accomplished much lately in my learning and moral cultivation, and I'm getting on in age. My life's goal is not being fulfilled. These feelings of disappointment are inexhaustible. I have no place to hide myself in shame. How distressing! (11:13b, no. 64)

This sense of anxiety with respect to his lack of progress might be seen as merely neurotic and morose introspection (which it often indeed is!) if taken separately from the overriding concern on his part to achieve sagehood, or from his sense that if he makes no progress he will not be able to conduct himself responsibly in the world. The issue of his progress, or the lack of it, takes on the emotional voltage it does because Wu feels the pressure of "TIME." He does not have forever to reach his goal but only his allotted span of years. The Journal reflects a real preoccupation—almost an obsession—with the passing of time. In the early years, it is a matter of whether he will ever in fact get on the right track. In his later years, having come to feel he is on the right track, he wonders how he can stay on it and reach the end of the road.

As he approaches the age of forty, Wu finds the passing of time to be especially burdensome. Confucius' words from *Analects* 17:26 continually haunt him: "When a person at forty is the object of dislike, he will continue to be that way." One of Wu's responses is: "As age forty approaches, I'm ending up a mean and petty person. Alas, I am overwhelmed with sadness!" (11:12a–b, no. 58). Confucius himself, in his chronicle of the stages of his life, said he had no doubts at forty.[37] Wu certainly still had his.

His fear of ending up a mean and petty person derives from having had high standards for himself in his youth, and he wonders what has happened that he has failed at these. One night, while looking over essays he wrote when he was twenty, he expresses his distress from this disconnect:

> I found myself overwhelmed with sighs of sadness. The reason is that, in the past, my goal in life was clear, based on the belief that the Way of the ancient sages and worthies could be learned, that it could be attained. Now it has been twenty years of vacillating and temporizing. . . . Not only can I not reach the point of being a sage or worthy, I cannot even succeed in my attempts to become somewhat of a person who has lessened his faults. What am I to do? What am I to do? (11:13a–b, no. 63)

The question for Wu is what to do with his sense of lost or wasted time. How can he move past his previous failings? How much will the past determine his future success? These questions are not trivial ones for Wu. We often find him engaging in retrospection over the past, most frequently when he has lain down for a rest or been looking over old papers of his.

Later in the Journal, the concern with time, although still present, has somewhat shifted in character. Things are not quite so dark; there is not such despair of ever making progress. Now he seems to feel that he is on

---

37. *Analects* 2:2.

the right track, but he is worried, because of his advanced years, that his efforts won't be brought to completion. Thus, when he writes of his progress in understanding the *Book of Changes*, he adds, "However, I regret that my vital energies are declining and that I have not much time left in my life" (11:31b, no. 208). And when he excitedly reports that he has learned the great value of reading the histories, his regret is "that there is not much time left in my life to devote to them" (11:32a, no. 214).

Although Wu rails thus at time, in another sense he owes his personal development and the gradual strengthening of his character to time and its cumulative power over a lifetime. Time brings not just decline and ill-health but also maturity and fulfillment. Confucius himself, in the outline of his own life from age fifteen to seventy, showed how a person could grow in sageliness over the course of a lifetime. It was only at age seventy that he felt he had achieved the perfect spontaneity that characterizes sagehood.

In the Journal, we can see that Wu is not the same person in 1469 at age seventy-seven that he had been in 1425 at age thirty-three, when he began the Journal. Definite shifts in tone and subject matter have taken place. In the earlier years, awed by the task before him, Wu talks more personally and emotionally about his life, especially about the difficulties he resents and with which he struggles. The tone is darker, filled as it is with intense concern over his faults and with the rigorous discipline needed to bring himself under control. At the same time, Wu experiences moments of exhilaration in his frequent encounters with the sages and the natural world. In fact, the frequent and abrupt shift in mood from entry to entry is one of the main characteristics of the early period.

In the later years, the tone tends to be lighter and more even, reflecting the life of a more tranquil, composed, and self-possessed person than in the earlier period. Wu has more self-confidence and understanding. The entries as a whole are far shorter and less personal. Rather than reflect upon specific incidents or problems in his life, he records passages from the sages or maxims he has made up for himself. These quotations convey to the reader indirectly what Wu has on his mind, and how he thinks he should conduct himself. There is not the same need to dwell too long on his own situation. In the later entries, he mentions reading certain books and the fact that he was quite affected by them, without specifying exactly what it was that moved him. The mood is more contemplative, as when he is enjoying nature, or resting and reflecting by his window. The number of recorded dreams increases for this later period. One might see this shift from a more self-absorbed to a somewhat more impersonal one as a measure of his success in expanding his personality beyond the confines of his more limited self, enabling him to participate in a larger order of things, both the natural world and the world of the sages.

That does not suggest that Wu changed dramatically from a totally depressed and angry young man to a completely tranquil and wise old man. From his very early years, Wu demonstrated his appreciation and capacity for tranquility and for enjoying the lighter, more joyful aspects of life. And even in his old age, Wu continued to struggle with himself and his life situation. In the very last year of his life, he complains about household matters ("I often feel oppressed by household business. Still, I must carry on, acting according to principle" [11:40a, no. 310]), and his lack of progress ("Time quickly passes by, yet I seem to be regressing instead of making progress in my learning and moral cultivation" [11:41a, no. 318]).

In the midst of these changes in mood, what strikes us is that he holds to the ideal of sagehood throughout. Even in old age, when he might be tempted to sit back and take it easy, enjoying his fame as a respected teacher, he continues to remind himself of his goal and the need to persevere in his efforts until the very end. Reminding himself, "As long as there is any breath remaining, a person must not tolerate the least bit of negligence with respect to his effort of the will," Wu asks himself, "How can I use the excuse of old age to feel wearied by events?" (11:32a, no. 211). He takes as his motto Zhu Xi's statement that "For every day that one is still alive, a person must undertake his responsibilities," and announces his determination to live out his remaining years trying to become a sage, subduing all within himself that is unbefitting of a sage. Even in one of the entries in the last year of his life, we find Wu still worrying about achieving his goal as his thinks back to the time when he first returned from the capital to life in the country in 1411:

> I had a poster on one of the pillars at my house in Shichuan that read, "If I wish to reach the realm of the great worthies, I must proceed from the results of 'studying things on the lower level.'" Looking back, I realize that that was almost sixty years ago. Alas! When will I ever reach that realm of the great worthies? (11:41b, no. 324)

## Wu's Role as a Teacher

Having made the decision to give up an official career in favor of a life outside the realm of active politics, Wu returned home to the country. There,
as he struggled in his pursuit of sagehood, he realized it could not be done
in isolation from other human beings. At the same time, alarmed over what
he saw as the decline of the Way (Dao) in his own age, especially when
compared to the Song, he developed a strong sense of mission to revitalize
the Way, and to lead others, not just himself, in the knowledge and practice of the Way, as far as it lay within his power. He was thus drawn to the
traditional Confucian role of moral teacher. Such a person undertook to
exemplify its teachings and embody the Way as a living tradition. This role
stressed the personal relationship between teacher and student as essential
for the type of transformation that the educational experience should bring
about. A later source described Wu in his role as teacher thus:

> Understanding that sagehood is something that can be reached
> through learning, Wu followed Master Cheng Hao's words and began
> his journey on the road to sagehood. Believing that the Way of the
> Teacher must be respected and propagated, he held to the methods of
> Cheng Yi as a means of enlightening others.[38]

One can take "Cheng Hao's words" here to refer to his saying that the
Learning of the Sages had not been transmitted since Mencius and that
the present age must heroically revive it,[39] and the "methods of Cheng
Yi" to refer to the basic program of cultivation advocated for the practice of reverence and the extension of knowledge.[40] Thus, the lessons Wu
sought to pass on to his students were those that he himself had learned
in his reading from the lives and teachings of the Song masters. What he
actually taught reflected not the full breadth of the Neo-Confucian tradition but a particular emphasis on practice that tended to be emotional

---

38. Chen Xianzhang, "Offering of a Funerary Piece to My Former Teacher Wu Yubi,"
in *Complete Works of Chen Xianzhang* (*Baisha quanshu*) 4:24b.

39. *Biographical Account of Cheng Hao,* in *Collected Works of Cheng Yi* 7:6b.

40. *Written Legacy of the Cheng Brothers* 18:5b.

and devotional. His approach was described by the late Ming thinker Liu Zongzhou as "deeply nourishing the nature and feelings through such concrete ways as mastering the self and resting content in a life of poverty."[41]

Wu's role as a teacher began slowly, with a few students from his own immediate area. Gradually, as his reputation spread, he began attracting a number of students from a wider area. He issued a set of "Standards for Learning," it has been suggested, because "By 1430, so many students had come to receive instruction that he instituted some rules for the younger ones."[42] As we saw in the Introduction, he lectured in the local official schools in the period from 1440 to 1442, even though he lacked an official degree. His frequent exchange of poems with persons who had official education titles in their names, especially as he got older, indicates the sizeable contact he had with those in the larger educational system. Students often came to him upon the recommendation of officials in their home areas. Those who recommended Wu for office did so on the basis of his ability as an outstanding teacher. One of them, Ho Zixue, was especially glowing in his praises of Wu as a teacher, citing how Wu's students "admire his righteous conduct and follow him with pleasure."[43]

As for what we know about Wu as a teacher, we rely on his letters and poems to friends and students rather than the Journal. The Journal concerns itself primarily with his own conduct and makes few references to his teaching. The letters and poems, on the other hand, contain exchanges of advice between Wu and his students, providing us with a picture of his philosophy of education as well as the nature of his personal relations with them.

The dominant theme in his writings on pedagogy to these people is, not surprisingly, the pursuit of sagehood. He wants students to be absolutely convinced of sagehood as a practical and achievable goal in the contemporary world, as well as to be firmly committed to that pursuit in their individual lives. He has nothing to offer students who lack such conviction and commitment. He calls on his students to have high expectations of themselves and not to be someone who "readily contents himself with easy

41. Liu Zongzhou, "Sayings of the Teacher," in *Case Studies of Ming Confucians* 2a–b.
42. Goodrich and Fang, eds., *Dictionary of Ming Biography,* p. 1498. "Standards of Learning" is included in the Translation Section.
43. His recommendation is included in "Appended Sources," CW 9a.

accomplishments in minor skills" (8:17b, Letter 3). The sages of the past became so because they constantly set high goals for themselves with regard to self-improvement.

Wu is careful to point out that there is no uniformity about sagehood, that each person has a unique path. He does not present himself as offering a formula for instant sagehood or any great insights into the deeper workings of the Way. Rather he presents himself as one ready to share in the pursuit of sagehood with anyone seeking help along the way. Inviting a friend to come study with him, Wu writes: "I live in a remote place, removed from everyday affairs. Every day with two or three students, I engage in the practices of book reading and plumbing principle, delighting in the Way of Yao and Shun—that is all. I dare make no claims of anything beyond this" (8:19a, Letter 4). In saying this, Wu was not just being modest. His basic curriculum really did not contain much that was original, only offering students the fundamental regimen of reading books and sitting in meditation that he himself practiced. And yet, as we shall see, there were elements of creativity in how Wu went about teaching the curriculum.

As for the importance of reading books, this was something Wu preached fervently as the essential part of self-cultivation, as we see from the lines in the poems he presented to his clansmen during his stay in Zhonghu in the early 1440s. Upon his arrival he wrote:

> My learning is ordinary and I have no other special abilities;
> Whenever I meet people, I encourage them to read books. (2:31b)

And upon his departure he wrote:

> Don't find the impractical nature of my parting words strange,
> But of the many human affairs, the reading of books comes
>     first. (3:8b)

And the list of books he recommended was a simple one, reflecting Zhu Xi's basic outline for education that had been adopted for the school system, first by Xu Heng of the Yuan dynasty, and then by the first emperor of the Ming. It begins with the *Elementary Learning* text, proceeds through the Four Books, is followed by the Five Classics, and then arrives at the writings of the Song Masters.

These had to be read in a particular order in order to derive the optimum benefit from them. "If a person, intent on penetrating the essence of these writings, doesn't follow this order but reads them in a careless, random way, he will fail in the end. He will have wasted his vital energies and passed the years in vain. What a great pity that would be!" (8:31a–b, Letter 15). In addition to the order of reading these books, the manner of reading them was also crucial, especially with the basic texts: "Recite them until they are committed to memory, causing the words to come out of your mouth as if they were your own. Then your own sense of their meaning will be special to you" (8:31a, Letter 15).

Just as in his own program of self-cultivation, the student must engage in the practice of self-reflection and meditation to achieve this. Wu's brother-in-law raised a pertinent question in this regard: "Even though I am able for a while to understand the words on paper, in the end what benefit does it have for my body and mind?" Wu answers:

> These words of yours raise an important issue which is precisely what you should reflect upon. Now the problem for people is that they don't know how to turn inward and seek within themselves. For them, books are just books, the self is just the self, and there is no connection between the two. When the books that a person reads only benefit his mouth and ears, then it is all a great failure. (8:29b, Letter 14)

Also connected with this question about the benefit to the self of reading books is one raised by an unnamed friend of Wu who fell sick from overdoing his reading of books. Here was a case of over-zealousness in reading that had a negative result, something with which Wu could readily identify since as a youth he had fallen into the same trap:

> I, myself, in the past, when I was inexperienced and green, was so eager to get ahead that I would over and over exhaust my energies in reading books. I would recite them aloud in a great loud voice, dissipating my vital energies until I reached the extreme of causing great harm to myself. (8:25a, Letter 11)

From his own experience, Wu tries to give his friends a sense of perspective as to what really matters in the overall enterprise of self-cultivation.

In what seems like a contradiction to what was just quoted above about the centrality of reading, he tells this friend that what counts is the type of interior attitude he brings to bear in every aspect of his life, not the quantity of the books he has read. That attitude is related to the all-important Neo-Confucian quality of reverence:

> On the whole, the essentials of what the sages and worthies transmitted are all contained in the one word "reverence" (*jing* 敬). If a person can put his attire in order, make his speech and actions correct and dignified, and conduct himself with a sense of propriety, then his mind naturally will be collected. Even if he does not read books, he still will gradually make progress in his self-cultivation. (8:25b, Letter 11)

Wu adds that if one is able to read books in addition to these things, it is all to the good, since reading when properly done helps to nourish the mind. However, he reiterates his point that a person who has not attempted to bring himself under control but rather "gives free rein to his passions," will not find any miraculous results in reading books.

Wu recommends a balance in effort such as is found in Mencius' dictum that there be "neither forgetting nor helping to grow," or in Cheng Yi's advice that one "be easy-going but thoroughly absorb when you learn."[44] The results of self-cultivation are cumulative and thus require a certain perseverance and patience. Because sagehood is a pursuit of a lifetime, continually challenging a person to push onward, and not some once-and-for-all achievement, a person has to pace himself in order to sustain his efforts and persevere in his commitment over a long period of time:

> As for the basis of learning, one must try for daily progress and monthly advance with a free and easy, unconstrained manner. Then and only then can one sustain his efforts over a long period of time. If one is in a hurry and presses for quick results, then he will only cause himself pain and end up in failure. (8:25b, Letter 11)

---

44. *Written Legacy of the Cheng Brothers* 15:2a (trans by Chan, *Reflections on Things at Hand,* p. 60).

Therefore, in rejoicing at the news of one student's progress in overcoming his faults, Wu hastens to caution, "Still, do not be too severe in the application of your mind to these things. As Mencius said, 'He who advances with precipitation will retire with speed'" (8:28b, Letter 13).

The effectiveness of Wu's ability as a teacher depended on how well he was able to gauge the particular needs of each student. We thus find him taking different approaches with different students, and even with the same student at different stages in his development. Above we see him recommend a gentle and patient approach to one student, but in other cases he takes a hard line, reminding students that they will never have their youth again and thus must exert themselves to the upmost in the present moment. In one letter to a friend, he does not mince words to express his strong disapproval of the man's son:

> The day before yesterday, your son, on the point of his departure from here, said that he might come back to see me in the mountains in the fourth month. This is now just the first month and he wants to wait until the fourth. He is lazy and not working to establish himself. . . . Moreover, from his use of the word "might," his laziness is even more apparent. Alas, it is clear that he is incapable of being taught! (8:20a, Letter 5)

Overall, Wu doesn't wish to berate his students. Even though he lets them know that a person is ultimately alone in his responsibility to realize sagehood, still, he is helped along the way by the support of friends. In Wu's approach to teaching and learning, an appreciation for the positive value of friendship constitutes one of its distinctive elements, along with two others, manual labor and recreation:

> On the twelfth of this month, you and I stayed up talking until midnight. The next day, the lingering joy was still special to me. It was just as a former worthy said, "In learning one needs to have discussion before one comes to understand the Way. And the friendship derived from teachers and friends is the way to get this." "Because the sages knew that the most benefit comes from friends, therefore they rejoiced when friends came to see them."[45]

---

45. Zhang Zai, "Discourse on the *Analects*." *Collected Writings of Zhang Zai* 14:4b.

The theme of friendship as a means of promoting virtue was not something new to Wu Yubi. It had been an important part of the Confucian tradition from earliest times, being one of the important themes of the *Analects*. Confucius spoke of *fu-ren* (輔仁), friends "helping to encourage virtue," when he said: "The noble person on grounds of culture meets with friends, and by their friendship helps his virtue to develop."[46] He also spoke of taking people around him as his teacher: "The Master said, 'When I walk along with two others, they may serve me as my teachers. I will select their good qualities and follow them, their bad qualities and avoid them.'"[47] The idea of learning in the context of friendship was so important that the teacher-student relationship did not constitute an additional relationship to that of the Five Cardinal Relationships[48] but was subsumed under the friend-friend relationship. This implied that the teacher-student relationship was a fluid rather than a fixed one, with mutual learning taking place for both people.

Letters between friends were particularly conducive vehicles for exchanging insights and advice for helping each other. In Wu's letters to friends and students, he attributes a good deal of his own progress to their helpful advice: "How marvelous are the results of friends 'helping to encourage goodness'" (8:16b, Letter 3). He is moved to offer his friends the benefit of his own insights in return: "The ancients placed much value on friends 'helping to encourage goodness' so how could I be selfish and not share with you what I have learned?" (8:15b, Letter 2).

Cognizant of the value of friendship in his own personal development, Wu exhorts his students to develop an appreciation for the power of friendship with each other in this regard. He encourages them to turn to each other, not just to him, taking advantage of the opportunities to discuss and clarify matters with each other, to encourage and reprove each other's conduct, and to share in each other's difficulties. On this point, Wu makes frequent references to hexagram 58 of the *Book of Changes, dui* 兌, "the joyous." The image of this hexagram is that of two lakes connected, one on top of the other: "Lake resting on the other: the image of the joyous. Thus

---

46. *Analects* 12:24.

47. *Analects* 7:21 (trans. Legge, *The Chinese Classics*, vol. 1, p. 202).

48. They are: the parent-child, ruler-minister, husband-wife, older brother-younger brother, and friend-friend.

the noble person joins with friends for discussion and practice."[49] Students are to nourish and enrich each other just as two connecting lakes do. We see this idea at work in the last lines of one of Wu's poems written while on an outing with students:

> With a group of my students out on an outing, leading each other along in pairs,
> We offer each other mutual advice in the spirit of "connecting lakes." (4:2b)

When students were about to leave to return home, Wu wrote essays or poems with allusions to the theme of "connecting lakes," to encourage them to seek out friends when they return home. He also encouraged them to follow a certain daily schedule, as can be seen in the following passage from a piece given to one student:

> Go home, and clean and sweep out a room. Set up some maxims of the ancient sages and worthies on your desk. In your free time from serving your parents, enter your chamber, straighten your clothing, and sit in a serious and proper manner. Thoroughly read and digest the writings of the sages and worthies, examining their application for yourself. Whether active or quiescent, whether talking or silent, always seek what is worthy of the sages and worthies, and get rid of whatever is not worthy. If you accumulate your efforts over a period of time, then the power of your tasting the Way and emulating the worthies will daily strengthen, and the power of your old habits and past defects will daily weaken. Don't worry that you will not reach the gate of the ancients! (8:42b, "Encouraging Learning")

One of his students, Hu Juren, provides a good example of how one student negotiated the difficulties of returning home by taking Wu's advice:

> For several years, I studied on and off with Wu, reaching a point where I felt I had some kind of anchor to hang on to. Still, my will and disposition remained coarse and mean. Ever since I parted from

---

49. *Book of Changes*, hexagram 58 (trans. by Wilhelm, *The I Ching, or Book of Changes*, vol. 1, p. 239).

him, I've been without his personal instruction on a regular basis. Worried that studying alone on my own, apart from him and other students, has been keeping me from any success in maintaining my efforts, I have therefore joined with several friends of like ambition to build this "Hall of Connecting Lakes," so we can share our common pursuit of sagehood.[50]

Next to this emphasis on "mutual help," another distinctive aspect of Wu's approach was his requirement of manual labor. Wu's school was considered a private "charity school" that charged no tuition: "Students from all over come to study under him. He divided what little he already had with them, providing them with food, drink, and instruction."[51] According to his student Lou Liang, he did not care about collecting any kind of stipend as a teacher,[52] even though his own situation was far from prosperous. What took its place was his requirement that students engage in manual labor on the farm when they came to study with him. Those early years when he had first returned to the countryside and was forced to struggle to make a living by farming had taught him valuable, important lessons about life. He alluded to this in a letter to his father when he heard of the possibility that his three younger brothers might be sent to study with him in the countryside:

> Not only is life in the country simple, honest, and frugal so that a person can advance in his learning and moral character, but also it allows a person early on to learn the toils and hardships of a farmer's life so that at a later time he will not fall in with the reckless and lazy. (8:27a, Letter 12b)

He wanted students to work hard in the fields so that they would also work hard in their pursuit of sagehood. Discipline in one area would help in the other. When he told them that all the progress he had made came only after difficulties and hardships, one of them declared that, "Only the Master could not be daunted by all this. The rest of us become discouraged and

---

50. *Collected Works of Hu Juren* (*Hu Jingzhai ji*), *juan* 2, p. 72.

51. Li Zhi, *Continuation of the Book to Be Hidden Away, juan* 21, p. 416.

52. *Biographical Account of Wu Yubi* 10:8b.

give up."[53] Shortly after the student Lou Liang arrived, Wu was out working in the fields. He signaled for Lou to come over to him. He told him quite directly and explicitly that he must make it a practice personally to attend to even the smallest details of his life. Lou realized that Wu wanted students to be grounded in the realities of everyday life, even those like Lou who had servants.[54] Wu himself worked side by side with his students in the fields:

> During a rainstorm, the Master would don his straw raincoat and hat, pull his plow over his shoulder, and join his various students in plowing. He would discuss with them the eight trigrams of the *Book of Changes*, starting with *qian* 乾 and *kun* 坤, and the six others, the principles of which could be observed in the plowing. Returning home, they would put up their equipment and eat coarse rice and wild vegetables.[55]

The manual work he had his students do was primarily farming. We find mention in his poetry of other jobs: helping to build a wall around his pond to keep the otters out, moving a gate house, and doing some land reclamation work.

Not all the students readily took to this particular requirement of the program. One famous example is that of Chen Xianzhang. Unlike many of Wu's students, Chen came from an affluent background and already had passed the first major level of the exam system:

> Chen Xianzhang came from Guangdong province to study with Wu. One day, just at daybreak, the Master began winnowing grain with his own hands. Since Baisha had not yet gotten up, the Master yelled in a loud voice, "If first degree students are as lazy as this, how will they ever expect eventually to reach the gate of Cheng Yi or Mencius?"[56]

Though he might have been criticized by Wu, Chen still retained an admiration for him. He recounts how once while they were reaping the grain,

---

53. Hu Jiushao, quoted in his biography in *Case Studies of Ming Confucians* 2:9b.

54. See biography of Lou Liang in *Case Studies of Ming Confucians* 1:8a.

55. *Case Studies of Ming Confucians* 1:1a.

56. Ibid., 1:1b. Baisha is Chen Xianzhang's sobriquet, or familiar name.

Wu cut his finger on the sickle. Bearing the pain stoically, not stopping his work because of it, Wu said, "How can I let myself be overcome by my environment?" Then he resumed his work as before.[57]

Engaging in farm labor was not just to toughen and discipline his students. It was also a way to teach them their connection to the larger working of the Way in the cosmic order. While out working in the fields, it is said Wu would teach his students the "eight trigrams" of the *Book of Changes*, explaining each of them in terms of the principles of agriculture. *Records of the Words and Deeds of Ming Confucians* includes an anecdote about Wu out inspecting the sowing of his fields by his students. When he asked them what they were doing, they replied that obviously they were planting seeds. With a slight smile, Wu corrected them: "No, not exactly. This is a matter of your assisting in what *Practicing the Mean* means by the 'transforming and nurturing processes of Heaven and earth.'"[58] Thus the benefit of exposure to farm work for students was that they could experience themselves as concretely participating in the working out of the Way in the world, as contributing to the creative nurturing of life through the cultivation of plant life. By penetrating the principles operative in the natural world, and then relating these to their own inner sense of principle, students could make the connection between the physical and moral aspects of the creativity of the Way.

But studying under Wu was by no means all hard work and rustic living conditions. To balance the hard work he had his students do, Wu saw that they had time for enjoyment and relaxation. His poetry is filled with descriptions of the frequent outings he took his students on in the local area, to climb mountains, view the flowers, and enjoy the pleasures of the natural world. Wine, poetry, singing, and even a few lessons were part of the program. In addition to these day outings, Wu would take a handful of students along with him on his various trips to other parts of the province or the country. For instance, he took a group to visit Hu Yan, his former teacher and head of the National University when Wu's father was Director of Instruction there. Hu made available to them for copying valuable editions of books in his vast library, books to which they would otherwise

---

57. Ibid.

58. *Records of the Words and Deeds of Ming Confucians* 3:3a. *Practicing the Mean* section 24.

have no access.[59] On these trips with his students, Wu wrote numerous poems for them and his son, both for their edification and to express his enjoyment of their company.

Wu describes himself as taking great delight in the company of his students, deriving pleasure from listening to them singing or reciting their lessons, from sharing with them the wonders of the natural world, and from supporting each other in the pursuit of sagehood. In his poem, "Listening to the Various Students of My Clan Reading in the Early Morning":

> The sound of the cock crowing is strident, the light of the morning sun still faint. I am pleased to hear the reciting of students on the other side of the wall. This then is really what "daily renewal" consists of. Bursting with pride, I write this poem for their edification. (2:46b–47a)

As for the particular students who studied under him, they represent a diverse group, some famous, some obscure. They differed in their career choices, some deciding against serving in government and others holding public office. Of those who didn't serve, many were farmer-teachers like Wu, with some financially well off and some even poorer than Wu. Of them all, Hu Jiushao, a relatively unknown figure, is the only one consistently mentioned in Wu's personal writings—his Journal, poetry, and letters.

Hu, who lived about thirty-five miles to the northeast of Wu, came from an extremely poor family and eked out a living by farming and teaching children. He began his studies with Wu in 1419. Right from the beginning, Wu and Hu shared a close relationship, as can be seen in the poems and letters Wu wrote to Hu, especially in the early years of their relationship, from 1419 to 1428. There are eight poems[60] written to Hu during this period, which range from expressions of joy upon the occasions of visits to Hu to those of sadness when inclement weather kept them apart. In a 1419 poem, even as Wu was dispensing advice, he saluted Hu as a "sworn family member (契家)" (1:11b). Wu shows concern when Hu does not show up for

---

59. China had already invented printing but widespread availability of many books was not yet a reality, especially in areas away from large cities. Students saw it as a great opportunity to be able to copy books from scholars with large personal libraries like this.

60. CW 1:10a, 1:11a, 1:11b, 1:11b–12a, 1:18a–b, 1:23b–24a, 1:36a–b, and 1:37a–b.

several evenings in a row for an appointed moon viewing, later confirmed in his suspicions that Hu had fallen sick from too much studying: "your being absent again caused me deep concern. Afterward, I still heard no news of you at all and feared that you had gotten sick" (8:21a–b, Letter 7). Hu is the only student mentioned in the Journal in any personal way. There Wu speaks of having derived much benefit on one occasion from having discussed an urgent matter with Hu "from every possible angle" (no. 59). He also tells of the several times they shared their respective difficulties in "conducting oneself in the world" (nos. 66 and 68).

That Wu came to depend on Hu Jiushao in special ways can be seen when Wu solicited Hu's help to accompany him to consult a doctor in the next county when his wife was seriously ill in 1421 (8:23a, Letter 9), and later in 1426, to go with him to Nanjing for the funeral of his father.[61] According to Hu's biography in the Fuzhou Gazetteer, his position was such that "when students first came to study with Wu, he would have them first see Hu Jiushao."[62] When Hu died in 1465, four years before Wu, Wu wrote a poem that ended with these lines:

> For the first time, my heart fully appreciates why, once Master
>     Zhong died and the sensitivity of his hearing was lost,
> That year, Master Bo's lute ceased being played.[63] (7:14a–b)

As mentioned in the Introduction, three of the most famous Neo-Confucian thinkers of the next generation all studied with Wu Yubi: Lou Liang (1422–1491), Chen Xianzhang (1428–1500), and Hu Juren (1434–1484). Interestingly, not only did all three differ in their own thinking, but they also engaged in disputes with each other in a decidedly sectarian atmosphere. Still, the one thing upon which they all were able to agree was their acknowledgement of Wu as a compelling teacher who had had a significant impact on their lives.

---

61. CW 3:1b and *Case Studies of Ming Confucians* 2:9b.

62. *Fuzhou Gazetteer* (*Fuzhoufu zhi*) 56:12b.

63. Allusion to the story of how Zhong Ziqi, with his sensitive appreciation, sustained the lute playing of the lute player Boyu. When Zhong died and Boyu no longer had such a sensitive person to understand his music, he stopped playing the lute entirely. The term *zhi-yin* 知音, to know or understand somebody's sound, has come to refer to a close relationship with the person who most understands one.

Lou, in praising Wu, wrote: "Wu tended to be self-effacing, never feeling satisfied with himself. His manner was lofty and awe-inspiring, his discussion of matters brilliant and impressive. He was good at opening up and leading students on, such that there was no one who heard his words that was not aroused to exert himself."[64] Chen, in turn, described how, "When I was twenty-seven, I traveled to Xiaopo where I heard Wu lecture on the learning of the sages. He taught the venerable teachings of the ancients, from the Song masters all the way back to Confucius and Mencius. He honored the Way of the Teacher and courageously undertook the responsibility for ensuring that the Way thrived. It was not a matter about which he was timid and docile. Like one standing on the summit of an eight thousand foot precipice, he became a hero for our whole age."[65]

The last of the three, Hu Juren, wrote of how, when he went to study under Wu, "for the first time I understood that the learning of the sages and worthies does not rest in the spoken word or in writings, but rather in the actual realization of it in one's moral conduct."[66] He exclaimed, "As for contemporary scholars in the world whose learning is clear and whose moral character can be admired, there is only Master Wu Yubi who is sufficient to serve as a model to be emulated."[67]

Tying up the discussion of Wu as a teacher, we can note that his great appeal and success as a teacher derived not so much from the content of what he taught. What he imparted was basically the core teachings of the Cheng-Zhu tradition as he saw them, with an emphasis on practice rather than theory. He had no sense of himself as presenting anything original, as starting a new school of thought, or as taking issue with past tradition in any way, as some of his students did. Rather, the source of his attractiveness to students was the power of his personality, the appeal of his personal style, which reflected his own integration of these teachings with his particular life situation.

Wu refrained from setting himself up as an aloof, perfectionist authority figure with all the answers. Rather he presented himself as one who was aware of his shortcomings and who continued to work to improve himself. Because he worked so hard in his own life to demonstrate the truth of the

---

64. *Biographical Account of Wu Yubi* 10:11b.

65. *Complete Works of Chen Xianzhang* 4:72b–73a.

66. *Collected Works of Hu Juren, juan* 1, p. 24.

67. Ibid., *juan* 2, p. 72.

*Great Learning* that peace in the world depends on cultivation of the individual, Wu developed a presence that others found compelling. He did not speak as one removed from what he taught, but as one who had struggled to make the teachings his own. Claiming no special access to the Way, he had to rediscover its truths for himself through hard efforts, through the ups and downs of everyday life: "The learning of the Master was obtained from hardship and vigorous effort and from the sweat and tears of late night reflection."[68] He was honest in admitting to his faults and weaknesses and in sharing his difficulties with his students and friends. Rather than proclaiming to his students that the Way to sagehood is easy, requiring only sincere faith in its possibility, Wu frankly told them that, on the contrary, such a goal was not at all easy. Indeed, it was the very difficulties of its pursuit that became the means of its realization. Yet, given the difficulties, Wu encouraged people to help each other with mutual support and guidance.

## Conclusion: Wu Yubi's Contributions to the Confucian Tradition

The value of Wu's Journal is that it helps us to understand Wu as a person, as a practitioner of Neo-Confucianism, and as a model for students. It is a valuable document attesting to how one individual, with his particular temperament and life situation, went about appropriating and integrating the teachings of Neo-Confucianism that had been shaped by men living in a different time under different circumstances. It provides us with a self-conscious expression of what a believer accepted as the imperatives of the tradition and the means by which to carry them out. It helps us to observe those elements in the tradition that could be most inspirational, and those most burdensome and oppressive. We can compare what Wu thought he was doing, strictly following the tradition, with what in many cases we see him actually doing, making important adaptations to the tradition.

If a return to the Song was a means of getting at the roots of the tradition for him, it also entailed a return to the root of his own self, his mind, as the basis of communication with the past. There he discovered

---

68. *Case Studies of Ming Confucians* 1:1a.

something more complex than the mere imitation of the sage models would suggest. While the latter models may have suggested possibilities for self-perfection, they were also reminders that he fell short of his own ideals. The issue was not so much the emulation of models in itself, but whether, in this process, he could manage the tension between the ideal and the real, whether he could avoid either giving up in discouragement or adopting an inflated, unrealistic identification with the past. This tension was something with which Wu struggled for most of his life, and in doing so, developed a greater self-consciousness of the interior processes of the mind, which moved him to record his life in a kind of detail that no other Neo-Confucian before him had attempted.

For Wu's time, the Journal represents a most distinctive document. As the Ming went on, Neo-Confucianism, under the leadership of Wang Yangming, turned against the Song tradition as too oppressive and rigid. It called for the celebration of the self and the great varieties of self-expression. Becoming a sage no longer was supposed to require reading a lot of books and doing a lot of self-examination. It only involved a spontaneous and natural expression of one's ordinary self. As a result of this new outlook, there was a proliferation of self-revelatory writing, and such a work as Wu's was not considered anything out of the ordinary.

But what is of significance is that such a self-revelatory document as Wu's Journal emerged before Wang Yangming, out of a school so often branded authoritarian, rigid, and uncreatively orthodox. Wu thought he was only keeping a journal to carry out more faithfully the teachings of the Cheng-Zhu school about paying close attention to one's state of mind, particularly to guard against selfish tendencies. Though the purpose was primarily negative at first, it was not such a big step for Wu to go beyond that to give vent to positive expressions of his feelings as well. In so doing, Wu's contribution to the increase of self-expression in the Ming should not be overlooked and undervalued. He showed that a greater sense of the self could emerge from the dynamics of the Cheng-Zhu school as from the Lu or Wang schools. His contributions can also be seen as not just in this emphasis on self-expression but also in the growing importance in the Ming of the independent teacher and the ideal of the sage as moral hero. Wu's life demonstrates that he was not merely reacting to his times, but putting his own mark on the age in which he lived.

This work cannot end without also mentioning one more point. Not only did Wu Yubi anticipate the more confessional, self-revelatory writings of the mid-Ming dynasty, he also anticipated the confessional diaries of Baptists and Quakers in sixteenth-century English writings, as well as the two great chronicles of the "dark night of the soul," by Teresa of Avila and John of the Cross in sixteenth-century Spain. A comparative study of all these offers intriguing possibilities. But for now, that is a story to be told in a future work.

# Glossary of People's Names

This is a list of the principal Neo-Confucian figures mentioned in the book. The names of local friends and acquaintances are not included, except for his student Hu Jiushao. Names in bold are those specifically mentioned by Wu Yubi in his Journal and Letters, with the parenthesis at the end indicating which entry in the Journal or which letter the person is mentioned in. Those names with an asterisk are mentioned or quoted so many times that their locations are not indicated. Chinese usually had at least two other names, a courtesy name (*zi* 字), and a sobriquet (*hao* 號), which was a kind of adult name that one chose for oneself. The title of a person's collected works usually used his *hao* rather than his ordinary name. I have indicated the *hao* (abbreviated "h.") of the most important Neo-Confucians after their names. This will help in locating their works in the Works Cited. Because of the different spellings of these men's names between the older Wade-Giles system of romanization and the now more commonly used pinyin system, I have given a conversion of the names from Wade-Giles to pinyin at the end of the Glossary.

**Chao Gongwu** 晁公武 (d. 1171)—Song dynasty scholar. (35)

Chen Xianzhang 陳獻章, h. Baisha 白沙 (1428–1500)—noted Neo-Confucian of the mid-Ming who studied under Wu Yubi in the mid-1450s. He moved away from Cheng-Zhu school teaching and put more emphasis on the mind-heart and meditation. Some regard him as the forerunner of Wang Yangming's School of the Mind.

**\*Cheng Hao** 程顥, h. Mingdao 明道 (1032–1085)—one of the principal Neo-Confucian thinkers of the Northern Song and the older brother of Cheng Yi. His thought is usually characterized as more intuitive and affective than his brother's more intellectual and philosophical approach. Next to Zhu Xi, he was one of the biggest influences as a role model on Wu Yubi.

**\*Cheng Yi** 程頤, h. Yichuan 伊川 (1033–1107)—leading Neo-Confucian thinker of the Northern Song, on whose ideas Zhu Xi drew heavily. His comments on the *Book of Changes* are widely quoted by Zhu in the anthology *Reflections on Things at Hand*. The younger brother of Cheng Hao by a year, he was more prolific and scholarly in his writings. The tradition usually speaks of them together as the Cheng brothers.

**\*Confucius** 孔子 (551–479 BCE)—Zhou dynasty philosopher and teacher who addressed the political and human issues of his times. His mission can best be summed up in his answer to a critic who suggested he drop out of society and stop the impossible task of trying to reform it: "I cannot herd together with the birds and beasts. If I am not a human being among other humans, what am I to do?" (*Analects* 18.6).

**Dong Zhongshu** 董仲舒 (179–104 BCE)—the most important Confucian of the Han dynasty who, as advisor to the emperor Han Wudi, was instrumental in making Confucianism the state orthodoxy. Reflecting the tenor of Han thought, he had a strong sense of the cosmological interpenetration of Heaven, earth, and the human. He is most famous for his commentary on the *Spring and Autumn Annals*. (77)

**Duke of Zhou** 周公 (c.1050 BCE)—brother of King Wu of the Zhou dynasty, he served as regent to his brother's son, King Cheng, promoting the idea of moral government in the concept of the Mandate of Heaven (*tian-ming*). Confucius felt a sense of closeness to him, once lamenting, "How extreme is my decline. It has been so long since I have seen the Duke of Zhou in my dreams" (*Analects* 7.7). (83) (Letter 3)

**Han Yu** 韓愈 h. Changli 昌黎 (768–824)—the most famous Tang dynasty Confucian, who is seen as the precursor of the revival of Confucianism in the Song. He championed the Confucian Way over that of the Buddhists and Daoists, calling for its revival. Placing a large emphasis on education as a means of reviving the Way, he championed the role of the Confucian teacher. (174, 175, 176)

**Hu Anguo** 胡安國 (1074–1138)—one of the most noted Confucians of the Southern Song whose specialty was the *Spring and Autumn Annals* text. His commentary on this text, heavily promoted by Zhu Xi, became part of the civil service examination curriculum. (197, 239)

**Hu Jiushao** 胡九邵 (fl. early-15th century)—was Wu's favorite student and closest friend. (59, 66, 71) (Letters 6, 7, 9, 14)

Hu Juren 胡居仁 h. Jingzhai 敬斋 (1434–1484)—one of Wu Yubi's students who put great emphasis on personal practice, especially the performance of Confucian rituals. Historians of thought such as Huang Zongxi paired him with Wu Yubi as members of the Cong-ren school of Zhu Xi's thought.

**Hu Yan** 胡儼 (1361–1443)—Ming dynasty scholar-official who headed the National University and appointed Wu Yubi's father to be the Director of Studies under him. Wu Yubi stayed in touch with him even after his father's death. (215)

Huang Zongxi 黃宗義 (1610–1695)—late-Ming and early-Qing Confucian thinker who compiled the all-important anthology of Ming thought, *Case Studies of Ming Confucians,* as well as the anthology *Case Studies of Song and Yuan Confucians.*

**King Cheng** 成王 (reigned c.1042–1021 BCE)—succeeded the throne from his father, King Wu, of the Zhou dynasty. Because of his young age, his uncle, the Duke of Zhou, served as his regent in the early years of his rule. (83)

**King Tang** 唐王 ("Tang, the Completer") (c.1675–1646 BCE)—founder of the Shang dynasty, virtuous ruler. (10, 83)

**King Wen** 文王 ("cultured") (c.1152–1056 BCE)—regarded as one of the founders of the Zhou dynasty, although it was his son, King Wu, who actually defeated the Shang for good. The Confucian tradition held him in highest esteem as the guardian of Chinese culture. (1)

King Wu 武王 ("martial") (r. 1046–1043 BCE)—son of King Wen who actually brought about the defeat of the Shang and founded the Zhou dynasty. Out of filial piety, he made his father the honorary founder.

**Li Ao** 李翱 (fl. 798)—Tang dynasty Confucian, who, along with Han Yu, is seen as one of the forerunners of Song Neo-Confucianism. (174)

**Li Tong** 李侗 h. Yan-ping 延平 (1093–1163)—Song dynasty scholar who is most famous as one of the principal teachers of Zhu Xi. Zhu Xi published Li's writings in the form of *Questions and Answers between Zhu Xi and Li Tong* (*Yan-ping da-wen* 延平答問). (10)

Li Zhi 李贄 (1527–1602)—radical Neo-Confucian of the late Ming who concerned himself with the assertion of the individual and who criticized the patterns of Confucianism he saw as repressive.

Lou Liang 婁諒 h. Yizhai 一斋 (1422–1491)—the student of Wu Yubi who was the most prominent both in terms of reputation and personal closeness to Wu. He is the author of Wu's biography, upon which most all others are based.

**Lu Dalin**  呂大臨 (1046/4–1092/3)—noted disciple of Zhang Zai and the Cheng brothers. (57)

Lu Zuqian  呂祖謙 (1137–1181)—prominent scholar and political figure of the Southern Song who was co-compiler of *Reflections on Things at Hand* (*Jinsilu*) with Zhu Xi.

**Lu Zhi**  陸贄 (754–805)—famous minister of the Tang dynasty, especially noted for his memorials to the throne. He served as advisor to Emperor Dezong (r. 779–805). (288)

**\*Mencius**  孟子 (372–289 BCE)—regarded as the first main successor of Confucius. He expanded Confucius' thought in two main areas: providing rulers with much more specific policies to show benevolent government, and addressing the deeper dimensions of human nature.

**\*Shao Yong**  邵雍 h. Kangjie 康節 (1011–1077)—considered one of the five principal Neo-Confucians of the Northern Song dynasty, who is most famous for his work on the *Book of Changes* and numerology. Wu Yubi was more interested in his poetry, especially those in the collection *Songs of Slapping an Old Gourd by the Yi River*.

**Song Taizong**  宋太宗 (r. 976–997)—second emperor of the Song dynasty, suspected by some to have killed his brother, the reigning emperor, Song Taizu, for the throne. (3)

**Shun**  舜 (22nd century BCE)—legendary sage ruler, to whom Yao passed on the throne. They are often spoken of together. (3) (Letters 3, 4, 5)

**Su Shi**  蘇軾 (1037–1101)—one of the most versatile and talented figures of the Northern Song, known for his abilities in statecraft, poetry, calligraphy, literature, and philosophy. (182)

**Tang, the Completer**  (*see* King Tang)

**Wang Dao**  王導 (276–339)—helped establish the Eastern Jin dynasty and served the two succeeding emperors as Assistant Grand Tutor. (83)

Wang Yangming  王陽明 (1472–1529)—courtesy name of Wang Shouren 王守仁, who was *the* most famous Neo-Confucian of the Ming, seen as having started the Lu-Wang school as opposed to the Cheng Zhu school.

**Wu Cheng** 吳澄 h. Caolu 草廬 (1249–1333)—foremost Neo-Confucian thinker during the Mongol-ruled Yuan dynasty, who hailed from an area of Jiangxi province near to where Wu Yubi lived. He is regarded as having kept the tradition alive during the Yuan period. (45)

**Wu Pu** 吳溥 h. Guai 古崖 (1363–1426)—father of Wu Yubi and the Director of Studies at the National University from 1408 to 1426. (Letters 1, 13a–d)

**Wu Yubi** 吳與弼 h. Kangzhai 康斋 (1392–1469)—Neo-Confucian of the early Ming.

Xue Xuan 薛瑄 (1389–1464)—Neo-Confucian thinker of the early Ming, who lived at the same time as Wu Yubi. The author of *Case Studies of Ming Confucians* put him in the category of the northern school. His thought was characterized as more philosophical than Wu's.

Yan Hui 顏回 (c.500 BCE)—favorite student of Confucius, known for his love of learning despite the straightened circumstances under which he lived.

**Yang Pu** 楊溥 (1372–1446)—held the position of Librarian in the Supervisorate of Instruction of the Heir Apparent. He was an important teacher of Wu and a close colleague of Wu's father. (13)

**Yang Shi** 楊時 (1053–1135)—regarded as one of the four Masters of the Cheng School. (182)

**Yao** 堯—legendary sage ruler of China, traditionally thought to have ruled around 2300 BCE. The Confucian tradition has regarded him as the greatest exemplar of benevolent rule and the standard to which contemporary rulers should aspire. (3) (Letters 3, 4, 5)

**Yi Yin** 伊尹 (1648–1549 BCE)—virtuous minister who served the founder of the Shang dynasty, King Tang. (83)

**You Zuo** 游酢 h. Chishan 廌山 (1053–1123)—Song Neo-Confucian scholar who was a disciple of Cheng Yi. (57)

**\*Zhang Zai** 張載 h. Hengqu 橫渠 (1020–1077)—one of the five principal Neo-Confucians of the Northern Song, famous for his theory of the monism of *qi* and for his "Western Inscription."

**Zhang Yi** 張繹 (b. 1081)—Song Neo-Confucian who was a disciple of Cheng Yi. (302)

**Zhen Dexiu** 真德秀 (1178–1235)—major proponent of Zhu Xi's thought after Zhu's death when his teachings were banned. Zhen helped raise the importance of the institution of the "classics mat," where emperors were lectured on Confucian values. He is most famous for his *Questions and Answers on the Great Learning.* (Letter 5)

*****Zhou Dunyi** 周敦頤 h. Lianxi 濂溪 (1017–1073)—one of the five principal Neo-Confucians of the Northern Song noted for his "Explanation of the Diagram of the Supreme Polarity," and *Penetrating the Book of Changes.* He was one of the teachers of the Cheng brothers. (Letter 8)

**Zhong Yu** 鐘繇 (151–230)—Wei dynasty literatus and famous calligrapher, known as the first and finest master of the regular script. (130)

*****Zhu Xi** 朱熹 h. Huian 晦菴 (1130–1200)—Neo-Confucian thinker of the Southern Song who is regarded as the principal architect of the Cheng-Zhu Neo-Confucian tradition. Prolific writer.

**Zisi** 子思 (c.481–402 BCE)—grandson of Confucius and the author of *Practicing the Mean.* (57, 75)

## Conversion of Names from Wade–Giles to Pinyin

| | |
|---|---|
| Chen Te-hsiu | Zhen Dexiu |
| Ch'eng I | Cheng Yi |
| Chang Tsai | Zhang Zai |
| Ch'en Hsien-chang | Chen Xianzhang |
| Chou Tun-i | Zhou Dunyi |
| Chu Hsi | Zhu Xi |
| Duke of Chou | Duke of Zhou |
| Hsüeh Hsüan | Xue Xuan |
| Hu Chü-jen | Hu Juren |
| Huang Tsung-hsi | Huang Zongxi |
| Li Chih | Li Zhi |
| Li T'ung | Li Tong |
| Ming T'ai-tsu | Ming Taizu |

| | |
|---|---|
| Shao Yung | Shao Yong |
| Tung Chung-shu | Dong Zhongshu |
| Tzu Ssu | Zisi |
| Wu Yü-pi | Wu Yubi |
| Yen Hui | Yan Hui |

# Glossary of Book Titles

This glossary lists the titles of books specifically mentioned in the Journal and Letters. Many of the titles, especially those of the Four Books, are frequently quoted by Wu, but I mention here only the times the title is mentioned. For the most part, I list them in alphabetical order by the English name given in the Journal and Letters, while also including their Chinese name. Those titles that are also included in Works Cited will be done so according to their Chinese name. Books that are quoted by Wu but not mentioned by specific name are not included here, but in Works Cited. The word *juan* 卷 is usually translated into English as "fascicle." Chinese books are divided into these.

Part I of the Glossary will focus on those texts that comprised the Neo-Confucian elementary program of study, presented in the order they are recommended to be read. While *Reflections on Things at Hand* is not specifically mentioned in the list, I include it here because it did serve as an important anthology of Neo-Confucian thought for students.

## I. Basic Texts of the Neo-Confucian Curriculum

***Elementary Learning*** (*Xiaoxue* 小學) in 6 *juan*—compiled by Zhu Xi with the help of Liu Qingzhi, and published in 1187. In Zhu's preface, he laments the lack of a text for beginners and hopes this text will remedy the situation. The text collects quotes from classical texts and Northern Song writings that give explicit guidelines for one's conduct, and present models from Chinese history that have embodied them. A majority of quotes are from the *Book of Rites* (*Liji*) and deal with teaching good manners and how to relate in social situations. Its purpose is to mold behavior more than provide philosophical discussions. That is why Wu Yubi insists so strongly that this text be the starting point of a young person's education. (Letters 12a, 15, "Standards for Learning")

174

**The Four Books** (*Sishu* 四書)—Although these four date from the classical period, they only came to be grouped together in the Song dynasty by Neo-Confucians. Regarded as encompassing all of the fundamental teachings of Confucianism, they constituted the dominant part of the core curriculum. Additionally, they, along with Zhu Xi's commentaries on them, became the basis of the civil service examinations from 1311 on. Here, they are presented in the order in which it was generally regarded they should be read.

> *Great Learning* (*Daxue* 大學)—a chapter from the *Book of Rites* that, along with *Practicing the Mean*, was taken out and published separately as an independent text. Reputed to have been edited by one of Confucius' students, Zengzi, Zhu Xi rearranged its content. He divided it into two parts: the "Text," which includes the so-called "Eight Items" (that relate cultivation of the individual person to peace in the cosmic order), and the "Commentary" in nine sections. (Letters 2, 3, 5, 11)

> *Analects* (*Lunyu* 論語)—in twenty chapters, it is our fullest record of the personality and teachings of Confucius (551–479 BCE). It includes a collection of his conversations with students, records of his behavior, and the sayings of some of his students, among other things. Compiled after his death, it is a miscellany of passages with no observable structure. Nevertheless, it is probably *the* most important single text in pre-modern China, if not all of East Asia, and one of the most frequently quoted in the Journal. (30, 62, 93) (Letters 1, 2, 3, 5)

> *Mencius* (*Mengzi* 孟子)—in seven chapters, with each chapter divided into two. It includes the conversations and sayings of Mencius (372–289 BCE), who is regarded as the first main successor of Confucius. He expanded Confucius' thought in two main areas, namely, providing rulers with much more specific policies to show benevolent government and addressing the deeper dimensions of human nature. Xunzi (c.312–230 BCE) was the other major successor to Confucius' thought, but Song Neo-Confucians preferred Mencius for his view that human nature was intrinsically good and for his passages on the interiority of the self. (12, 43, 46, 117) (Letters 1, 2, 3)

> *Practicing the Mean* (*Zhongyong* 中庸)—in thirty-one sections, thought to have been written by Confucius' grandson, Zisi. Like the *Great Learning*, it was originally a chapter of the *Book of Rites*.

It focuses on the achievement of "the mean," or balance among the myriad affairs of life. The text also stresses the importance of authenticity *cheng* 誠 and the cosmic dimensions of sagehood. Of the Four Books, this has produced the most variations in the translations of its title. The most widely used is the *Doctrine of the Mean*. Others include *The Mean, Centrality and Equilibrium*, the *Constant Balance, Maintaining Perfect Balance*, the *Constant Mean*, and *Centrality and Commonality*. After much thought, I decided for purposes of Wu's use of it on *Practicing the Mean*, inspired by Andrew Plaks translation, *On the Practice of the Mean*. Wu was not reading it for its ideas as a philosopher or scholar, but for its help with self-cultivation in everyday life. "Practicing" in the title gives it a dynamic sense the other translations lack. (48, 49, 50, 52, 57, 68, 75, 86, 127) (Letters 1, 2, 3, 6)

**The Five Classics** (*Wujing* 五經) These are texts first canonized as the Confucian classics back in the time of the Han dynasty. Before the Song, they were regarded more highly than the Four Books. The tradition believes that Confucius had something to do with either their compiling, editing, or even writing.

*Book of Changes* (*Yijing* 易經)—the most important of the five classics in terms of its influence on Neo-Confucian cosmology and self-cultivation. Originally a divination text, it had much commentary added to it over time. Neo-Confucians drew upon many of its ideas found in the Ten Wings, especially the "Commentary on the Appended Phrases" in two parts. (35, 67, 208, 281, 288, 322)

*Book of History* (*Shujing* 書經)—a collection of speeches, decrees, and documents that are said to have come from as far back as the sage rulers Yao and Shun up until the early Zhou. Other translations of its title include *Book of Documents* and *Classic of History*. Wu Yubi doesn't mention reading it specifically but alludes to it in entries 10 and 224.

*Book of Odes* (*Shijing* 詩經)—the first anthology of poetry in China, which includes a little more than three hundred poems, ranging from folk songs to highly ceremonial ones for court. It is also known as the *Book of Poetry*, the *Book of Songs*, and the *Classic of Odes*. (172, 266)

*Book of Rites* (*Liji* 禮記)—its content ranges from general principles about the cosmos to very specific rules for behavior, such as table manners. As noted about the Four Books, two of its chapters (the *Great Learning* and *Practicing the Mean*) later became regarded as texts in their own right and were published separately. (106)

**Spring and Autumn Annals** (*Chunqiu* 春秋)—a record of the affairs of the state of Lu, the home of Confucius, from 722 to 481, said to have been written by Confucius himself. Written in a terse style, it is usually only read with commentaries, the three principal ones being the Gongyang 公羊, Guliang 穀梁, and Zuo 左傳. (164) (Letter 9)

**Reflections on Things at Hand** (*Jinsilu* 近思錄)—anthology compiled by Zhu Xi and Lu Zuqian, in 14 *juan*, of the sayings of the major Northern Song Neo-Confucians, and published in 1175. In the Preface, Zhu Xi states, "Fearing that a beginner may not know where to start, we have selected passages concerned with fundamentals and closely related to daily application to constitute this volume. . . . So if a young man in an isolated village has the will to learn but no teacher, this is for him." (Trans. by Chan, *Reflections on Things at Hand*, p. 2.) It was one of the key educational texts for Neo-Confucians, in addition to the Four Books. (27, 28, 98, 111, 144) (Letter 12a)

## II. Other Titles

**Answers to Questions on the Great Learning** (*Daxue huowen* 大學 或問)—a short text in 2 *juan*. Written by Zhu Xi to clarify and answer questions about his more extensive *Commentary on the Great Learning* (*Daxue zhangzhu*). (Letter 5)

**Biographical Account of Cheng Hao** (*Mingdao xingzhuang* 明道行 狀)—by Cheng Yi, in *Collected Works of Cheng Yi* (*Yichuan wenji* 伊川文 集) 7:1a–7a. (117, 136)

**Case Studies of Ming Confucians** (*Mingru xuean* 明儒學案)—compiled by Huang Zongxi, it is one of the most important anthologies of Ming thought.

**Catalogue of the Imperial Manuscript Library** (*Siku quanshu zongmu* 四庫全書總目). This is an annotated catalog to the great governmental compilation project in the eighteenth century of all the books in

China. One translation of the compilation is *Complete Library of the Four Treasuries*.

**Chronological Biography of Zhu Xi**   (*Zhuzi nianpu* 朱子年譜)—by Yuan Zhonghui in 1 *juan*. (107)

**Classified Conversations of Zhu Xi**   (*Zhuzi yulei* 朱子語類)—compiled by Li Jingde (fl. 1263) in 140 *juan*, published in 1270. Also known by Zhu's *hao*, as the *Huian xiansheng yulu* 晦菴先生語錄 (Classified Conversations of Master Huian). (185, 215, 282, 298) (Letter 12a)

**Collected Commentaries on the Analects**   (*Lunyu jizhu* 論語集 注)—by Zhu Xi in 10 *juan*. (Letter 12b)

**Collected Works of Lu Zhi**   (*Lu Xuangong ji* 陸宣公集)—his collected writings in 15 *juan*. (288)

**Collected Works of Wu Cheng**   (*Caolu wenji* 草廬文集)—his collected writings in 100 *juan*. (45)

**Collected Works of Zhu Xi**   (*Huian wenji* 晦菴文集, or *Zhuzi wenji* 朱子文集, or *Zhuzi daquan* 朱子大全)— his collected writings edited by Zhu's disciple Zhu Zai, in 100 *juan*. (117, 127, 150, 179, 184, 307, 309; Letters 12a, b)

**Compilation of Exemplary Biographies to Alert the Self**   (*Zijing bian* 自警編)—edited by Chao Shanliao (fl. 1231), in 9 *juan*. Offers exemplary words and deeds of virtuous men in anecdotal style. (207, 240)

**Complete Works of Han Yu**   (*Han Changli quanshu* 昌黎全書)—his collected writings. (174, 175, 176)

**Correct Models for Literature**   (*Wenzhang zhengzong* 文章正宗)— edited by Zhen Dexiu in 24 *juan*; presents literature from the point of view of principle. (58)

**Diagrams to the Yi Rituals**   (*Yilitu* 儀禮図)—compiled by Yang Fu (fl. 1230) in 17 *juan*. (270)

**Digest of the Recorded Conversations of Zhu Xi**   (*Zhuzi yulue* 朱子 語略)—compiled by Zhu Xi's student Yang Yuli to provide a simple selection of Zhu Xi's sayings. (107) (Letter 12a)

**Extended Meaning of the Great Learning**   (*Daxue yanyi* 大學演 意)—by Zhen Dexiu in 43 *juan*. This was not an ordinary commentary on the *Great Learning* but a guide for correct moral behavior, especially for the emperor. It not only emphasizes the importance of self-cultivation for the emperor but draws on historical cases from the past to illustrate what would be deemed exemplary or bad actions. (Letter 5)

**History of the Jin Dynasty** (*Jin shi* 金史)—history of the Jin dynasty (265–419) in 130 *juan*. (83)

**"Letting My Feelings Arise While Resting in My Studio" Poems** (*Zhaiju ganxing shi* 斎居感興詩)—in 20 *shou* 首 (quantifier for poetry), these are poems by Zhu Xi in his *Collected Works* 4:6b–9a. He said he wrote them after reading some poems of the Tang poet Chen Ziang, which he thought were too Buddhist. (139)

**Master Zhu's Works on the Management of Human Affairs and Providing a Standard for Literature** (*Zhuzi jingji wenheng* 朱子經濟文衡)—a collection of selections from Zhu Xi's *Recorded Conversations* and his *Collected Works*, divided into categories, edited by Teng Gong of the late 12th century. (Letter 13)

**Record of the Origins of the School of the Two Chengs** (*Yi Luo yuanyuanlu* 伊洛淵源錄)—a collection of biographies of key Neo-Confucians of the Northern Song period in 14 *juan*, compiled by Zhu Xi. This is the text that sparked Wu Yubi's conversion experience. (Letter 3, Colophon)

**Records of the Words and Deeds of Eminent Officials of the Song Dynasty** (*Song mingchen yanxinglu* 宋名臣言行錄)—edited by Zhu Xi, a collection of biographies of Northern Song officials, with a focus more on social-political aspects than self-cultivation. (118, 182) (Letter 12a)

**Records of the Words and Deeds of the Song Confucian Masters** (*Yi Lo Guan Min yanxinglu* 伊洛關閩言行錄)—The title more literally is the "Records of the Words and Deeds of Zhou Dunyi, the Cheng Brothers, Zhang Zai, and Zhu Xi." I have not been able to find anything about this text, which from its title seems to have been modeled on the format of Zhu Xi's biographical collection just discussed in the entry above. (193)

**Written Legacy of the Cheng Brothers** (*Chengzi yishu* 程子遺書)—in *Er Cheng quanshu* (*Complete Works of the Two Chengs*) in 25 *juan* with one appended *juan*. It was edited by Zhu Xi in 1168. An alternate translation of its title is *Surviving Works of the Cheng Brothers*. (183, 189, 272, 279, 288, 319) (Letter 12a)

**Zhu Xi's *Classified Conversations*** See *Classified Conversations of Zhu Xi.*

**Zhu Xi's *Collected Works*** See *Collected Works of Zhu Xi.*

## Conversion of Book Titles in Wade–Giles to Pinyin

| | |
|---|---|
| *Chang Tzu ch'üan-shu* | *Zhangzi quanshu* |
| *Cheng-meng* | *Zhengmeng* |
| *Ch'eng Tzu i-shu* | *Chengzi yishu* |
| *Chou Tzu ch'üan-shu* | *Zhouzi quanshu* |
| *Chin-ssu lu* | *Jinsilu* |
| *Chung-yung* | *Zhongyong* |
| *Chu Tzu Ta-ch'üan* | *Zhuzi Daquan* |
| *Chu Tzu nien-p'u* | *Zhuzi nianpu* |
| *Chu Tzu yü-lei* | *Zhuzi yulei* |
| *Erh-Ch'eng ch'üan-shu* | *Er Cheng quanshu* |
| *Hsiao-hsüeh* | *Xiaoxue* |
| *I Ching* | *Yijing* |
| *I-ch'uan wen-chi* | *Yichuan wenji* |
| *I-shu* | *Yishu* |
| *K'ang-chai hsien-sheng hsing-chuang* | *Kangzhai xiansheng xingzhuang* |
| *Ming-dao hsing-chuang* | *Mingdao xingzhuang* |
| *Ming-ju hsüeh-an* | *Mingru xuean* |
| *Shih-ching* | *Shijing* |
| *Ssu-k'u ch'üan-shu tsung-mu* | *Siku quanshu zongmu* |
| *Ssu-shu* | *Sishu* |
| *Ta-hsüeh* | *Daxue* |
| *Ta-hsüeh yen-i* | *Daxue yanyi* |
| *T'ung-shu* | *Tongshu* |

# Works Cited

## Chinese Pre-1900

Chao Gongwu晁公武. *Zhaode xiansheng junzhai tushuzhi* 昭德先生郡斋 讀書志 (Catalogue of the Library of Master Chao Gongwu). Guoxue jiben zongshu edition.

Chen Xianzhang 陳獻章. *Baisha quanshu*白沙全書(Complete Works of Chen Xianzhang). Taipei: Commercial Press, 1973.

Cheng Hao 程顥. *Mingdao wenji* 明道文集 (Collected Works of Cheng Hao). In Cheng Hao and Cheng Yi, *Er Cheng quanshu* (Collected Works of the Two Chengs). Edited by Wang Xiaoyu. Beijing: Zhonghua shuji, 1981.

———, and Cheng Yi 程頤. *Er Cheng quanshu* 二程全書 (Collected Works of the Two Chengs). Edited by Wang Xiaoyu. Beijing: Zhonghua shuji, 1981.

———. *Chengzi yishu* 程子遺書 (Written Legacy of the Cheng Brothers). In Cheng Hao and Cheng Yi, *Er Cheng quanshu*.

Cheng Yi. *Mingdao xingzhuang* 明道行狀 (Biographical Account of Cheng Hao). In *Yichuan wenji* (Collected Works of Cheng Yi) 7:1a–7a.

———. *Yichuan wenji* 伊川文集 (Collected Works of Cheng Yi). In Cheng Hao and Cheng Yi, *Er Cheng quanshu*.

*Fuzhoufu zhi* 撫州府志 (Fuzhou Gazatteer) 1876 edition.

*Han Shu* 漢書 (History of the Han). Hanfenlou 1739 edition.

Han Yu 韓愈. *Han Changli quanshu* 昌黎全書 (Complete Works of Han Yu). Sibu beiyao edition.

*Hou Han Shu* 後漢書 (History of the Later Han). Hanfenlou 1739 edition.

Hu Juren 胡局仁. *Hu Jingzhai ji* 胡敬斎集 (Collected Works of Hu Juren). Congshu jicheng edition.

Huang Zongxi 黃宗羲. *Mingru xuean* 明儒學案 (Case Studies of Ming Confucians). Sibu beiyao edition.

*Jin Shi* 金史 (History of the Jin). Hanfenlou 1739 edition.

Li Zhi 李贄. *Xu cangshu* 續藏書 (Continuation of the Book to Be Hidden Away). Beijing: Zhonghua Press, 1959.

Lou Liang 婁諒. *Kangzhai xiansheng xingzhuang* 康齋先生行狀 (Biographical Account of Wu Yubi). In Xu Hong, *Ming mingchen wanyan lu*.

*Ming Shi* 明史 (History of the Ming). Taipei: Guofang yanjiu yuan, 1962.

Shao Yong 邵雍. *Yichuan jirang ji* 伊川擊壤集 (Songs of Slapping an Old Gourd by the Yi River). Sibu conggao edition, vols. 497–498.

Shen Jia 沈佳. *Mingru yanxing lu* 明儒言行錄 (Records of the Words and Deeds of Ming Confucians). Siku quanshu zhenben edition, series 3, vol. 143.

*Siku quanshu zongmu* 四庫全書總目 (Catalogue of the Imperial Manuscript Library). Shanghai: Dadong Press, 1930.

Wu Cheng 吳澄. *Wu Wenzheng ji* 吳文正集 (Collected Works of Wu Cheng). Siku quanshu zhenben edition, series 2, vols. 319–328. (Also known as *Caolu wenji* 草廬文集)

Wu Yubi 吳與弼. *Kangzhai ji* 康齋集 (Collected Works of Wu Yubi). Siku quanshu zhenben edition, series 4, vols. 335–336.

———. *Kangzhai xiansheng wenji, fulu* 康齋先生文集附錄 (Collected Works of Master Wu Yubi, with Appended Sources). Gest Library photocopy of Naikaku Library 1526 edition.

———. *Kangzhai xiansheng wenji, fulu* 康齋先生文集附錄. (Collected Works of Master Wu Yubi, with Appended Sources). National Library of Rare Books Microfilm of 1590 edition.

Xu Hong 徐紘. *Ming mingchen wanyan lu* 明名臣琬琰錄 (Records of the Noble Conduct of Famous Officials of the Ming). Siku quanshu zhenben edition, series 6, vols. 103–104.

Yang Rong 楊榮. *Yang wenmin gong ji* 楊文敏公集 (Collected Works of Yang Rong). Taipei: Wen-hua Press, 1970.

Yang Shiqi 楊士奇. "Wu xiansheng muzhi ming" 吳先生墓誌銘 (Funeral Piece for Master Wu Pu). In Xu Hong, *Ming mingchen wanyan lu*.

Yin Zhi 尹直. *Jianzhai suojiu lu* 謇齋瑣綴錄 (Record of Bits and Pieces Put Together by Yin Zhi). In *Shuoku* 說庫 (Treasury of Prose). Edited by Wang Wenru 王文濡. Taipei: Hsin-hsing Press, 1963.

You Zuo 游酢. *You Chishan ji* 游廌山集 (Collected Works of You Zuo). Siku quanshu zhenben edition, series 4, vol. 253.

Zhang Zai 張載. "*Lunyu xuo*" (Discourse on the *Analects*) 論語說 in *Zhangzi quanshu.*

———. *Zhangzi quanshu* 張子全書 (Complete Works of Zhang Zai). Sibu beiyao edition.

———. *Zhengmeng* 正蒙 (Correcting Youthful Ignorance) in *Zhangzi quanshu.*

Zhen Dexiu 真德秀. *Wenzhang zhengzong* 文章正宗 (Correct Models for Literature). Sibu zongkan edition.

Zhou Dunyi 周敦頤. *Tongshu* 通書 (Penetrating the *Book of Changes*) in *Zhouzi quanshu.*

———. *Zhouzi quanshu* 周子全書 (Complete Works of Zhou Dunyi). Sibu beiyao edition.

Zhu Xi 朱熹 *Sishu jizhu* 四書集注 (Collected Commentaries on the Four Books). Sibu beiyao edition.

———. *Song mingchen yanxinglu* 宋名臣言行錄 (Records of the Words and Deeds of Eminent Officials of the Song Dynasty). Columbia University East Asian Library, 1830 edition.

———. *Zhuzi yulei* 朱子語類 (Classified Conversations of Zhu Xi). 1970 Reprint of 1437 edition. Zhengzhong Book Co.

———. *Zhuzi wenji* 朱子文集 (Collected Works of Zhu Xi). Sibu beiyao edition, entitled *Zhuzi daquan* 朱子大全 (Great Compendium of Zhu Xi's Works).

———. *Yiluo yuanyuan lu* 伊洛淵源錄 (Record of the Origins of the School of the Two Chengs). Taipei: Sung Historical Materials edition, series 2.

———. and Lu Zuqian 呂祖謙, eds. *Jinsilu* 近思錄 (Reflections on Things at Hand). Sibu beiyao edition.

## Modern

Bloom, Irene, trans. *Mencius.* Edited by Philip J. Ivanhoe. New York: Columbia University Press, 2009.

Chan, Wing-tsit, trans. *Reflections on Things at Hand: The Neo-Confucian Anthology.* New York: Columbia University Press, 1967.

————, compiler and trans. *Source Book in Chinese Philosophy.* Princeton, NJ: Princeton University Press, 1963.

————. "Neo-Confucian Philosophical Poems." *Renditions* 4 (1975): 5–12.

de Bary, Wm. Theodore. *Learning for One's Self: Essays on the Individual in Neo-Confucian Thought.* New York: Columbia University Press, 1991.

————. *Neo-Confucian Orthodoxy and the Learning of the Mind-and-Heart.* New York: Columbia University Press, 1981.

Goodrich, L. Carrington, and Fang Chao-ying, eds. *Dictionary of Ming Biography.* 2 vols. New York: Columbia University Press, 1976.

Fang Chao-ying, Julia Ching, and Huang P'ei. "Wu Yü-pi" entry. In Goodrich and Fang, eds. *Dictionary of Ming Biography.* 2 vols. New York: Columbia University Press, 1976.

Fang Lienche Tu. "Ming Dreams." *The Tsing Hua Journal of Chinese Studies,* New Series X, no. 1 (June 1973): 55–73.

Lau, D. C., trans. *Confucius, the Analects.* Harmondsworth, England: Penguin Books, 1979.

Slingerland, Edward, trans. *Confucius: Analects, with Selections from Traditional Commentaries.* Indianapolis, IN: Hackett Publishing Co., 2003.

Legge, James, trans. *The Confucian Analects, the Great Learning, and the Doctrine of the Mean.* (*The Chinese Classics*, vol. 1). Taipei 1971 reprint of 1893 original.

————, trans. *The She King or the Book of Odes.* (*The Chinese Classics*, vol. IV). Taipei 1971 reprint of 1871 original.

————, trans. *The Shoo King or the Book of Historical Documents.* (*The Chinese Classics*, vol. III). Taipei 1971 reprint of 1865 original.

————, trans. *The Works of Mencius.* (*The Chinese Classics*, vol. II). Taipei 1971 reprint of 1894 original.

Qian Mu. "Study of the Currents of Thought in the Early Ming Chu Hsi School." In *Collection of Discussions of the History of Chinese Scholarship and Thought,* vol. 7. Taipei: Far Eastern Library Co., 1979.

Wilhelm, Richard, trans. *The I Ching, or Book of Changes.* Rendered into English by Cary F. Baynes. 2 vols. New York: Bollingen, 1950.

Wu Pei-yi. *The Confucian's Progress: Autobiographical Writings in Traditional China.* Princeton, NJ: Princeton University Press, 1990.

# Suggested Further Reading

## For Background on the Ming Dynasty

Brook, Timothy. *The Troubled Empire: China in the Yuan and Ming Dynasties*. Cambridge, MA: Harvard University Press, 2010. Interesting new approach that includes the effect of climate change on political changes, and topics on material culture and women.

Dardess, John W. *Ming China 1368–1644: A Concise History of a Resilient Empire*. Lanham, MD: Rowman & Littlefield Publishers, 2012. Short history arranged around a variety of topics, including emperors, governance, and outlaws.

Goodrich, L. Carrington, and Fang Chao-ying, eds. *Dictionary of Ming Biography.* 2 vols. New York: Columbia University Press, 1976. Valuable reference book, offering biographies of a wide variety of people who lived or traveled to China in the Ming dynasty, including Mongols and Westerners.

## For More on Neo-Confucianism

Bol, Peter K. *Neo-Confucianism in History*. Cambridge, MA: Harvard University Asia Center, 2008. (Includes an exhaustive bibliography for further reading.)

Chaffee, John. W, and Wm. Theodore de Bary, *Neo-Confucian Education: The Formative Stage.* Berkeley: University of California Press, 1989. See especially, "Chu Hsi's Aims as an Educator" by W. T. de Bary, and "Back to Basics: Chu Hsi's *Elementary Learning (Hsiao-hsüeh)*" by M. T. Kelleher.

de Bary, Wm. Theodore. *Learning for One's Self: Essays on the Individual in Neo-Confucian Thought.* New York: Columbia University Press, 1991. See especially, chapters 1–5.

Gardner, Daniel K. *The Four Books: The Basic Teachings of the Later Confucian Tradition*. Indianapolis, IN: Hackett Publishing Co., 2007.

Graham, Angus C. *Two Chinese Philosophers.* 1958. Reprint, Open Court Books, 1991. Valuable study on the Cheng brothers with translations of their writings.

Keenan, Barry. *Neo-Confucian Self-Cultivation.* Honolulu, HI: University of Hawaii Press, 2011.

Tu Wei-ming. *Neo-Confucian Thought in Action: Wang Yang-Ming's Youth (1472–1509).* This presents the autobiographical account of the struggles with sagehood that Wang, who came after Wu Yubi, had.

## For Translations of Neo-Confucian Writings in English

Chan, Wing-tsit, trans. *Reflections on Things at Hand: The Neo-Confucian Anthology.* New York: Columbia University Press, 1967. Chapters 2–5, "The Essentials of Learning," "The Investigation of Things," "Preserving One's Mind," and "Correcting Mistakes" are quite helpful aids in reading Wu's Journal.

———. *Source Book in Chinese Philosophy.* Princeton, NJ: Princeton University Press, 1963.

de Bary, Wm. Theodore, and Irene Bloom, eds. *Sources of Chinese Tradition.* Vol. 1, 2nd ed. New York: Columbia University Press, 1999. This is the largest compilation of Confucian and Neo-Confucian sources in print. The revised edition includes more sources for Neo-Confucianism, especially from Zhu Xi's writing, with other material on education, including that of women, and social institutions.

Gardner, Daniel K., trans. *Learning to be a Sage: Selections from the Conversations of Master Chu, Arranged Topically.* Berkeley, CA: University of California Press, 1990. This is a good complement to studying Wu's Journal.

## Some of the English Translations Available for the Four Books: *Analects, Great Learning, Mencius,* and *Practicing the Mean*

Ames, Roger T., and Rosemont, Henry, trans. *The Analects of Confucius: A Philosophical Translation.* New York: Ballantine Books, 1998.

Bloom, Irene, trans., and Philip J. Ivanhoe, ed. *Mencius.* New York: Columbia University Press, 2009.

Lau, D. C., trans. *Confucius, the Analects.* Harmondsworth, England: Penguin Books, 1979.

————, trans. *Mencius.* Harmondsworth, England: Penguin Books, 1970.

Legge, James, trans. *The Analects of Confucius, the Great Learning, and the Doctrine of the Mean.* 1893. Reprint, Taiwan SMC Publishing, 1991.

————, trans. *The Works of Mencius.* 1894. Reprint, New York: Dover Books, 1971.

Plaks, Andrew H., trans. *Ta-hsüeh* and *Chung Yung: The Highest Order of Cultivation* and *On the Practice of the Mean.* New York: Penguin USA, 2003.

Slingerland, Edward, trans. *Confucius Analects, with Selections from Traditional Commentaries.* Indianapolis, IN: Hackett Publishing Co., 2003.

Van Nordon, Bryan W., trans. *Mengzi, with Selections from Traditional Commentaries.* Indianapolis, IN: Hackett Publishing Co., 2008.

Waley, Arthur, trans. *The Analects of Confucius.* 1938. Reprint, New York: Vintage Books, 1989.

Watson, Burton, trans. *The Analects of Confucius.* New York: Columbia University Press, 2007.